TABLE OF CONTENTS FOREX TRADING 2021

Table of Contents Swing and Day Trading 2021

TABLE OF CONTENTS OPTIONS TRADING 2021

Copyright © 2020

Forex Trading contains the information you need to take the first step in trading the world's currencies:

Chapter 1: What is the Forex Market? It presents the global forex market and gives an idea of its size and scope.

Chapter 2: The Mechanics of Currency Trading observes how currencies are traded in the foreign exchange market: what currency pairs are exchanged, what price quote implies, how profits and losses are calculated, and how the global trading day flows.

Chapter 3: How to Develop a Profitable Forex Trading Mindset analyzes the different approaches used by professional currency traders to develop a profitable mindset.

Chapter 4: Getting Started Along with Your Practice Account guides you through the different ways you can establish a market position, how to manage your transaction during the open, how to close your position, and how to critically evaluate your results.

Chapter 5: Choosing Your Trading Style reviews the different approaches used by expert currency traders and how they impact trading decisions, as well as how to craft a disciplined trading plan and stick to it.

The second part of the book **(chapters 6 to 10)** deals more with the following topics:

- Basic Forex Strategies
- Brokers to avoid
- Dealing with loss
- Techniques to earn $ 15,000 per month in 2021
- Strategies for creating passive
income with cryptocurrencies

FOREX TRADING 2021

CHAPTER ONE   WHAT IS FOREX MARKET?

The foreign exchange market - usually called the forex market, or simply refer to as the FX market - is the commonly traded financial market in the globe. We like to see the foreign exchange market as the "Big Kahuna" of the financial markets. The foreign exchange market is the crossroads of international capital, the crossroads through which global trade and investment flows must move. International trade flows, like when a Swiss electronics company buys components made in Japan, were originally the basis for the development of foreign exchange markets.

Today, however, the global investment and financial flows dominate trade as the main non-speculative source of foreign exchange market volume. Whether it is an Australian pension fund that invests in US Treasury bonds or a British insurer that allocates assets on the Japanese stock market or a German conglomerate that buys a Canadian-made facility, every international transaction goes through the foreign exchange market at some point.

More than anything, the foreign exchange market is a commercial market. It's a 24/7 market, allowing traders to act on news and events as they see fit. It's a market where half a billion dollars can be executed in a matter of seconds and may not even move prices in a remarkable way. Try to buy or sell half a billion products in another market and see how prices react.

GETTING INSIDE THE NUMBERS

The average daily volume of currency trading exceeds $ 2 trillion per day. That's an impressive number, right? $ 2,000,000,000 - it's a lot of zeros, no matter how you cut them. To give you such a perspective, it's about 10 to 15 times the size of the daily trading volume on all the stock markets of the world together.

SPECULATING IN THE CURRENCY MARKET

Although commercial and financial transactions on the money markets represent huge nominal amounts, they remain pale compared to values based on speculation. The vast majority of currency market volume is by far speculative - traders who buy and sell for short-term gains based on minute-to-minute, hour-to-hour, and day-to-day price fluctuations.

It is assessed that more than 90% of daily trading volume is derived from speculation (i.e., investment-based foreign exchange transactions or transactions represent less than 10% of the daily trading volume). The breadth and depth of the speculative market mean that the liquidity of the global currency market is unmatched among global financial markets.

Most spot currency trading, about 75 percent by volume, takes place in so-called "major currencies," which represent the largest and most developed economies in the world. In addition, foreign exchange activity often operates on the basis of the regional "currency bloc," where most of the negotiations take place between the

USD block, the JPY block, and the EUR block, representing the three largest economic regions. world.

GETTING LIQUID WITHOUT GETTING SOAKED

Liquidity is known as the level of market interest - the buying and selling volume - available at any time for a particular security or asset. The greater the liquidity or, the deeper the trade, the easier and faster it is to buy or sell a security.

From a business perspective, liquidity is a critical consideration as it determines the speed at which prices move between trades and over time. A very liquid market such as forex can see large volumes of traded trades with relatively low price changes. A non-liquid or weak market tends to see prices rise faster in relatively lower trading volumes. A market that trades only for certain hours (futures, for example) also represents a less liquid and thinner market.

AROUND THE GLOBE IN A TRADING DAY

The forex market is active and opens 24 hours a day, from the opening hours on Monday morning in Asia-Pacific to the closing hours on Friday in New York. At any given time, according to the time zone, dozens of global financial centers - such as London. Sydney, or Tokyo - is open, and the exchange offices of these financial centers are active in the market.

Currency trading does not stop even on holidays, when other financial markets, such as stocks or futures exchanges, can be closed. Even if it is a vacation in Japan, for example, Sydney, Singapore, and Hong Kong can always be open. It may be July 4th in the United States, but if it's a business day, Tokyo, London, Toronto, and other financial centers will continue to trade currencies. The only common holiday in the world is New Year's Day, and even that depends on the day of the week it falls.

THE OPENING OF THE TRADING WEEK

There is no officially designated start time for the trading day or week, but for all intents and purposes, market action begins when Wellington, New Zealand, the first financial center to the west from the international data line, opens Monday morning, a local hour. Depending on if daylight saving time is in effect in its own time zone, it is approximately the beginning of Sunday afternoon in North America, Sunday night in Europe, and early Monday morning in Asia.

Sunday's opening is the starting point for a recovery in money markets after Friday's closing in North America (5 pm ET). This is the currency market's first chance to react to news and events that may have occurred over the weekend. Prices may have closed trades in New York at one level, but depending on the circumstances, they may start trading at different levels on open Sunday.

Trading In The Asia-Pacific Session

Trading volumes of currencies in the Asia-Pacific session represent about 21% of the world's total daily volume, according to a 2004 survey. The main centers business are Wellington, New Zealand; Sydney, Australia; Tokyo, Japan; Hong Kong; and Singapore. In terms of the most traded currency pairs, this means that news and data reports from New Zealand, Australia, and Japan will come to the market during this session.

Due to the size of the Japanese market and the importance of Japanese data in the market, much of the trade during the Asia-Pacific session focuses on Japanese Yen currency pairs (explained in more detail in Chapter 2), for example, USD / JPY - forex. to the US dollar / Japanese yen - and the JPY crosses, such as EUR / JPY and AUD / JPY. Of course, Japanese financial institutions are also more active during this session, so you can often understand what the Japanese market is doing based on price movements.

For individual traders, overall liquidity in major currency pairs is more than adequate, with generally orderly price movements. In some less liquid non-regional currencies such as GBP / USD or USD / CAD, price movements may be more irregular or non-existent depending on the environment.

Trading in the European/London session

In the middle of the Asian session, European financial centers are starting to open the market and are booming. The center's European financial account and London for over 50% of the total daily volume of world trade, with London representative alone for about a third of the total daily global volume, according to the survey in 2004.

The European session spans half of the Asian trade and half of the US trade, which means that market interest and liquidity peak in this session.

Current events and data from the euro area (and from countries such as Germany and France), Switzerland, and the United Kingdom are generally reported in the early hours of the European session. As a result, some of the most active and largest active deals are in European currencies (EUR, GBP, and CHF) and cross currency pairs (EUR / CHF and EUR / GBP).

The Asian trading centers are beginning to slow down in the early hours of the European session in the morning, and US financial centers arrive a few hours later, about 7 am Brasilia time.

Trading In The North American Session

Due to the overlap between the US and European trading sessions, trading volumes are much larger. Some of the largest and most important directional price movements occur during this transition period. In itself, however, the US trading session is about the same share of world trade volume in the Asia-Pacific market, about 22% of the world's daily trading volume.

The American morning is the time when the main US economic data are released, and the foreign exchange market makes many of its most important decisions on the value of the dollar. Most US data reports are published at 8:30 am ET, while others are published later (between 9am and 10am ET). Canadian data reports are also published in the morning, usually between 7 am and 9 am Brasilia time. There are also US economic reports that come out at noon or 2 pm ET, animating the New York market afternoon. London and the Centers European financial start to close their daily trading operations at noon Eastern Time (ET) each day. London, or the closure of Europe, as we know, can often generate volatile business upheavals.

Most days, the liquidity and interest rates drop significantly in the afternoon of New York, which can lead to difficult trading conditions. In calm weather, a general decline in market interest often leads to stagnation of price action. On more active days, when prices may have changed more significantly, a decline in liquidity may trigger additional excessive price movements as fewer traders strive for similar prices and liquidity. As with the closing of London, there is never a precise way to move the New York afternoon market, so traders need to be aware that lower liquidity conditions tend to prevail and that adapt accordingly.

CURRENCIES AND SOME FINANCIAL MARKETS

As much as we like to refer to the forex market as a whole and at the end of all financial markets, it does not exist in a vacuum. You may have even heard of some of these other markets: gold, oil, stocks, and bonds.

There are several misinformation and noise about the supposed interdependence between these markets and individual currencies or currency pairs. To be sure, you can still find a correlation between two different markets over a period of time, even if it is just zero (i.e., the two markets are not correlated).

Always remember that all the different financial markets are markets in their own right and operate according to their internal dynamics based on feelings, data, news, and positioning. Do the markets sometimes overlap and have different degrees of correlation? Of course, and it's always important to know what's happening in other financial markets. But it is also essential to consider each market from its own point of view and to negotiate each market individually.

Let's dive into some of the other major financial markets and see what conclusions we can draw for currency trading.

Gold

Gold is commonly known as a hedge against inflation, an alternative to the US dollar, and a store of value in the period of political or economic uncertainty. In the long run, the relationship is almost reversed, with a weaker dollar generally accompanying a higher gold price and a stronger dollar accompanying a lower gold price. However, in the short term, each market has its own dynamics and liquidity, which makes short-term trading relationships generally fragile.

Overall, the gold market is much smaller than the foreign exchange market, so if we were gold traders, we would keep an eye on what is happening with the dollar, not the other way around. With this observed, extreme movements in gold prices tend to grab the attention of currency traders and generally influence the dollar upside down.

Oil

There are tons of wrong information on the internet about the supposed relationship between oil and the US dollar or other currencies such as CAD or JPY. The idea is that, as some countries are oil producers, their currencies are positively (or negatively) affected by increases (or decreases) in oil prices. If the country is an oil importer (and which countries are not today?), The theory is that your currency will be affected (or aided) by higher (or lower) oil prices.

Correlation studies show no appreciable relationships in this sense, especially in the short term, which is central to most trading currencies. When there is a long-term relationship, it is as obvious to the dollar as one or more than any single currency, whether it is an importer or an exporter of black gold .

The most effective way to look at oil is as an inflation factor and a limiting factor in overall economic development. The greater the price of oil, the higher the inflation, and the more likely the economy will slow down. The lesser the price of oil, the less inflationary pressures are likely (but not necessarily). We like to take into account changes in oil prices in our expectations of inflation and growth, and then draw conclusions about the evolution of the dollar. Above all, oil is just one of many.

Stock

Equities are microeconomic bonds, which rise and fall in response to the results and prospects of individual firms, while currencies are essentially macroeconomic bonds, fluctuating in response to broader economic and political developments. As such, there are few intuitive reasons for equity markets to be linked to currencies. Long-term correlation studies confirm this, with essentially zero correlation coefficients between major US pairs and US equity markets over the last five years.

The two markets sometimes intersect, although this usually occurs only at extremes and for very short periods. For example, when stock market volatility reaches extraordinary levels (for example, Standard & Poor's loses more than 2% in one day), the dollar may be subject to more pressure than otherwise - but there is no guarantee. The US stock market may have fallen into an unexpected rise in US interest rates, while the US dollar may rise with the surprise action.

Bond

Bond markets or fixed income have a more intuitive link with the foreign exchange market because both are strongly influenced by interest rate expectations. However, the dynamics of short-term market supply and demand disrupt most attempts to establish a viable link between the two markets in the short term. Sometimes, the foreign exchange market reacts first and faster, depending on the evolution of interest rate expectations. At most times, the bond market more accurately shows changes in interest rate expectations as the currency market bounces back later.

Overall, as currency traders, you should definitely keep an eye on the benchmark returns of major currency countries to better track the expectations of the interest rate market. Changes in interest rates (interest rate differentials) have a major influence on foreign exchange markets.

The forex market possesses its own set of trading conventions and the associated language, just like any financial market. If you are new to currency trading, mechanics and terminology may take a while to get used to. But in the end, most currency trading conventions are quite simple.

BUYING AND SELLING SIMULTANEOUSLY

The biggest mental barrier that newcomers face in currencies, especially those in many other markets, is that each transaction consists of a simultaneous purchase and sale. On the stock market, for example, if you buy 100 shares of Google, you have 100, and you expect to see the price increase. When you want to get out of this position, you are simply selling what you bought previously. Easy no?

But in currencies, the purchase of currency involves the simultaneous sale of another currency. This is the exchange of foreign currency. Succinctly put, if you are looking for a rise in the dollar, the question is "bigger against what?"

The answer is another motto. In relative terms, if the dollar appreciates against another currency, this other currency will also fall against the dollar. If you think about it in stock market terms, when you buy a stock, you sell money, and when you sell a stock, you buy money.

CURRENCIES COME IN PAIRS

To make matters easier, the exchange markets refer to currencies traded in pairs, with names that combine the two different currencies exchanged or "traded" against each other.

In addition, the currency markets have given nicknames or abbreviations to most currency pairs, which refer to the pair and not necessarily to the different currencies involved.

Major currency pairs

The main currency pairs involve the US dollar on one side of the business. The main currency denominations are expressed using the International Organization for Standardization (ISO) codes for each currency. Table 2-1 lists the most traded currency pairs, what they are called in conventional terms, and what nicknames gave them the market.

Table 2-1	The Major U.S. Dollar Currency Pa		
ISO Currency Pair	**Countries**	**Long Name**	
EUR/USD	Eurozone*/U.S.	Euro-dollar	N
USD/JPY	U.S./Japan	Dollar-yen	N
GBP/USD	United Kingdom/U.S.	Sterling-dollar	S
USD/CHF	U.S./Switzerland	Dollar-Swiss	S
USD/CAD	U.S./Canada	Dollar-Canada	L
AUD/USD	Australia/U.S.	Australian-dollar	A
NZD/USD	New Zealand/U.S.	New Zealand-dollar	

The Eurozone is made up of all the countries in the European Union that adopted the euro as their currency.

Major cross-currency pairs

While the vast majority of currency trading takes place in pairs of dollars, cross-currency pairs serve as an alternative to always trading the US dollar. A cross-currency pair, or *cross* or *cross* for short, is a currency pair that does not include the US dollar. Crossed rates are derived from the respective dollar pairs, but are quoted independently.

Crosses allow traders to direct trades more directly to specific individual currencies to make the most of events and news.

For instance, your analysis may propose that the Japanese yen has the worst outlook for all current major currencies, based on interest rates or economic prospects. To take advantage of it, you want to sell JPY, but against what another motto? You are considering the USD, potentially buying USD / JPY (buying USD / selling JPY), but then concluding that the USD outlook is not much better than JPY. Future research from you could point to another currency with much better prospects (such as high or rising interest rates or signs of strengthening the economy), says the Australian dollar (AUD). In this example, you would try to buy the AUD / JPY cross for your opinion that AUD has the best prospects between the major currencies and the worst JPY.

The most vigorously traded crosses focus on the three major currencies other than the USD (i.e., EUR, JPY, and GBP) and are called Euro Crosses, Yen Crosses, and Sterling Crosses. Table 2-2 presents the most actively traded cross currency pairs.

Table 2-2	Most Actively Traded Cross Pairs	
ISO Currency Pair	Countries	Market N
EUR/CHF	Eurozone/Switzerland	Euro-Swis
EUR/GBP	Eurozone/United Kingdom	Euro-sterl
EUR/JPY	Eurozone/Japan	Euro-yen
GBP/JPY	United Kingdom/Japan	Sterling-y
AUD/JPY	Australia/Japan	Aussie-ye
NZD/JPY	New Zealand/Japan	Kiwi-yen

THE LONG AND THE SHORT OF IT

Foreign exchange markets make use of the same terms to express the market positioning of most other financial markets. But as currency trading involves simultaneous buying and selling, clarity of terms helps - especially if you are completely new to the financial market.

Going long

No, we are not talking about running away for a football pass. A long position, or simply a long position, refers to a position in the market in which you purchased security. In foreign currency means the purchase of a currency pair. When you buy, you are looking for higher prices in order to sell at a higher price than what you purchase. When you decide to close a long position, you have to sell what you bought. If you shop at different price levels, you increase the lengths, and you get longer.

Getting short

A short, or simply a short position, refers to a position in the market in which you sold a stock you never owned. On the stock market, selling short stocks requires you to borrow stock (and pay a fee to the loan broker) before you can sell it. In the currency markets, this means that you have sold a currency pair, which means that you sold the base currency and bought the counter currency. You make so always an exchange, only in reverse order and according to the listing requirements of the currency pair. When you trade a currency pair, it's called a short sale or a short sale, and that means you're looking for the price of the pair to go down so you can buy it in a profitable way. If you sell at different price levels, you add shorts, and you shorten.

In currency trading, shorts are as common in the long run. "Sell high and buy low" is a standard currency trading strategy.

Currency pair rates show relative values between two currencies, not the absolute price of a single stock or commodity. Since currencies can fall or increase in relation to each other in medium and long-term trends and minute-by-minute fluctuations, currency pair prices are likely to fall at any time. To take advantage of these movements, foreign investors often use short positions to exploit the fall in currency prices. Traders in other markets may feel ill at ease with the sales out, but it is something you must understand.

Squaring up

To have no position in the market is called a square or a flat. If you have an open position and want to close it, it's called square. If you are small, you must buy to make a square. If you are long, you will have to sell to stay stable. The only time you have no exposure to the market or financial risk is when you are up to date.

PROFITS AND LOSSES

Profit and Loss (P & L) is the way traders measure failure and success. A clear understanding of how Profit & Loss works are particularly critical for online margin trading, where your Profit & Loss directly affects the amount of margin you need to work with. Changes to your margin balance determine how much you can trade and how much time you can trade if prices change against you.

MARGIN BALANCES AND LIQUIDATIONS

When opening an online currency trading account, you will have to pay money as collateral to meet the margin requirements set by your dealer. This initial margin deposit becomes your opening margin balance and is the basis on which all your subsequent transactions are guaranteed. Unlike futures markets or margin-based stock trading, online forex brokers do not issue margin calls (requests for additional collateral to support open positions). Instead, they establish margin balance indices for open positions that must be upheld at all times.

Here's an instance to help you understand how the required margin indices work. Suppose you have an account with a leverage ratio of 100: 1 (so that a $ 1 margin in your own account can control a $ 100 position size), but your broker requires a 100% margin rate, which means you have to maintain 100% of the required margin at any time. The ratio varies depending on the size of the account, but a 100% margin requirement is typical for small accounts. This means that to have a $ 10,000 position size, you will need $ 100 in your account because when you divide $ 10,000 by the leverage ratio of $ 100 is $ 100. If your account margin falls below the required rate, your broker is probably entitled to terminate your positions without notice. If your broker liquidates your position, it usually means that your losses are blocked, and your margin balance has become smaller.

Make sure you understand your broker's margin requirements and settlement policies. The requirements may differ depending on the size of the account and whether you are negotiating mini lot sizes (10,000 units) or standard lot sizes (100,000 currency units). Some broker settlement policies allow you to liquidate all positions if you do not meet the margin requirements. Others close the most significant losses or parts of losses until the required proportion is satisfied again. You can find the details in the small print of the account opening contract that you sign. Always went through the fine print to ensure you understand the margins and trade policies of your broker.

UNREALIZED AND REALIZED PROFIT AND LOSS

Most online forex brokers provide real-time valuation calculations showing your margin balance. Mark-to-market is the calculation that shows unrealized results based on where you can close your open positions in the market at that time. Depending on your broker's market platform, if you are long, the calculation will usually be based on where you could sell at that time. If you are small, the price used will be the one where you can buy at that time. Your margin balance is the total sum of your unrealized profit, your initial margin deposit, and your realized profit.

The realized P & L is what you get when you close a trade position or part of a trade position. If you close the full position and become stable, everything you have done or lost will disappear from the unrealized profit calculation and will enter your margin balance. If you close only a portion of your open positions, only this portion of the trading result is realized and enters the margin balance. Your unrealized profit continues to fluctuate based on the remaining open positions, as well as the balance of the total margin.

If you have an open winning position, your unrealized profit is positive, and your margin balance increases. If the market changes relative to your positions, your unrealized result is negative, and your margin balance is reduced. Forex prices change constantly, so the result of your mark-to-market and the balance of the total margin also change constantly.

Calculation of profit and loss with pips

Profit and loss calculations are quite simple in terms of mathematics - all based on the size of the position and the number of pips you make or lose. A pip is the smallest increase in currency price fluctuations . The glitches can also be called points; we use both terms interchangeably.

Examining certain currency pairs helps you get an idea of what a pip is. Most currency pairs are quoted by making use of five digits. The appointment of the decimal point depends on whether it is a JPY currency pair; In this case, there are two digits behind the decimal point. All other currency pairs have four digits behind the decimal point. In all cases, this last figure is the pip.

Here are some of the main currency pairs and crosses, with the pip underlined:

EUR / USD: 1.2853

USD / CHF: 1.2267

USD / JPY: 117.23

EUR / JPY: 150.65

Focus first on the EUR / USD price. Looking at EUR / USD, if the price went from 1.2885 to 1.2873, it went up 20 pips. If it goes from 1.2853 to 1.2792, it drops by 61 pips. The glitches make it easy to calculate the results. To turn this pip movement into a profit and loss calculation, all you need to know is the size of the position. For a position of 100 000 EUR / USD, the movement of 20 pip equals $ 200 (100,000 EUR × 0.0020 = 200 $). For a position of 50,000 EUR / USD, the 61-point movement translates to $ 305 (50,000 EUR × 0.0061 = $ 305).

Whether the values are negative or positive depends on whether you were long or short for each movement. If you were small for the highest blow, it's a - in front of $ 200, if you were long, it was a +. EUR / USD is not difficult to calculate, especially for USD-based traders, because the result is accumulated in US dollars.

If you use USD / CHF, you will need to do another calculation before understanding the meaning. Indeed, the result will be denominated in Swiss francs (CHF), because CHF is the counter-currency. If the USD / CHF goes from 1.22267 to 1.2233 and you have less than $ 100,000 for the lowest movement, you just get a 34-pips drop. This is a profit of CHF 340 ($ 100,000 × 0.0034 = CHF 340). Yes, but how much does it represent in real money? To convert to USD, you must divide CHF 340 by the USD / CHF rate. Use the closing rate of transactions

(1.2233) because that's the position of the market the last time, and you get $ 277.94.

Even the venerable pip is being updated as e-commerce continues to grow. A few paragraphs ago, we say that pip is the smallest increase in currency price fluctuations. Not so fast. The online market is growing rapidly to decimal pips (trading at 1/10 pips), and half-pip prices have been the norm in some inter-bank currency pairs for many years.

Factoring profit and loss on margin calculations

The great news is that online FX trading platforms automatically calculate the outcome for you, both unrealized when trading is open and when trading is closed. So why did we just drag it through a mathematical calculation of results using pips? As online brokers, do not start calculating your result for you until after you complete a transaction.

To structure your trading and effectively manage your risk (what is the size of a position, what is the margin of risk?), You will have to calculate your P & L results before entering the trade.

Understanding the P & L implications of a trading strategy you are considering is essential to maintaining your margin balance and keeping control of your transactions. This simple exercise can help you avoid costly mistakes, such as making very large transactions or placing stop-loss orders beyond price when your account falls below the margin requirement. At a minimum, you must calculate the price at which your position will be settled when your margin balance falls below the required rate.

UNDERSTANDING ROLLOVERS AND INTEREST RATES

An exclusive market convention for foreign currencies scrolls. A rollover is a transaction in which an open position from a value date (settlement date) is postponed to the next value date. Rollovers represent the intersection of interest rate and currency markets.

After all, the currency is money.

The turnover rates are based on the difference in interest rates of the two currencies of the pair you are trading. This is because what you really exchange is good old-fashioned money. When you have a long currency, it's like having a bank deposit. If you have a short currency, it's like borrowing a loan. Just as you expect to earn interest on a bank deposit or pay interest on a loan, you should expect a gain / interest charge to maintain a foreign currency position on the change in value.

Consider an open currency position as an account with a positive balance (the currency you buy) and one with a -ve balance (the currency you buy). However, as your accounts are in two different currencies, the two interest rates for different countries apply.

The difference between interest rates in both countries is called the interest rate differential. The higher the interest rate differential, the greater the impact of bearings. The narrower the interest rate spread, the lower the effect of rollovers. You can find the relevant interest rate levels of major currencies on a number of financial markets sites. Look for basic or reference loan rates in each country.

Application of rollovers

Rollover transactions are usually done automatically by your forex broker if you hold an open position after the date of the change in value.

Overlaps are applied to your open position by two clearing operations that result in the same open position. Some online forex brokers apply scroll rates by adjusting the average rate of your open position. Other forex brokers apply turnover rates by applying the credit or debit roll directly to your margin balance.

Understanding currency rates

Here we look at how online brokers display currency prices and what they mean for trading and order execution. Remember that different online forex brokers use different formats to display prices on their trading platforms.

Offers and Bids

When you are in front of the screen, and you are looking at the trading platform of an online forex broker, you will see two prices for each currency pair. The price on the left is called the offer, and the right price is called the offer (some call it asking). The bid is the cost at which you can trade the base currency. The "offer" is the cost at which you can buy the base currency.

Some brokers display prices on top of each other, with supply down and supply up. The simplest way to know the difference is that the offer price is always lower than the offer price.

The listing of each offer and offer you see will have two components: the overview and the trading price. The large figure refers to the first three digits of the overall exchange rate and is usually displayed in a smaller font size or even in the shadow. The negotiated price refers to the last two digits of the price of the general currency and is brilliantly displayed in larger font size.

Spreads

A difference is a difference between the bid price and the bid price. Most online forex brokers use spread-based trading platforms for individual traders. Look at the gap as the compensation that the broker receives to be the market maker and perform his trade.

The spreads vary from one broker to another and in currency pairs in each broker as well. As a general rule, the more liquid the currency pair, the smaller the spread; The less the currency pair is liquid, the larger the gap. This is particularly the case for some of the less traded passages.

CHAPTER THREE - HOW TO DEVELOP A PROFITABLE FOREX TRADING MINDSET

It is an inevitable reality that your success or failure in forex trading will largely depend on your state of mind. In other words, if your psychology of Forex trading is not correct, you will not earn money! Unfortunately, most dealers ignore this important fact or do not know how important it is to have an appropriate mindset for the success of Forex trading. If you do not have the right trading mentality, whatever the quality of your trading strategy, because no strategy will ever make cash if it is used by a professional with bad psychology.

Note: I would like to know how you plan to use the points discussed here to improve your Forex trading mindset. Leave me your comments and comments below after reading today's lesson!

Many people seem to be unaware that they are negotiating with a state of mind that stops them from making money in the markets. Instead, they think that if they find the right system or indicator, they will magically start printing money on their computers. Success in business is the end result of developing good business habits, and habits are the end result of good business psychology. Today's lesson will give you the information you need to develop a profitable business mindset; So read this lesson carefully and do not ignore it, because I promise you that the reason you are having problems in the markets is that your mindset works against you rather than for you.

Step 1: You must have realistic expectations

The first thing you must do to develop the right Forex trading mentality is to have realistic expectations of trading. I mean this; Do not think that you will leave your job and start earning $ 1 million a year after two months of live trading with your $ 5,000 account. It doesn't work this way, and the sooner you base your expectations, the sooner you start making money consistently. You must accept that you can not negotiate and leverage the path to business success. If you do both, you can make money fast, but you will soon lose everything and more. Accept the reality of the money you have on your trading account and the amount you are willing to lose by trading. Here are some other things to consider:

• **Trade only with disposable risk capital** - The **capital** disposable is money you do not need for your living expenses, including retirement and other long-term things. If you do not have capital available or risky, keep doing demos until you have, or stop trading together, but whatever you do, do not trade with money because you will be delighted of the loss. Always assume that you can lose the money you have on your account or in a trade ... if you really agree with that, then you should go, just make sure not to lie to you ... REALLY OK, Exchanging "scared" money (money you can not afford to lose) will cause intense emotional pressure and loss.

• **Make sure you can always sleep at night** - This is related to the point above about available capital. But the major difference is that you must ask EVERY transaction, whether you are 100% neutral or OK, with the possibility of losing the money you are about to risk. If you can not sleep at night because you think about your business, you risk doing too much. No one can dictate how much you risk in trading; it depends on how comfortable you are personally. If you trade 4 times per month, you can obviously risk a little more per transaction than someone who deals 30 times a month ... it's about your trading frequency, your skills as a trader, and your tolerance for personal risk.

• **Understand that each transaction is independent of the previous one** - This is important because I know that many traders are overly influenced by their previous trades. The fact is that your last company has absolutely nothing to do with your next business. You must avoid becoming euphoric or overconfident after a winning or vengeful negotiation after a lost negotiation. The fact is that every time you trade, this should only be considered as a new execution of your trading margin; If you only had three consecutive winners, avoid risking more than usual in your next exchange, simply because you feel very confident and avoid returning to the market immediately after a lost exchange, just to try What You Lost. When you do these things, you operate 100% with emotions rather than logic and objectivity.

• **Do not get too focused on your trades** - If you follow the three points we've just discussed, it's unlikely that you'll focus too much on your business. Do not take trades in person; it's not because you lose in a few trades in a row that you're bad at trading, even if you win in three trades in a row, it does not mean you're a negotiator "God" safe from losing. If you do not risk a lot by negotiating and do not trade with the money you require for other things in your life, you are probably not very attached to your business.

Step 2: Understand the power of patience

I think one of the biggest achievements that allowed me to turn my own operations is that I did not have to trade a lot to get a decent monthly return. Think about it; most people consider an annual return of 6% is very good for an account of savings, and if you value your retirement fund to 12% per year, you are very happy. So, why do most traders expect 100% per month or some other unrealistic return? What is the problem of winning 5 or 10% per month? It's still exceptional over a year. Although I can not suggest that you make a certain percentage per month, if you understand that slower and more consistent profits are the path to long-term market success, you will be much better at the end of each year. negotiation. Here are some other things to consider about patience:

• **Learn how to trade on daily charts first** - By learning to trade first on daily chart periods, you will naturally take a broader approach to markets and avoid the temptation to over-trade. the delays induce. Beginning traders must especially slow down and learn to trade the daily charts first. Daily charts give the most practical and relevant view of the market. You do not have to trade every day to get a solid return every month.

45

• **Quality rather than quantity** - I consider myself a "sniper" on the market; I wait for days or even a week without negotiating when I see a price action parameter that triggers my alarm "it's obvious" ... I shoot the trigger with ZERO emotion. I am always ready to lose the money I risked in any profession because I negotiated that if I am 100% convinced that my room for negotiation on the price action is present.

Use Your Bullets Wisely - To truly harness the power of patience in developing the right business mindset, you need to understand that patience will instill you with positive business habits. Patience strengthens positive trading patterns, while emotional negotiation reinforces negative ones. Once you have begun to negotiate patiently, you will see how the judicious use of your "bullets" ... you just need a few good transactions a month to get a respectable return on the markets; Once you have it patiently, you will learn to appreciate NOT being in the markets ... because then you are "looking for prey." This contrasts with the frustrated and frustrated trader who stays up all night watching the graphics as a zombie who simply does not accept that he has to trade less often.

Step 3: Be ordered in your approach to the markets

You MUST have a business plan, a business journal, and you must plan the bulk of your stock market before you can enter. The more you plan before you register, the more likely you are to make money in the long run. You will ALWAYS interpret the market more precisely when you are not in business ... so planning everything increases your chances of making money because you work more on logic than on emotion.

• **Adopt a trading plan** - I know it can be boring, I know you might think you do not "need" to make one, but if you do not make a trading plan and you really use and adjust as you learn, you will start to negotiate in a disorganized and possibly emotional way. A business plan should not be a very dry and boring document; You can be creative with that. Your trading plan may be that you write your own weekly comment before the start of each week, plan what you will do and look for next week ... just make sure you have a "plan of attack" already before you begin all trading.

• **Keep a professional trading log** - You need a history, you have to record your transactions, you must do it in a forex trading journal. This is an essential element to forge the right Forex trading mentality as it provides a tangible document that you can view and instantly get rough feedback on the performance of your trading. Once you begin to keep a journal of your trades, it will become a habit, and you will not want to see any emotional results you look at in your corporate journal. Finally, you will see your trading diary as a work of art that proves your capability to trade with dignity as well as your capacity to follow your trading plan. This is something that any serious investor will want to see if he is considering trading other people's money.

• **Think before shooting, not after** - All the planning and pre-emption I just mentioned is akin to thinking before shooting. A weapon is a very powerful weapon, we all know we have to think before we shoot, even if we just hunt or shoot at close range. Similarly, markets can be very powerful "weapons" to win or lose money. So, you want to think as much as possible before starting a job, because once you enter, you will naturally become more emotional and will not want to be able to conclude pitiful transactions constantly. If you plan your actions before joining, you should not regret your operations, even when you lose trades. I never regret the exchanges I receive because I only negotiate if my advantage is present, and I am always comfortable with the amount of money I have risked in any transaction.

Step 4: Do not have doubts about your business advantage

Finally, do not start trading for real money if you do not know how to trade your advantage. Obviously, you will not develop the appropriate trading mindset if you enter the trading of an active account without being 100% sure of what you are looking for. Whatever your benefit, make sure you can redeem it on a demo account for at least three months or more before uploading it. Not just "dive " without feeling completely comfortable with your approach ... that's what most traders do, and most of them also lose money.

• **Have 100% confidence in your advantage** - I have 100% confidence in my price action trading strategies ... that does not mean I'm fool enough to believe that ALL trades will win, but I am completely confident that every time I negotiate my advantage is really present. I do not compromise my business advantage by making settings that seem "almost" good enough ... I just do not work in this case. I take only the price action patterns that I feel in my instincts as valid high-probability representations of my benefit. Therefore, I am never afraid or worried about the negotiations I enter, even if I lose.

• **Do not gamble** - There are skilled traders and people who play in the markets. If you take a calculated and calm approach to your trading and wait patiently for your trading margin to appear as a sniper, then you are a skilled trader. If you "run and shoot" and deviate from your trading plan, you are a player. So, are you a Foreign exchange trader or a player?

• **Price action trading helps develop an appropriate trading mindset** - My benefit is price action, and I am convinced that the simplicity of price share trading has helped me develop and maintain a mindset of proper Forex trading. We do not need tons of confusing indicators on our charts, and we do not need Forex trading robots or other expensive software. All we need is the raw action of market prices and our magnificent human spirit to interpret it; it is up to us to exploit this power.

The action on market prices gives us a map to follow, and of course, if we can ignore the emotional temptations that pop up in our minds, we will have no problem taking advantage of this price action card. I believe that today's lesson has provided some tips on how to develop the right mindset, ignore the emotions, and ditch the habits that destroy the success of your business.

CHAPTER FOUR – GETTING STARTED WITH YOUR PRACTICE ACCOUNT

The best way for beginners to understand currency trading is to open a practice account.

Almost all forex brokers offer a free practice account to potential customers; Simply register on the broker's website. The practice accounts are funded with "virtual" money, so you can do real money trading and gain experience with how margin trading works.

Practice Accounts give you an excellent opportunity to experience the Foreign exchange market. You can see how prices fluctuate at different times of the day, how different currency pairs may differ, and how the forex market reacts to new information when big news and economic data are released. You can also start trading in real market conditions without fear of losing money, trying different trading strategies to see how they work, acquire experience using different orders and manage open positions, improve your understanding of how trading and margin leverage. work and start by analyzing the graphs and following the technical indicators.

Practice accounts are a great way to get to know the Forex market closely and in person. They are also a great way to test all the features and functionality of a broker's platform. However, the only thing you can not simulate is the pleasure of managing real money. To get the most out of your practice account experience, treat your practice account as if it were real money.

PULLING THE TRIGGER

It's time to pull the trigger, buddy. This section assumes that you have registered for a practice account with an online forex broker and that you are ready to start some hands-on operations.

You trade on the foreign exchange market in two ways: you can trade *on the market* or at the current price using the click and auction function of your broker's platform, or you can use commands such as limited commands and commands with another cancellation (OCO).

CLICKING AND DEALING

Most traders like the idea of opening a trading position rather than leaving an order that may or may not be executed. They prefer to make sure they are on the market. Active buying and selling are also elements that make trading and speculation as fun as hard.

Most foreign exchange brokers provide live streaming prices that you can manage with a single click of your computer mouse. To trade on these platforms:

- **Specify the amount of trade you want to perform.**
- **Click the Buy or Sell button to carry out the operation.**

The forex trading platform responds, usually in one or two seconds, to let you know if the transaction has succeeded:

If the transaction is complete, you will receive a contextual confirmation of the platform, and your open list will be updated to reflect the new transaction.

If trading fails because the trading price has changed before receiving your request, you will receive a response stating "changed rates," "unavailable price," or something in that sense. You must repeat the steps to make a new trading attempt.

Sometimes attempts to trade on the market may fail in rapidly changing markets when prices adjust rapidly, for example, after the publication of data or the violation of a relevant technical level or price. Part of this stems from the *effect* of *the latency* Internet commerce, which refers to the delay in time between the price of the flat - form that comes to your computer and your trade request to the flat - form server.

If trading fails because trading was too much, depending on your margin, you will have to reduce the size of the trade.

Understand from the start that any action you take on a trading platform is your responsibility. You may want to click Buy instead of Sell, but no one knows for sure, except you.

USING ORDERS

Orders are essential trading tools in the foreign exchange market. Think of them as a company waiting for realization, because that's exactly what they are. If you enter an order and a successive price action triggers its execution, you will be in the market, so be very careful when placing your orders on the market.

Currency traders use orders to capture market movements when they are not in front of their screens. **Don't Forget:** the foreign exchange market is open 24 hours a day, five days a week. A change in the market is likely to occur while you sleep or shower while watching the screen. If you are a part-time trader, you will probably have a full-time job that requires attention when you are at work. (At least, your boss *expects* to *what* it retains your attention.) The orders are the way you can act on the market without being. Experienced Forex traders also regularly use orders to:

- Implement a business strategy from entry to exit
- Capture sudden fluctuations in short-term prices
- Limit risk in volatile or uncertain markets
- Preserve the commercial capital of unwanted losses
- Maintain commercial discipline
- Protect profits and minimize losses

We can not emphasize enough the importance of order in currency trading. Foreign exchange markets can be notoriously volatile and difficult to predict. The use of orders makes it possible to capitalize on short-term market movements by limiting the impact of any unfavorable price movement. While there is no guarantee that using orders will limit your losses or protect your profits in all market conditions, disciplined use of orders helps to quantify the risk you are taking and, with a little luck, gives you peace of mind. your negotiation. Bottom Line: If you do not use orders, you probably do not have a well-thought-out trading strategy - and it's a painful recipe.

Types of Orders

Several types of orders are available on the foreign exchange market. Remember that not all order types are available from all online brokers; therefore, add order types to the questions to ask your potential forex broker.

Take-profit orders

Do not you just like that name? An old market saying says, "You can not fail to make a profit." Use *profit orders* to make gains when you have an open position in the market. If you have a short USD / JPY at 117.20, your profit order would be to buy back the position and be somewhere below that price, for example, 116.80. If you buy GBP / USD at 1.8840, your profit order will be to sell the position somewhere higher, maybe 1.8875.

Limit orders

Limit orders are orders that trigger the trade-in levels more favorable than the price
of the *current* market. Think about buying low, selling high. If the limit order is to purchase, it must be entered at a price lower than the current market price. If the limit order is sold, it must be placed at a price higher than the current market price.

Stop-Loss Orders

Boo! The sound is bad, right? In fact, stop-loss orders are essential to the survival of trading. The traditional *stop-loss order* does exactly that: it stops losses by closing an open position that loses money. Make use of stop-loss orders to limit your losses if the market moves against your position. Otherwise, you leave for the market, which is dangerous.

Stop-loss orders are on a different side of the current price of profit orders, but in a similar direction (in terms of buying or selling). If you go long, your stop-loss order will sell, but at a price lower than the current market price. If you are small, your stop-loss order will purchase but at a higher price than the present market.

Trailing stop-loss orders

You may have been told that one of the keys to successful trading is to reduce lost positions and let winning positions run quickly. A final stop-loss order lets you do just that. The logic is that when you have a winning job, you expect the market to reverse and withdraw, instead of trying to choose the right level to get out of it.

A stop-loss order is a stop-loss order that you set to a fixed number of pips from your entry rate. The last stop adjusts the order rate as the market price changes, *but only in the direction of your transaction.* For example, if you bought EUR / CHF at 1.5750 and set the mobile stop at 30 pips, the stop will initially be activated at 1.5720 (1.5750-30 pips).

If the EUR / CHF price rises to 1.5760, the stop adjusts higher pip by pip with the price and is active on

1.5730. The trailing stop continues to adjust as the market continues to grow. When the market reaches the top, your last stop will be 30 pips (or the distance you specify) below that peak, wherever you are.

If the market drops by 30 pips, as in this example, your stop will be triggered, and your position will close. Therefore , in this case, if you have a time of 1.5750 and set a mobile stop of 30 pip, the shutdown becomes initially active at 1.5720. If the market never goes up and down, you will be stopped at

1.5720. If the price goes up first to 1.5775 then decreases by 60 points, your final stop will have increased to 1.5745 (1.5775-30 pips), and that's where you will be stopped. Very cool, no?

One-cancels-the-other orders

A *one-cancels-the-other order* (better known as the OCO order) is a stop-loss order associated with a profit order. An OCO claim is the definitive insurance policy for any open position. Your position remains open until one of the order levels is reached by the market and closes your position.

When one command level is reached and triggered, the other command is automatically canceled.

Say you have a short USD / JPY at 117.00. Do you think that if you go over 117.50, you will continue to increase, so that's where you wish to place your stop loss buy order? At the same time, you think the USD / JPY has a negative potential

116.25, this is where you set your purchase order cost-effectively. You now have two bracketing orders on the market, and your risk is clearly defined. As long as the market is trading between 116.26 and 117.49, its position will remain open. If 116.25 is reached first, your profit is triggered, and you redeem with profit. If 117.50 is reached first, your position will be interrupted.

OCO orders are strongly recommended for all open positions.

Contingent orders

A *contingent order* is a sophisticated term for combining different types of orders to create a comprehensive currency trading strategy. Use contingent orders to negotiate while you are asleep or sick, knowing that your contingent order has all the bases taken care of, and your risks are defined. Contingency commands are also called *if/then* commands. The if/then requests require that the request *if* one *makes* first and *then* the second part of the application becomes active; therefore, they are sometimes called *if done/then* requests .

The main feature of an order of most political brokers is that their orders are executed based on the *difference* in *prices* of the trading platform. This means that your limited purchase order is executed only if the offer price of the trading platform reaches your purchase rate. A sell limit order is triggered only if the bid price of the trading platform reaches its selling rate.

In practice, say you have a EUR / USD buy order at 1.2855, and the broker's EUR / USD spread is 3 pips. Your purchase order will only be filled if the price of the platform is 1.2852 / 55. If the least price is 1.2853 / 56, no cigar because the lowest offer of the broker of 56 has never reached its purchase rate of 55 The same goes for limited sales orders.

The stop loss execution policies are slightly different from those of stock trading.

Stop-loss orders for sale are triggered if the broker 's *bid* price reaches its stop-loss order rate. Specifically, if your stop-loss order is sold at 1.2820 and the broker's lowest price is 1.2820 / 23, your stop will get filled at 1.2820.

The stop-loss orders are triggered if the price of the *offer of* the platform reaches its stop-loss rate. If your stop order is at 1.2875 and the dealer's high rate is 1.2872 / 75, your stop will get filled at 1.2875.

The advantage of this practice is that some companies guarantee against the slippage of their stop-loss orders under normal commercial conditions. (Rarely, if ever, a broker will guarantee losses by publishing economic reports.) The disadvantage is that your order will likely be triggered earlier than orders with losses in other markets, so you'll need to add a little more cushion by placing them on your forex platform.

Managing the Trade

So, you pulled the trigger and the open position, and you are now on the market. It's time to relax and let the market do what's right, right? Not so fast, my friend. The forex market is not a roulette where you place your bets, watch the wheel spin, and simply get the results. It is a dynamic and fluid environment where new information and price developments create new opportunities and change previous expectations.

We hope you will deliberate on our recommendations to always negotiate with a plan - by identifying beforehand where to enter and where to exit all transactions based on stop loss and profit. Conclusion: You increase your overall chances of commercial success (and minimize the risks involved) by carefully planning each transaction before engaging with the emotions and noise of the market.

Depending on the trading style you are looking for (short term versus medium and long term) and general market conditions (range versus trend limit), you will have more or less to do when managing an open position. If you follow a medium and long-term strategy with generally broader stop-loss and profit-taking parameters, you may prefer to follow the established and forgotten business plan that you have developed. But many things can happen between the moment you open a transaction, and the prices reach one of your trading levels. Therefore, staying at the top of the market is always a good idea, even for long-term trading.

Monitor the market while your transaction is active

Whichever trading style you follow, it's worth keeping up with market news and price developments while your trading is active. Unexpected news affecting your position could hit the market at any time. The news is news; By definition, you could not have explained this in your trading plan, so new news may require changes in your trading plan.

When we are talking about carrying out changes on the market plan, we are simply referring to reducing the risk of global trading by making a profit (total or partial) or by moving the stop loss in the way of trading. The idea is to be dynamic and fluid in one way: to make a profit and to reduce risks. Keep your breakpoint where you decided to go before you enter the trade.

Stay tuned for news and data

If your business logic depends on certain data or event expectations, you should be particularly careful about future reports on these topics.

Part of its calculation of shortening the EUR / USD, for example, may be based on the idea that inflationary pressures in the euro area are retreating, suggesting a decline in interest rates in the euro area to come. If the ratio of the price index for consumption (CPI) for the euro area the next day confirms his view, the fundamental basis of maintaining the strategy will be strengthened. You can determine if you want to increase your profit target based on the market reaction. Similarly, if the CPI report comes out unexpectedly, the fundamental basis of its trade is seriously compromised and serves as a clue to exit trade earlier than expected.

Each trading strategy must take into account news and upcoming data events before opening the position. Ideally, you should be aware of any data reports and news events that must occur during the expected time horizon of your trading strategy. You must also have a good understanding of what the market expects in terms of event results to anticipate the likely market reaction.

Look at other financial markets

Forex markets operate alongside other major financial markets such as stocks, bonds, and commodities (e.g., gold, oil, etc.). There are important psychological and fundamental relationships (discussed in more detail in Chapter 1) between other markets and currencies, especially the US dollar, so look for developments in other financial markets to see if they confirm or contradict the price movements of the pairs of dollars.

Evaluate your trading results

Whatever the outcome of any negotiation, you want to review the whole process to understand what you have done right and wrong. In particular, ask yourself the following questions:

How did you identify the business opportunity? Was it based on fundamental analysis, a technical vision, or a combination of both? Looking at your business in this way helps you identify your strengths and weaknesses as a technical or fundamental trader. For instance, if technical analysis generates more of your winning trades, you will probably want to devote more energy to this approach.

How was your business plan? Was the size of the position sufficient to match the risk and reward scenarios, or was it too big or too small? Could you have reached a better level? What tools did you use to improve entry time? Have you been patient enough, or have you been quick to think that you have never had the opportunity again? Was your profit realistic or twisted in the sky? Has the market respected your choice of profit levels, or have prices reached this value? Ask the same questions about your stop loss level. Use the answers to refine the size of your position, entry-level, and order placement in the future.

How well did you carry out the trade after it opened? Have you been able to monitor the market while your transaction was active effectively? If yes, how? If not, why not? The solutions to these questions show volumes about the time and dedication you can devote to your trading. Have you changed your business plan along the way? Have you adjusted stop-loss orders to protect profits? Did you make a partial profit? Have you closed the deal based on your trading plan, or have you been surprised by the market? Based on your answers, you will learn what role your emotions can play and what a professional's discipline is.

There are no good and bad answers in this review process; be as honest with yourself as possible. No one else will know your answers, and you have everything to gain by identifying what you are good at, what is not so good, and how you, as a currency trader, should get closer to the market.

Currency trading is about getting what you put in it. Regularly evaluating your trading results is an essential step to improve your trading skills, refine your trading styles, maximize your trading strengths, and minimize your trading weaknesses.

Before getting involved in trading actively forex market, take a step back, and think about how you want to approach the market. There is much more to currency trading than it seems, and we believe that the trading style you pick is one of the most important determinants of the overall success of trading.

This chapter presents the main points to consider when defining your own approach to currency trading. We analyze the characteristics of some of the most commonly applied trading styles and discuss their concrete meaning. We also present the essential elements of developing and adhering to a business plan.

FINDING THE RIGHT TRADING STYLE FOR YOU

We are often questioned, "What is the best way to trade on the foreign exchange market?" This is a delicate question that seems to imply that there is a good and a bad way to trade currencies. Unfortunately, there is no easy answer. Better to say, there is no *model* answer - that applies to everyone.

The characteristics of forex trading have something to offer to all styles of trading (long term, medium-term, or short term) and the approach (technical, fundamental, or mixed). Therefore, in deciding the style or approach that best suits the currencies, the starting point is not the exchange market itself, but its individual situation and thinking.

REAL-WORLD AND LIFESTYLE CONSIDERATIONS

Before you begin to identify the style and approach to trading that's right for you, think carefully about the resources you have to support your trading. As in most of the efforts of life , when it comes to trading on the financial market, there are two main features that people seem never enough: time and money. Deciding how much each one you can spend on currency trading helps to establish how you are pursuing your trading goals.

If you are a full-time trader, you have a lot of time to devote to market analysis and trading in the market. But as currencies are traded nonstop, you must always know which trading session you are trading in and the daily peaks and valleys of activity and liquidity. (See Chapter 1 for specific session details.) Just because the market is always open does not mean it's always a perfect time to trade.

If you own a full-time job, your boss may not like to take the time to follow charts or economic data reports while you are at work. This implies that you will have to use your free time to do your market research. Be realistic in thinking about how much time you can regularly spend, taking into account family obligations and other personal circumstances.

As far as money is concerned, we can not emphasize enough that commercial capital must be venture capital, and you should never risk money that you can not afford to lose. The default definition of *venture capital* is money that, if lost, will not significantly affect your standard of living. Needless to say, borrowed money is not ventured capital - you should never use borrowed money for speculative transactions.

By determining the amount of venture capital you have for trading, you'll have a better idea of the size of the account you can trade and the size of the position you can manage. Most online trading platforms usually offer generous leverage ratios that let you control a larger position with less margin required. But it's not because they offer high leverage that you need to use it fully.

MAKING TIME FOR MARKET ANALYSIS

Calculating the amount of data and news that flows through the forex market on a daily basis can be really overwhelming. So, how can a trader track all the data and news?

The key is to develop an effective daily market analysis routine. Through the internet and online currency brokers, independent traders can access a variety of information.

TECHNICAL VERSUS FUNDAMENTAL ANALYSIS

Ask yourself on what basis will you make your business decisions - fundamental analysis or technical analysis?

The bottom line is the large pool of news and information that reflects the macroeconomic and political fortunes of countries whose currencies are traded. In most cases, when you hear someone talking about the fundamentals of a currency, it refers to economic fundamentals. Economic fundamentals are based on:

- Economic data reports
- Interest rate levels
- Monetary Policy
- International trade flows
- International investment flows

The *technical* term refers to *technical analysis,* a form of market analysis that typically involves graphical analysis, trend line analysis, and mathematical studies of price behavior, such as momentum or moving averages. to name a few.

We do not know many currency traders who do not follow any form of technical analysis in their trading. Even stereotypical marketers who practice anything are probably aware of the technical price levels identified by others. If you are a trader active in other financial markets, you have probably done a technical analysis or at least heard about it.

The followers of each discipline have always debated the approach that works best. Instead of taking sides, we suggest following an approach that combines the two disciplines. In our knowledge, macroeconomic factors such as relative growth rates, interest rates, and market sentiment determine the general direction of exchange rates. But currencies seldom move in a straight line, which means that there are many short-term price movements to take advantage of - and some of them may be important.

Technical analysis can provide insights into the path of major price changes, allowing traders to predict the scope and direction of future price changes more accurately. More importantly, technical analysis is the key to building a well-defined trading strategy. For instance, your fundamental analysis, data expectations, or simple instinct may lead you to conclude that the USD / JPY is down. But where exactly do you fail? Where do you make profits, and where do you reduce your losses? You can use technical analysis to refine the points of entry and exit of trading and decide if and where to add positions or reduce them.

Sometimes foreign markets seem to be more due to fundamental factors such as current economic data and comments from a central bank official. At that time, the foundations provide the catalysts for breaks and technical reversals. At other times, technical growth seems to be leading the charge - an interruption in trend line support can trigger long-term stop-loss sales and incorporate system models that are sold according to the interruption of support. Later economic reports may be against directional theft, but the data must be damaged - the media is finished, and the market is selling.

The market approach with a mix of fundamental and technical analysis increases your chances of detecting business opportunities and managing your business more effectively. You will also be better prepared to deal with markets that react alternatively to key technical developments or a combination of both.

DIFFERENT STROKES FOR DIFFERENT FOLKS

Once you have thought about the time and resources you can devote to currency trading and the approach you favor (technical, fundamental, or mixed), the next step is to choose the trading style that you want. is best. corresponds to these choices

There are as many trading styles and different market approaches to the foreign exchange market as there are individuals in the foreign exchange market. But most marketing styles can be grouped into three major categories that boil down to varying degrees of market risk exposure. The two major elements of trade risk are time and relative price movements. How much more you hold a position, the higher the risk is exposed. The more you anticipate a price change, the more you are exposed to risk.

In the following segments, we detail the three main trading styles and what they really mean for individual traders. Our goal here is not to advocate a particular trading style because styles often overlap, and you can adopt different styles for different business opportunities or different market conditions. Instead, our goal is to give an idea of the different approaches used by forex traders so that you can fully understand the basis of each style.

SHORT-TERM, HIGH-FREQUENCY DAY TRADING

Short-term currency trading is different from short-term trading in most other markets. Short-Term trading of stocks or commodities usually means holding a position for one day for at least several days. However, due to liquidity and low spreads of supply and supply in currencies, prices fluctuate constantly in small increments. Constant and fluid currency price action allows speculators to trade on a very short-term basis and only want to capture a few pips (explained in Chapter 2) in each transaction.

Short-term forex trading usually involves maintaining a position for a few seconds or minutes and rarely more than an hour. But the time factor is not the defining quality of short-term currency trading. Instead, pip fluctuations are important. Traders who follow a short-term trading style seek to profit by opening and closing positions multiple times after winning only a few pips, often as little as 1 or 2 pips.

In the interbank market, very short-term incoming and outgoing exchanges are called *jobbing the market;* Online currency traders call it *scalping*. (We use terms interchangeably.) Traders who follow this style should be among the fastest and most disciplined traders because they only want to capture a few pips in each trade. In terms of speed, quick response and instant decision-making are essential to succeed in the job market.

When it comes to discipline, stockbrokers must be absolutely cruel when they make profits and losses. If you only wish to make a few pips in each trade, you can not lose much more than a few pips in each trade.

Working on the market requires an intuitive understanding of the market. (Some practitioners call this *rhythm trading.*) Money changers do not care much about fundamentals. If you ask a scalper for his opinion on a specific currency pair, she is likely to respond to the "Looks *Bid* " or "Looks *Offered* " lines (that is, she feels buying or underlying sales in the market - but at that time). If you ask again a few minutes later, she can answer in the opposite direction.

Successful stockbrokers have absolutely no loyalty to one position. They would not care less if the currency pair went up or down. They are strictly focused on next glitches. Their position works for them, or they come out faster than you can blink. All they need is volatility and liquidity.

Retail traders are generally faced with discrepancies between offers and offers between 2 and 5 pips. While this makes the job a bit more difficult, it does not mean that you can not still engage in short-term negotiations - it simply means that you will need to adjust the risk parameters of the style. Instead of trying to make 1 to 2 pips in each transaction, you need to get a pip gain at least as big as the spread with which you trade in each currency pair. The other basic rules of only minimal losses and not staying in the same position for a long time still apply.

Here are some other essential guidelines to bear in mind when following a short-term trading strategy:

- **Only trade in the most liquid currency pairs such as EUR / USD, USD / JPY, EUR / GBP, EUR / JPY, and EUR / CHF.** The most liquid pairs have the narrowest trading spreads and the least sudden price jumps.
- **Only trade during peak periods of liquidity and market interest.** Constant liquidity and smooth market interest are essential for short-term trading strategies. Market liquidity is deeper in the course of the European session when the centers business in Asia and America north to overshadow European areas of time - about two in the morning to noon (the Eastern States - the US). Trading in other sessions may leave you with less predictable short-term price movements that you can take advantage of.
- **Concentrate your trading on one pair at a time.** If you plan to capture price movements from second to second or minute to minute, you need to focus fully on one pair at a time. This will also improve your perception of the pair if this pair is everything you look at.
- **You have predefined your default trading size, so you do not have to specify it in each transaction.**
- **Find a brokerage firm that offers clicks and transactions, so you do not experience delays or foreclosures.**
- **Modify your risk and reward expectations to reflect the trading spread of the currency pair you are trading.** With spreads of 2 to 5 pip on most major pairs, you will likely need to capture

3 to 10 pip per transaction to make up for losses if the market moves against you.

• **Avoid trading around dice throwing.** Taking a short-term position in a data publication is very risky because prices can skyrocket after launch, throwing a short-term strategy out of the water. Markets are also subject to rapid price adjustments between 15 and 30 minutes prior to the release of key data when closing orders are triggered. This can result in a rapid change of position, which may not be resolved before the data is released.

MEDIUM-TERM DIRECTIONAL TRADING

Medium-term positions are generally busy for periods ranging from minutes to hours, but usually not much more than a day. As with short-term trading, the main distinction of medium-term trading is not the opening time of the position, but the number of pips you seek / risk.

When short-term traders seek to take advantage of the routine noise of small price movements, almost disregarding the general direction of the market, medium-term transactions seek to gain the right direction and benefit from more favorable exchange rate movements. important.

Almost as many currency investors fall into the medium-term category (sometimes called *momentum trading* and *swing trading*) as in the short-term category. Medium-term trading needs many of the same skills as short-term trading, particularly with respect to entry / exit positions, but it also requires a broader perspective, a greater analysis effort, and a lot more patience.

Capturing intraday price movements for maximum effect

The benefit of medium-term trading is to determine where a currency pair is likely to move in the next hours or days and developing a trading strategy to exploit that vision. Medium-term traders usually follow one of the following general approaches, with plenty of room to combine strategies:

- **Trading a View:** Have a basic opinion about how a currency pair will likely evolve. The display operations are generally based on prevailing market themes, such as interest rate expectations or economic growth trends. Display traders must always be aware of technical levels as part of a global trading plan.
- **Trading the technical:** Base your market perspective on graphical models, trend lines, support and resistance levels, and momentum studies. Technical traders usually identify a trading opportunity in their charts, but they must always be aware of key events because they are the catalyst for many technical breaks.
- **Trading Events and Data:** Base your positions on the results of expected events, such as a rate decision from the central bank or a G7 meeting or individual data reports. Event / data traders usually

open positions well in advance and close them when the result is known.

• **Trading with the flow:** Trading based on the general direction of the market (trend) or on the main purchases and sales (flows). To trade with feed information, look for a broker that offers feedback on the market flow, such as the one found on FOREX.com *Forex Insider* (www.forex.com/forex_research.html). Flo w traders tend to be excluded from limited markets at short-term intervals and only enter when market movement is underway.

WHEN IS A TREND NOT A TREND?

When it's a trading range, a *range* or *market-related to* a *range* is a market that remains confined to a relatively narrow price range. In currency pairs, a short-term trading range (in the next few hours) may have a width of 20 to 50 pips, while a long-term trading range (in the next few days or weeks) may have a range of 20 to 50 pips. width from 200 to 400 pips.

Despite all the hype that trends have in various market publications, the reality is that most markets do not tend to be over a third of the time. The rest of the time, they jump at intervals, consolidate, and exchange laterally.

While mid-term traders seek to capture larger relative price movements - say, 50 to 100 pips or more - they also quickly realize smaller profits on the basis of short-term price behavior. For example, if a violation of a technical resistance level suggests a higher target price move of 80 pips toward the next resistance level, the medium-term trader will be more than happy to capture 70% to 80% of the next resistance level. Expected price movement. They will not stay in position in search of the exact price to reach.

LONG-TERM MACROECONOMIC TRADING

Long-term currency trading is generally reserved for hedge funds and other institutional types. Long-term currency trading may involve holding positions for weeks, months, and potentially years at a time. Holding positions over this period necessarily involves being exposed to significant short-term volatility that can quickly overwhelm margin trading accounts.

With appropriate risk management, individual margin traders can seek to capture long-term trends. The key is to maintain a small enough position relative to your margin balance to withstand the volatility of up to 5% or more.

CARRY TRADE STRATEGIES

A *carry trade* occurs when you buy a high yielding currency and sell a lower-yielding currency. The strategy profits in two ways:

- **Being long the highest yielding currency and short the lowest yielding currency, you can get the interest rate differential between**

the two currencies, called *carry*. If you have the opposite position - buy the smallest and the smallest - the interest rate differential is against you and is known as the *cost of shipping*.

• **Spot prices rise in the direction of the interest rate differential.** Currency pairs with large interest rate differentials tend to move in favor of the higher-yielding currency as long traders are rewarded, increasing buying interests, and short traders are penalized, reducing the interest of sale.

So, let me clarify: you may be thinking: all I have to do is buy the most profitable currency / sell the worst-performing currency, sit down, earn the carry, and to watch the spot price rise? What is the question?

The problem is that the negative volatility of spot prices can quickly erase any gain in the carry trade differential. The risk can be exacerbated by the over-positioning of the market in favor of the carry trade, which means that they carry trade has become so popular that everyone gets into it.

Carry trades generally work best in low volatility environments, for example, when the financial markets are relatively steady, and investors are forced to chase yield. Remember that carry trades need to have a significant differential in interest rates between the two currencies (usually over 2%) to make them attractive. And carry trade is certainly a long-term strategy because depending on when you enter, you can be caught in a downdraft that can take days or weeks to relax   before   the   trade   becomes   profitable again.

DEVELOPING A DISCIPLINED TRADING PLAN

Whatever trading style you decide to adopt, you need an organized trading plan, or it does not go very far. The difference between losing cash and making cash in the foreign exchange market can be as simple as trading without a plan or trading with it. A *trading plan* is a prepared approach to execute a trading strategy that you have developed based on your analysis and market outlook.

Here are the main elements of any business plan:

- **Determine the size of the position:** what is the size of your position for each trading strategy? The size of the position is half the equation to determine how much money is involved in each transaction.
- **Decide where to get into the position:** where exactly are you going to try to open the desired position? What happens if your entry-level is not reached?
- **Setting Stop Loss and Take Profit Levels:** Where exactly will you leave the position if it is a winning position (make a profit) and if it is a stop position? The stop-loss and take-profit levels are the second half of the equation that determines

how much money is involved in each
transaction.

That's it - just three simple components. But it's amazing
how many new and seasoned traders open positions
without ever thinking fully about their game plan. Of
course, there are several tricky points to consider when
developing a trading plan. But for the
moment, we just want to get back to the point where
negotiating without an organized plan is like flying a
plane blindfolded - you can take off, but how are you
going to land?

And regardless of how good your trading plan is, it will
not work if you do not follow it. Sometimes, emotions
arise and distract traders from their trading plans. Other
times, unexpected news or a price movement forces
traders to abandon their trading strategy halfway, or in
the middle of trading , as the case may be. Anyway, when
that happens, it's the same as never having a business
plan in the first place.

Developing a market plan and sticking to it are the two
main ingredients of *corporate discipline*. If we name the
trait that defines successful traders, it would not be
technical analysis skills, instinct, or aggression - although
they are all important. No, it would be a commercial
discipline. Traders who follow a disciplined approach are
those who survive year after year and cycle
aftermarket. They can even make mistakes more often
and continue to make money because they follow a
disciplined approach.

TAKING THE EMOTION OUT OF TRADING

If the key to fruitful trading is a disciplined tactic - developing a trading plan and making use of it - why is it so difficult for many traders to practice trading discipline? The answer is complex, but it usually comes down to a simple case of human emotions that takes them away. Do not underestimate the power of emotions to distract and disturb.

So, how do you get the thrill of trading? The answer is simple: you can not. As far as your heart beats and your synapses fly away, the emotions will flow. And, to be honest, the high emotional levels of business are one of the reasons people get attracted to it in the first place. There is no hurry to doing business successfully and withdrawing money from the market. So accept that you will experience quite intense emotions during the negotiation.

The long answer is that because you can not block emotions, the best you hope to achieve is to understand where the emotions come from, recognize them when they hit, and limit the impact on your negotiations. It's very easy to say, but bear in mind some of the following to keep your emotions under control:

> • **Concentrate on pips, not on dollars and cents.** Do not be distracted by the exact amount of money earned or lost in the exchange. Instead, focus on where the prices are and how they behave. The market has no idea how big your

business is and how much you win or lose, but you know where the present price is.

• **It's not about being wrong or right; It's about making money.** The market does not care whether you are right or wrong, and you should not either. The only real method used to measure a company's success is in dollars and cents.

• **You will lose in a reasonable number of transactions.** No operator is always right. Taking losses is as routine as making profits. You can always succeed over time with a solid risk management plan.

Technical and fundamental analysis are the two major areas of the FOREX market strategy, which is exactly the same as in the stock market. However, technical analysis is the most common strategy used by individual FOREX traders. Here is a brief summary of both forms of analysis and how they apply directly to forex trading:

FUNDAMENTAL ANALYSIS

If you have trouble evaluating a company, try to evaluate an entire country. Fundamental analysis of the foreign exchange market is often extremely difficult and is generally only used as a means of predicting long-term trends. However, it is essential to mention that some traders negotiate strictly in the short term in press releases. There are many different fundamental indicators of monetary values published at many different times. Here are some to help you get started:

- Non-agricultural payroll
- Purchasing Managers Index (PMI)
- Consumer Price Index (CPI)
- Retail sales
- Durable goods

You should know that these reports are not the only fundamental factors to note. There are also a variety of meetings where you can get quotes and comments that can affect the markets as much as any report. These meetings are often held to discuss interest rates, inflation, and other issues that may affect the value of currencies.

Even changes in the way things are formulated to solve certain problems, such as the comments of the Chairman of the Federal Reserve on interest rates, can cause a volatile market. Two vital meetings to note are the Federal Open Market Committee and the Humphrey Hawkins Hearings.

By reading the reports and reviewing the comments, you can help FOREX's fundamental analysts better understand all the long-term market trends and also allow short-term traders to take advantage of extraordinary events. If you decide to follow a key strategy, always keep an economic calendar at hand to know when these reports will be published. Your broker may also provide you with real-time access to this type of information.

TECHNICAL ANALYSIS

Like their counterparts in the stock markets, FOREX technical analysts analyze price trends. The only major difference between technical analysis in FOREX and technical analysis in stocks is the period involved in the 24-hour FOREX markets.

For this reason, some time-sensitive forms of technical analysis need to be modified to work with the 24-hour FOREX market. Some of the major forms of technical analysis used in FOREX are:

- Elliott's waves
- Fibonacci studies
- Parabolic SAR
- Pivot points

Many technical analysts tend to combine technical studies to make more accurate predictions on their behalf. (The most common technique for them is merging the Fibonacci studies with Elliott Waves.) Others prefer to set up the systems negotiation in order to locate repeatedly conditions of purchase and sale of similar. Using a profitable trading system with a demo account for a few weeks is a great way to get an accurate "feel" of Forex trading - without risking your own money!

BEST FOREX TRADING STRATEGIES THAT WORK

You may have been told that maintaining your discipline is an essential aspect of trading. While this is true, how can you make sure that you apply this discipline during a negotiation? One way to help is to possess a trading strategy that you can follow. If it is well-founded and retested, you can be sure that you are using one of the successful Forex trading strategies. This trust will allow you to follow the rules of your strategy more easily - so maintain your discipline.

Often, when people talk about Forex strategies, they talk about a specific trading technique that is usually just one facet of a whole trading plan. A consistent Forex trading strategy gives beneficial input signals, but it is also essential to consider:

- Position sizing
- Risk management
- How to exit a trade

CHOOSING THE BEST FOREX AND CFD STRATEGY FOR YOU IN 2021

When it comes to clarifying what the most profitable and best forex trading strategy is, there is really no single answer. Here's why. The best exchange strategies will be adapted to the individual. This means that you have to consider your personality and find the best Forex strategy for you. What can work for someone else can be a disaster for you.

On the other hand, a strategy that has been ignored by others may be right for you. Therefore, it may be necessary to experiment to discover the Forex trading strategies that work. Conversely, it can remove those that do not work for you. One of the major factors to consider is a delay in your trading style.

There are different types of trading styles (as discussed in the previous chapter), short-term, and these have been widely used in previous years and still remain a popular option on the list of best trading strategies Forex on the market. 2021. The best forex traders are always aware of the different styles and strategies in their quest to know how to trade forex successfully so they can pick the right one based on current market conditions.

50-Pips a Day Forex Strategy

This strategy is based on the initial market movements of certain highly liquid currency pairs. The GBPUSD and EURUSD currency pairs are among the best currencies to trade using this particular strategy. After the candlestick closes at 7:00 GMT, traders place two opposing positions or two orders on hold. When one of them is activated by the price movements, the other position is automatically canceled.

The profit target is placed at 50 pips, while the stop-loss order is placed between 5 and 10 pips above or below the candlestick at 7:00 GMT after its formation. This is implemented to manage the risks. Once these conditions are set, it is now up to the market to take over. Day trading and scalping are short-term trading strategies. However, keep in mind that shorter time frames imply a higher risk; Therefore, effective risk management is essential.

Forex Daily Charts Strategy

The best forex traders swear on daily charts of shorter-term strategies. Compared to the one-hour forex trading strategy or even shorter deadlines, there is less market noise involved in daily charts. These charts can provide more than 100 pips a day because of their long run, which can result in some of the best forex deals.

Trading signals are more reliable, and the profit potential is much higher. The trader also doesn't need to worry about daily needs and random price fluctuations. The method is based on three main principles:

- Spot the trend: Markets tend to consolidate, and this process is repeated in cycles. The first feature of this style is to find prolonged movements in the currency markets. One way to identify forex trends is to study 180 periods in forex data. Identifying the ups and downs of the balance sheet will be the next step. By referencing these price data on the current charts, you can identify the direction of the market.
- Stay focused: it requires patience, and you will have to get rid of the desire to enter the market immediately. You must stay away and preserve your capital for a greater opportunity.
- Less leverage and more downtime: be aware of the large intraday market fluctuations. However, using larger stops does not mean endangering large amounts of capital.

Although there are many trading strategies guides available for professional forex traders, the best Forex strategy for consistent earnings can only be obtained through in-depth practice. Here are some other strategies you can try:

Forex 1-Hour Trading Strategy

You can take advantage of the 60-minute delay in this strategy. The greatest currency pairs to trade using this strategy are EUR / USD, USD / JPY, GBP / USD, and AUD / USD. You would need a 100pip moment indicator and indicator arrows, both available in MetaTrader 4.

Rules of buy trade:

You can enter a long position once both conditions are met:

- The Momentum 100 pips indicator triggers a buy signal when its blue line crosses the red line below
- The indicator arrow emits a green arrow signal

In this case, you can place the stop loss under the red indicator line or the most recent support line. You can close trading after 30 pips or make a profit when the indicator arrows emit a red arrow signal.

Rules of Sell Trade:

You may enter a short position once the following conditions are true:

- The Momentum 100 pips indicator triggers a sell signal when its blue line crosses the red line above
- Indicator arrows emit a red arrow signal

Place the stop loss above the red indicator line or the most recent resistance line. Close trading after 30 points, or when the indicator arrows give a green arrow signal.

Forex weekly trading strategy

While many forex traders prefer intraday trading, as market volatility offers more profit opportunities in the shorter term, weekly forex trading strategies can offer more flexibility and stability. A weekly candlestick provides complete information on the market. It contains five daily candles and changes that reflect the actual market trends. The weekly forex trading strategies are based on lower position sizes and avoid excessive risk.

For this strategy, we will make use of the exponential moving average (EMA) indicator. The last daily candlestick of the previous week should close at a level above the EMA value. Now, we have to search for the moment when the high level of the previous week was broken. Then a buy stop order is placed in the H4 closed candlestick at the broken level price level.

The stop loss should be put at the nearest minimum point, between 50 and 105 pips. The previous extreme value is used for calculations if the nearest minimum point is closer to 50 pips. Here, last week's range of motion is considered the profit range.

The role of stock price trading in Forex strategies

The extent to which fundamentals are used varies from trader to trader. At the same time, the best strategy invariably utilizes action. This also is known as technical analysis. As far as technical currency trading strategies are concerned, there are two main styles: tracking trends and counter-trend trading. Both currency trading strategies attempt to profit by recognizing and exploiting price models.

In terms of price models, the most important concepts include concepts such as support and resistance. In simple terms, these terms represent a market's tendency to recover from previous highs and lows. Support is the market trend to increase from a previously established minimum level. Resistance is the ability of the market to fall from a previously established high. Indeed, market players tend to judge subsequent prices against recent lows and highs.

What transpires when the market is approaching recent lows? In other words, buyers will be attracted by what they consider cheap. What happens when the trade approaches recent highs? Sellers will be attracted by what they consider to be expensive or a good place to make a profit. As a result, recent ups and downs are the criteria by which current prices are valued.

There is also a self-fulfilling aspect of the support and resistance levels. Indeed, market players anticipate some price action at these points and act accordingly. Therefore, their actions can contribute to market behavior as expected.

However, these three things should be noted:

- Support and resistance levels do not have strict rules; they are simply a common consequence of the natural behavior of market players.
- Trend tracking systems aim to take advantage of times when levels of support and resistance are deteriorating.
- Counter-trend trading styles are the opposite of trend tracking - they are meant to sell when there is a new higher and buy when there is a new low.

Trend-Following Forex Strategies

Sometimes a market comes out of the beach, moving under the rack or over the resistance to start a trend. How does this happen? As support breaks and the market moves to new lows, buyers begin to postpone. In fact, buyers constantly realize lower prices and want to wait for a fund to be reached. Similarly, there will be traders who sell in panic or are simply forced to leave their positions.

The trend remains until the end of the sale, and the belief begins to return to buyers when it is determined that prices will no longer fall. Trend tracking strategies encourage traders to buy in the markets after breaking resistance and selling markets, and when they fall into support levels.

In addition, trends can also be dramatic and prolonged. Due to the magnitude of the movements involved, this type of system has the potential to be the most successful Forex trading strategy. Trend tracking systems use indicators to inform traders when a new trend may have started, but there is no sure way to know, of course.

Here is the good news:

If the indicator can set a time when it is more likely that a trend has started, you are tipping the odds in your favor. The indication that a trend can form is called a leak. An interruption occurs when the price exceeds the highest or lowest maximum for a specified number of days. For example, a 20-day break occurs when the price exceeds the highest peak of the last 20 days.

Trend monitoring systems require a specific state of mind because of the long duration - during which the benefits may disappear as the market swings - these trades may be more psychologically demanding. When markets are volatile, trends tend to be more disguised, and price fluctuations are greater. Therefore, a trend tracking system is the best trading strategy for Forex markets that are calm and trendy.

A good example of a simple trend tracking strategy is the Donchian Trend system. The Donchian channels wer e invented by futures trader Richard Donchian and are trend indicators in the process of being established. The Donchian channel's parameter can be altered as you see fit, but in this example, we will see a leak of 20 days.

Basically, Donchian channel breakout suggests two things:

- Buy if the market price exceeds the highest of the last 20 days

- Sell if the price falls below the 20-day low.

There is an additional rule for trade when the market condition is more favorable to the system. This rule is designed to filter leaks that go against the long-term trend. In summary, you analyze the 25-day moving average (MA) and the 300-day moving average. The direction of the shortest moving average determines the allowed direction. This rule allows you only to go:

- Short if the 25-day moving average is below the 300-day moving average

OR

- Long if the 25-day moving average is above the 300-day moving average
- The negotiations end similarly to the entry but only with a 10-day break. This implies that if you open a long position and the market falls below the previous 10-day low, you can sell to exit the trade - and vice versa.

4-Hour Forex Trading Strategy

A potentially beneficial and profitable Forex trading strategy is the 4-hour trend strategy. However, the four-hour delay makes it more appropriate for swing traders. This strategy makes use of a 4-hour base chart to track the potential locations of trading signals. The one-hour graph is used as a signal graph to determine where the actual positions will be taken.

Always remember that the time period for the signal graph must be at least one hour shorter than the basic graph. Two sets of MA lines will be selected. One will be the MA of 34 periods, while the other will be the MA of 55 periods. To see if a trend is worth exchanging, MA lines will have to be linked to price action.

In the case of an uptrend, the conditions that will be fulfilled are as follows:

- The price will remain higher than the MA lines
- Line 34-MA will remain above line 55-MA and continue to do so.
- MA lines tilt-up for the maximum duration during an uptrend
- In the case of a downtrend, the following conditions will be met:
- Price action will remain below two MA lines
- Line 34-MA will remain below line 55-MA and continue to do so.
- MA lines go down for a maximum duration

The MA lines will become a support zone during bullish trends, and there will be resistance zones during downtrends. It is in and around this area that the best positions for the trend strategy can be found. Learn how to negotiate step by step with our new educational course, Forex 101, with important information from industry experts.

Counter-Trend Forex Strategies

Counter-trend forex strategies are based on the fact that most leaks do not turn into long-term trends. Therefore, a trader using this strategy seeks to take advantage of the price trend to reflect the previously established-ups and downs. On paper, counter-trend forex strategies are the best Forex trading strategies to boost confidence because they have a high success rate.

However, it is essential to note that tight reins are needed on the risk management side. These Forex trading strategies are accompanied by levels of support and resistance. But there is also a risk of major disadvantages when these levels deteriorate. Continuous monitoring of the market is a good idea. The state of the market that best fits this type of strategy is stable and volatile. This type of environment provides market oscillations healthy pre ç is ã the limit in a range. It is important to note that the market may change state.

For example, a stable and calm market can start the trend, remain stable, become volatile as the trend develops. How the state of a market can change is uncertain. You need to look for evidence of the current state to find out if it fits your trading style.

CHOOSING YOUR STRATEGY

The most successful traders will develop a strategy and refine it for a specific period of time. Some people will focus on a specific study or calculation, while others will use a broad-based analysis to determine their business. Most experts probably suggest that you try to use a combination of fundamental and technical analysis, with which you can make long-term projections as well as determine the entry and exit points. Obviously, in the end, it is the professional who must decide what suits him best.

When you're ready to go into the FOREX market, open a demo account and paper exchange so you can practice until you make a steady profit . Many people who fail tend to enter the FOREX market and quickly lose a lot of money for lack of experience. It's important to take your time and learn how to trade properly before you start hiring capital.

You must also be able to exchange without emotion. You can not track all stop-loss points if you do not have the option to run them on time. You must always set your breakpoints and profit-taking points so that they automatically run and change them only when absolutely necessary. Make your decisions and stick to them. Otherwise, you will become crazy (and your brokers).

You must also realize that you must follow the trends. If you are against the trend, you are just playing with your money because the FOREX market tends to evolve more often than anything else, and you are more likely to succeed in trading with the trend.

The foreign exchange market is the largest market in the world, and every day people are more interested in it. But before you begin to trade, make sure your broker meets certain criteria and take the time to find a trading strategy that's right for you.

Learning to choose the right trading strategy for you can be difficult for beginners. Most Forex traders want to become rich in a short time from the time they start trading, but this is sometimes unrealistic.

You should also consider high-risk, high-return strategies versus low-risk, low-return strategies during the selection process to get the best trading strategy. Another important factor to consider is to test your strategy on a demo account.

Below you will find a list of Forex beginners strategy trading tips that will help you throughout your journey.

Select a strategy and stick to it.

This is very crucial for beginners. Avoid trading strategies all the time because it generates less profit. This is the tip that forex savvy traders use to make higher profits. They select a trading strategy and adhere to their specific strategy. So why do not you learn the hacks of experienced Forex traders and do not stick to your specific strategy?

Choose your broker wisely

This is another tip that can help you. Make sure to check the reviews and recommendations for choosing a reliable broker that fits your trading personality well. Remember that choosing the right broker is half the hassle. For your information, expect to find fake brokers who will stand in your way but choose an authorized broker with a license. You can do this by setting strict standards to be met by the broker you choose to protect your money.

Do not let your emotions take over.

You must always take control of your emotions, even if it is not easy, especially after suffering a series of defeats. If you let your emotions take you away, you expose yourself. Make sure you eliminate emotions, especially after deciding on your specific trading strategy. Traders who earn higher profits are generally calm all the time, whether the market is volatile or not. It allows them to make good decisions.

Make your own strategy.

The most common errors made by novice traders do not create their own action plans. You must know what you expect from trading. Make sure you have a well-thought-out end goal in mind to succeed in your trading discipline. In fact, it is suggested to use a Forex trading strategy consistent with your goals in order to quickly build your success.

Always practice.

They say that practice leads to perfection, and this is one of the crucial tips and tricks for novice traders. By practicing constantly, you increase the chances of consistently higher results. You may not want to lose money learning the basics, but the good thing is that testing your strategy on a demo account does not cost you anything to set up. Therefore, you must begin to learn the basics and slowly graduate until you understand the rules of the game.

Refrain from stressing yourself.

This is one of the Foreign exchange hacks, which is obvious. You must discover the source of your stress and try to eliminate it or minimize its influence on you. Breathing deeply and focusing on something else can be beneficial at this stage. You can use different ways to overcome stress, such as listening to music or exercising.

Currency trading can be devastating, especially for new traders who have no idea of the rules involved. There are different types of Forex trading strategies that you can decide to adopt. If you want to venture into Forex trading, there are many strategies to choose from. You must know what suits you.

However, you should know the advantages and disadvantages of each strategy, as well as the risks involved in each strategy.

This will help you evaluate the performance of the strategy of your choice. Most professional traders choose the trading day because it presents less risk of events that may have an impact on the share price aftermarket hours.

Conclusion

By following these hacks, during the process of choosing your Forex trading strategy, you need to know that without risk, there is no success. Therefore, when you choose to become a Forex trader, you must have already accepted the probability of failure.

WHAT IS A FOREX BROKER?

The brokers Forex are companies that provide specialist marketing with access to a flat - form that allows them to trade foreign currencies. Transactions on this market are always between a pair of two different currencies, so currency traders buy or sell the specific pair they wish to trade.

Forex brokers can also be called retail forex brokers or currency brokers. Most forex brokers only manage a very small portion of the overall volume of the foreign exchange market. Retail currency traders use these brokers to access the 24-hour currency market for speculative purposes. Forex brokerage services are also provided to institutional clients by large companies such as investment banks.

Main conclusions:

- Forex brokers allow traders to access the foreign exchange market.
- Most brokers serve retail clients, although large banking companies also serve institutional clients.
- Forex brokers let clients trade with very high leverage.
- Forex brokers make money primarily on buy and sell spreads, but may also have other ways to do so.

UNDERSTANDING THE ROLE OF A FOREX BROKER

Forex brokers give access to trading in all major currency pairs; EUR / USD, GBP / USD, USD / JPY, and USD / CHF, as well as other G10 currencies and all exchange rates between them. In addition, most brokers will allow clients to trade emerging market currencies.

A forex broker allows a trader to open a transaction by buying a currency pair and closing the deal by selling the same pair. For instance, if traders want to exchange euros for US dollars, they buy the EUR / USD pair. This is equivalent to buying euros in US dollars for the purchase. When they close the deal, they sell the pair, which is equivalent to buying US dollars and using euros to buy. If exchange rates were higher when traders closed, they would maintain profits. Otherwise, traders would notice a loss.

Forex brokers have improved their customer service over the years. Opening a forex trading account is usually quite simple and can be done online. Before trading, a forex broker will ask clients to deposit money into their accounts as collateral. However, the brokerage firm also provides its customers with effect from leverage so they can negotiate larger amounts than is deposited into their account. Depending on the trading country of the trader, this leverage can be 30 to 400 times the amount available on the trading account. High leverage makes forex trading very risky, and most traders lose money trying to trade this way.

HOW FOREX BROKERS MAKE MONEY

Forex brokers are compensated in two ways; First, through it's spread of buying and selling a currency pair. For example, when the euro-dollar pair is quoted at 1.120010 and 1.120022 ask, the difference between these two prices is 0.00012 or 1.2 pips. When a retail customer opens a position at the selling price and then closes the position in the offer price, the forex broker will have collected this spread value. Second, brokers may charge additional fees. Some may charge transaction fees or monthly fees for accessing a specific software interface, or fees for access to special commercial products such as exotic options. However, the competition between forex brokers is very intense, and most companies serving retail customers think they should attract customers by eliminating as many fees as possible. This has led many people to propose free or very low transaction costs beyond the spread.

Some forex brokers also earn money through their own trading operations. This can be problematic if your negotiations create a conflict of interest with your clients, but regulation in this area has helped to reduce this practice significantly.

REGULATION BETWEEN FOREX BROKERS

Two entities exercise regulatory functions between forex brokers to discourage and eliminate fraudulent practices: The National Futures Association and CFTC (Commodity Futures Trading Commission). These organizations pursue lawsuits against which their practices are considered fraudulent or intentionally prejudicial to their clients.

It is important to research whether a broker has an excellent reputation and the functionality you are looking for at a broker. This search can be done by visiting the NFA home page and reviewing the opinions of Investopedia brokers.

Most major forex brokers will allow potential customers to use a convenient account to understand better what the system looks like. It's a great idea to test as many platforms as possible before deciding which broker to use.

In addition, as the foreign exchange market is open 24 hours a day, most quality forex brokers will provide 24-hour service.

6 CRUCIAL THINGS TO TAKE INTO ACCOUNT TO CHOOSE A FOREX BROKER

The retail foreign exchange market is so competitive that just having to look at all the available brokers can cause a big headache.

Choosing the forex broker to trade can be a very overwhelming task, especially if you do not know what to look for.

In this part, we will discuss the features you should look for when choosing a forex broker.

1. Security

The first and foremost feature that a good broker should have is a high level of security. After all, you will not hand over thousands of dollars to someone who simply claims to be legitimate, right?

Fortunately, checking out the credibility of a forex broker is not very difficult. There are regulatory agencies around the world that separate fraudulent trust.

Here is a list of countries with their corresponding regulatory bodies:

- United Kingdom: Prudential Regulation Authority (PRA) and Financial Conduct Authority (FCA)
- United States of America: Commodity Futures Trading Commission (CFTC) and National Futures Association (NFA)
- Australia: Australian Securities and Investments Commission (ASIC)
- Germany: Bundesanstalt für Finanzdienstleistung saufsicht (BaFin)
- Switzerland: Swiss Federal Banking Commission (SFBC)
- France: Autorité des Marchés Financiers (AMF)
- Before you even consider putting your money in a broker, make sure he is a member of the regulatory bodies mentioned above.

- Canada: Investment Information Regulatory Organization of Canada (IIROC)

2. Transaction costs

No matter what type of trader you are, whether you like it or not, you will still be subject to transaction fees.

Whenever you enter a trade, you will have to pay the spread or commission, so it is natural to look for the cheapest and cheapest rates.

Sometimes, you may have to sacrifice small transactions for a more reliable broker.

Make sure you need tight spreads for your type of trading and review the available options. It's about discovering the right balance between security and low transaction costs.

3. Deposit and withdrawal

Good currency brokers allow you to deposit funds and withdraw your winnings without complications.

Brokers have really no reason to make it difficult to withdraw their profits because the only reason they keep their funds is to facilitate transactions.

Your broker only holds your money to facilitate transactions, so there is no reason for you to have trouble getting the profits you have made. Your broker must ensure that the withdrawal process is fast and smooth.

4. Trading platform

In online forex trading, most trading activities are done through the broker's trading platform. This means that your broker's trading platform must be user-friendly and stable.

When searching for a broker, always look for what their trading platform has to offer.

Offer a free news feed? How about easy-to-use technical and graphical tools? Provides all the information you need to trade correctly?

5. Execution

Your broker must inform you at the best possible price for your orders.

Under normal market conditions (for instance, normal liquidity , no surprise events, or major press releases), there is no reason for your broker not to inform you of the market price you see when you pick on the "Buy" button or the button. "sell."

For instance, assuming you have a steady internet connection, if you click "buy" EUR / USD for 1.3000, it should be filled at this price or inside micro-pips. The speed at which your orders are executed is very important, especially if you change money.

A difference of a few pips in the price can make it very difficult to win this offer.

6. Customer service

Brokers are not perfect, so you must choose a broker that you can easily contact in case of problems.

Brokers' competence when dealing with the account or technical support issues is as important as their performance in executing trades.

Brokers can be helpful and kind during the account opening process, but they enjoy terrific after-sales support.

BROKERS YOU MUST AVOID

Just as there are brokers you want, there are also brokers you want to avoid. For example, brokers who are likely to buy or prematurely sell near predefined points (usually called sniping and hunting) are insignificant things that are done by brokers who are simply trying to increase their profits.

Obviously, no broker would agree to do this, but there are ways to know if a broker has committed this crime.

Unfortunately, the only way to really determine which brokers are doing this and which ones are not talking to other traders. There is no actual list or organization reporting this type of activity. The major point here is that you have to visit online discussion forums or talk to others in person to find out who is an honest broker.

Strict margin rules

When negotiating with borrowed money, your broker should have an opinion on the level of risk you can take. With this in mind, your broker can purchase or sell at your discretion, which can be a very bad thing for you.

Let's assume you own a margin account, and your position drops sharply before you start recovering at unprecedented highs. Even if you have enough money to cover it, some brokers will settle your position on a margin call at this low. This action on their part can be expensive. You talk to other people in person or visit online discussion forums to find out who the honest brokers are.

Registering for a FOREX account is very similar to obtaining a balance sheet account. The only big difference is that for FOREX accounts, you have to sign a margin contract.

This contract essentially says that you are dealing with borrowed money, and, For this reason, the brokerage organization has the right to interfere with its activities to protect its interests. Once registered, simply deposit on your account, and you are ready to trade immediately.

For most traders, the most difficult part of Forex trading is dealing with financial losses. It's not just a matter of pain and anguish, but it's also a fact that losses are usually the catalyst that leads traders to make their worst mistakes, which can result in even greater losses, creating a vicious spiral in which the account of the merchant turns. out of control.

It follows that a forex trader must have a strategy on how to manage the losses and be able to execute this adaptation strategy. There is no point in "knowing" that your losses are under control and how to keep them under control if you can not use knowledge. Your coping strategy must be real. You must understand the logic behind your knowledge of losses and believe the truth in faith.

Losses are inevitable

The loss of negotiations is inevitable; In fact, it is often more difficult to make money with strategies that try to ensure a very high victory rate. It's just the nature of how the market evolves.

Some traders follow a methodology that tries to reduce or even eliminate losses dramatically. There are only two methods to do it, and it is important to understand them perfectly:

> • Adding to a lost negotiation, the belief that you were right in the original commercial entry, and

that the timing was wrong. You can even add a larger amount to the next entry for easier recovery. The simple fact is that while this may work as a method, it's usually not ideal, and you'll usually get better results by simply accepting the first loss and closing the trade rather than attempting a "bailout." After all, if your original stop was reached, why would the second exchange be better than the first?

• "Turn in the wind" and open a trade in the opposite direction. In fact, it does not prevent a loss; In fact, it crystallizes a loss by changing its net position. If you have 1 long lot then buy 2 short lots, you end up with 1 short liquid lot with a crystallized loss in this 1 lot.

There is one more particular thing you can do: do not close the lost trades and let them run against you more and more. If you do that, you will close your account.

Fortunately, until now, I've convinced you that you have to accept a losing business. If I have not done so, please go back and read and re-read it until you are convinced. If you are not convinced, write to me and explain your reasons: I hope to convince you by email!

Know how many losses you can tolerate

If you have accepted, lost trades, and risk losing (called "downgrades"), you must decide how psychologically you can tolerate losing without losing your courage. To do this, you must have an honest conversation with

113

yourself. You might think that you could handle something like a withdrawal of 50% on your trading account, but in reality, you do can not possibly manage 25% when it actually occurs. Try to visualize what's going on, close your eyes, and put yourself there.

Another second thing to consider is that as any reduction in your account increases, the amount you need to recover to get the amount you started increases. For example, if you lose 10%, you will need to increase the remaining 90% by 11.11% just to recover the original 100%. When you arrive at a very low 50% draw, you must earn 100% just to return to the original 100%. It is a bitter truth that the deeper your losses are, the harder it will be to get back to where you started.

After considering this, on the other hand, it is also true that the less risk you have, the less you will earn when trading is favorable.

Use a trading method that you really believe in.

After you are sure of the maximum loss you can tolerate, it is necessary that any method you use to decide when to go in and out of a trade and what to negotiate is a good method that generates a positive "wait." This means that in a large business sample, he earns more money than he loses.

You must believe that it is a lucrative method and also submit it to a functional test over several years of historical data.

This is important because when you hit an inevitable losing streak, you have the courage to continue. If you do not do it and stop trading, nor lose courage and excessive trading, you will lose the winning sequence after the losing sequence.

Another benefit of a backward test is that you can use a long-term backtest to determine the worst drawdown and the number of consecutive missed transactions. You can use it to make sure you can survive stretch marks lost. For instance, if the worst performance of your strategy in the last 10 years and thousands of transactions have lost 50 consecutive transactions and the maximum withdrawal you think you can tolerate is 25%, this suggests that if you risk 0, 50% of your capital per transaction, you probably suffer a downward revision over the next 10 years. If you reduce the risk by 0.25% per transaction, you reduce the probability of this depth of reduction.

You should also use a fractional share risk management system, which gives you greater peace of mind knowing that there is a buffer to reduce total losses. You can also decide that if you have a withdrawal much worse than the last 10 years, you will stop trading and reconsider your strategy.

Catastrophic losses

Sometimes events happen on the market to trigger price movements that are so large and so violent that even if you use a stop loss, your broker will not (or pretend not to be able to) execute it. This means that when the shutdown is finally triggered, you may experience much larger losses than you expected. The evolution of the

Swiss franc 2015 is a good example. The Brexit vote last week is a much milder example.

You can avoid this problem by not negotiating any currency that central banks adopt the policy of swimming against the market, attaching the value to another currency, and not being in a position immediately before the high risk of something planned, like a referendum.

Peace of mind will help you cope

After taking these steps, you can be sure to risk money on transactions in the settings you set. You'll know pretty much what percentage of deals they tend to lose, how long the tracks tend to be, and, most importantly, ultimately, they tend to go ahead. At this point, you must accept that lost trades are natural and are just necessary sacrifices that you must make to the market to make money: a "cost to do business."

4 STAGES OF LOSS IN FOREX TRADE

I have already mentioned that loss is as much a part of negotiations as a victory. After all, forex trading is usually a game of zero-sum . Someone is definitely on the other side of your job, and it's only a matter of time before you get on the wrong side.

But while this is part of the overall bargaining process, losing is something that many traders - both beginners and professionals - are struggling with.

Losing in a game where absolute nothing is at stake is difficult enough, what else when there is real money for which you worked hard is involved?

I believe that the main reason for the difficulty in managing losses is the lack of understanding of their nature and impact on business psychology rather than actual psychological problems.

In this book, I would like to address this lack of knowledge with loss. I will talk about the four stages of currency loss, namely, denial, rationalization, depression, and acceptance.

Do you think the terms are familiar? They should because they are similar to the four stages of grief. Note that they are applied differently in the forex.

Knowing the four steps, I hope you are better able to handle trading losses.

Step 1: denial

The first step of the loss allows you to deal with the loss of transactions.

At this point, you deny to yourself and others that your trading idea was wrong and that the loss was not your fault. Reasons like "I stopped hunting" and "I do not really care about this job" are commonly used. There is nothing wrong with feeling this, especially if you are young. It's a way to mitigate the blow to your ego, survive the loss, and move on.

Step 2: Streamlining

After the rejection phase, you streamline your trading setup. This is the moment when you point out everything that is right in your business idea and does not even think about what you have done wrong.

You cite the relevance of your trading plan, your profit target, your stop loss, and your point of entry, but you are totally unaware that you have actually lost your trading and made a mistake somewhere.

Step 3: Depression

At this point, you have examined all the possible external explanations for your loss. You then turn inward and contemplate on the idea that the loss was entirely caused by your own action.

While it is reasonable to take responsibility for your loss, blaming yourself too much can hurt your career in the market if you constantly doubt yourself.

You may ask yourself, "Is forex trading really for me?" And "Why continue?" You can even withdraw from the company if you do not find enough reasons to keep moving.

Anyone who has experienced this kind of doubt can attest that the longer the defeat sequence, the more intense the feeling of despair. Some even think of pursuing other opportunities and giving up forex trading altogether!

Step 4: Acceptance

At this point, you begin to understand that it is unhealthy to blame you for everything that went wrong.

Even if you have accepted that the loss was partly your fault, you are also aware that the foreign exchange market is a wild and wild animal and that there are many factors of the market out of your control.

Let me clarify, however, that acceptance does not simply mean that the loss is good. In fact, acceptance is more about aligning with reality and realizing that loss can not be undone.

When you reach this level, you accept that you have made mistakes, but there are also things that you can not control.

Some even say that acceptance is a mixture of rationalization and depression when you combine the two before you can continue.

After everything, it's essential to remember that you can never really reverse what has been lost, but you can catch up with it.

One obvious technique to do this is to have a winning job and recover financially, but you can also recover mentally.

You can make improvements to your trading strategy, exercise better risk management, or simply discover how to better manage your losses.

Instead of denying the loss, you have to move forward, adapt, and grow.

BOUNCING BACK AFTER A BIG TRADING LOSS

Whether it's a technological collapse, a lack of discipline, or simply a continuous flight of commercial capital, almost all traders will face a major loss (or many) in their careers. How to recover after a big loss is not complex; This can be done in a few simple steps. The hard part is to repair the mental damage caused, especially the damage to the trust.

While overconfidence is blinding, successful traders do not exchange fear because fear is also blinding. This level of trust in which you see the market for what it is intervenes whenever there is an opportunity, reduces your losses when they do not happen, and puts your hand when the conditions are not good - it is the trust that can be lost after a sequence of defeats.

After a series of losses or a big loss, you can start asking yourself, which leads to all the typical problems of many new traders, such as withdrawing too quickly from trading, holding them back for a long time, ignoring the scary trades to lose, or enter more trades than it should, in order to win winning trades. If you encounter these problems or experience a significant loss of capital, there are ways to get you back on track.

The day of your loss

Every trader has bad days. In general, never let a bad day cost more than you earn a profitable average day. If you win an average of $ 700 on the days of victory, do not miss a lot more on a bad day. Check the inconvenience.

A great loss causes all kinds of internal conflicts - the need for revenge, fear, anger, frustration, self-hatred, market hatred, and the list goes on. After a big loss, there is no way to negotiate with a clear head. There are more than 250 trading days a year, so there is no hurry to return; Today is not the day of return.

Accept responsibility

Maybe it was a few bad days, maybe it was your biggest personal loss of all time, or maybe it's a life-changing loss. In the latter case - faced with financial ruin - there is not much to do. Do not negotiate until the problem is solved. Once it is, you can proceed with the steps below, but not before. Do not treat a huge debt over your head with the intention of using it to abolish this debt; It's a lot of pressure and can lead to a worse situation.

If you have withdrawn your account, suffered a defeat sequence, or suffered a sudden loss, it's different. You are still in the game, just a little beat. Everyone loves a story back, and every professional who has been around for a while has one (or more). It does not matter if a surprise announcement has pushed the price beyond your stop loss or if a technological failure has made you lose your connection, and the market has evolved against you.

There is always an excuse for a lost job. Some are very good excuses, but as traders, we must finally accept all the risks. Until we accept responsibility for everything that happens to our requests, history will probably be repeated, and the same thing will happen again.

Accept responsibility and find out what could have been done differently. This will help reduce the chances of re-offending. It is also healthier than swallowing hostility and blaming others for their misfortunes. To blame others is to admit that you do not control your own trading, and if so, why are you trading? If you control your trading, you can correct it; If other people control your trading, you can not fix anything.

There's always something to do. This may involve changing markets, connecting backup data, stopping losses, and automatically submitting targets when an exchange is initiated, or you can configure your platform to settle your transactions if you reach a loss limit daily. The solution is there; You just need to discover it. The best way to find it is to admit that the loss is the result of something wrong, and then to take steps to correct it.

The correction of the specific problem causing the loss is the first step. There remains the question of trust. Even with the problem solved, your confidence may be low after a hard blow.

Reorient your concentration

When you started, you were probably too confident, but the market put you in its place. You have developed a healthy trust over time by building your trading system, testing and practicing it, and finally using it for real money trading. Trust is created by accomplishing difficult tasks and improving these tasks. In trading, our aim is to implement our trading plan. Trust is growing as we see positive results from this business plan.

After suffering from a big loss, get back to basics. Concentrate on the trading plan (with any adjustments made) and its implementation. Return to what attracted you to the business first: develop or learn a strategy that has always made money. Negotiation is difficult, so like and accept the challenge again. Many good times can make us lazy, and often a big loss wakes up. It is the market that informs us that we have gone astray.

Practice and regain confidence

After a big loss, confidence can below. This means that the mind may not be right to negotiate. Not having a clear mind can make you skip negotiations, panic (do not negotiate not to lose), or be too aggressive in trying to return to your old winning methods quickly. None of this is good. Go back and swap a demo account for a few days. If you lose, it will probably save you money. Since this is not real money, there is also less pressure on a demo account, so it is easier to concentrate on trading and not worry about the financial aspect.

Start small

A few winning days on the demo account will increase your confidence level and put you in a better mental space to re-enter the market with real money. After a sequence of defeats, start small; Do not go back to the same position size that you traded before. On the first day of return, negotiate a small position size. A winning day accompanied by a small position size will help build confidence, and you can increase the size of your position the next day. If you have a lost day, the loss with small position sizes is easier to manage than another day with the loss of full position sizes.

Come back to live to trade at a slow pace. If you're really upset, spend at least 2 to 5 days in simulation and when you return to the floor, start small and increase the size of the position when you have winning days. Regardless of winning a few days in a row, gradually increase the size of your position, so it takes about a week to return to the maximum size of your position. I saw people trying to resume live trading after a big loss, and they were not ready. They ended up losing more. Some forex traders repeat this cycle and never recover.

After negotiating larger position sizes, it's annoying to start with a small position size, but it's the best. Recover from a string of losses is back to basics and to work well a strategy, not make money. The money comes from implementing a good strategy. Demonstration trading and small trading allow you to focus on what's important so you can start building trust again. The money will come on its own without being forced.

The essential

If you have just suffered a big blow, stop trading for a few days. When you return, review your trading plan and trading problems and solve the problem and make the necessary changes to the trading plan. Then redeem a demo account for a few sessions to build trust. Just switch to live to trade after a few profitable days and look more like your old and successful one.

HOW MUCH CAN I EARN FOREX DAY TRADING?

Many people like to trade foreign currency on the foreign exchange market because it requires the least capital to start day trading. Foreign exchange trades 24 hours a day during the week and offers a lot of profit potential because of the leverage provided by foreign exchange brokers. Forex trading can be very volatile, and an inexperienced trader can lose substantial amounts.

The following scenario shows the potential of using a forex day trading strategy controlled by risk.

Forex Day Trading Risk Management

Every successful day forex trader manages his risks; This is one, if not the most crucial, of continued profitability.

For starters, you have to keep the risk in every job very small, and 1% or less is typical. This means that if you have a $ 3,000 account, you should not lose more than $ 30 in a single transaction. This may seem weak, but the losses increase and even a good trading strategy of a day will see loss sequences. The risk is managed using a stop-loss order.

Forex Day Trading Strategy

While a strategy can possibly have many elements and can be analyzed for profitability in a number of ways, a strategy is often categorized by its rate of return and its risk / reward ratio.

Win rate

Your win rate represents the number of transactions you earn in a given total number of transactions. Let's say you earn 55 trades out of 100; your win rate is 55%. While not mandatory, having a win rate of over 50% is ideal for most daily traders, and 55% is acceptable and achievable.

Risk/Reward

Risk / reward means how much capital is risky to make a certain profit. If a trader loses 10 pips to lose trades but earns 15 pips to win, he wins more winners than losers. This implies that even if the trader only earns 50% of his trade, he will be profitable. Therefore, winning more winning deals is also a strategic element that many forex traders strive for.

A higher business gain rate means more flexibility with your risk / reward, and a higher risk / reward means that your win rate may be lower, and you will still be profitable.

Hypothetical scenario

Suppose an operator has $ 5,000 inequity and a decent 55% success rate in their trades. They take the risk of only 1% of their capital or $ 50 per transaction. This is done using a stop-loss order. In this scenario, a stop-loss order is placed at 5 pips from the entry price and a goal at 8 pips.

This implies that the potential reward for each transaction is 1.6 times higher than the risk (8/5). Remember, you want the winners to be bigger than the losers.

While trading a currency pair for two hours during an active hour of the day, it is usually possible to perform about five round transactions (the round includes the inputs and outputs) using the above parameters. If there are twenty trading days in a month, the trader will make 100 trades on average in a month.

Trading Leverage

Forex brokers offer leverage up to 50: 1 (more in some countries). In this example, suppose the trader uses a 30: 1 leverage, as it is usually more than enough for forex day traders. Because the dealer has $ 5,000 and a leverage of 30: 1, he can take positions worth up to $ 150,000. The risk is always based on the original $ 5,000; This limits the risk to a small portion of the deposited capital.

Forex brokers generally do not charge a commission, but increase the gap between supply and purchase, making

128

profitable trading more difficult. ECN brokers offer a very small gap, which facilitates profitable trading, but they typically charge about $ 2.50 for every $ 100,000 exchanged ($ 5 shifts).

Trading Currency Pairs

If you trade a currency pair like GBP / USD daily, you can risk $ 50 on each transaction, and each move pip is worth $ 10 with a standard lot (100,000 currency units). Therefore, you can take a position on a standard lot with a 5 pip stop-loss order, which will keep the risk of loss at $ 50 in trading. It also means that a winning offer is worth $ 80 (8 pips x $ 10).

This evaluation can show how much a forex day trader could earn in a month by performing 100 trades:

- 55 profitable trades: 55 x $ 80 = $ 4,400
- 45 trades were losing: 45 x ($ 50) = ($ 2250)

Gross profit is $ 4400 - $ 2250 = $ 2150 if there are no commissions (the rate of gain would probably be lower)

Net income is $ 2150 - $ 500 = $ 1650 if you use a commission broker (the rate of profit would be higher)

Assuming a net income of $ 1,650, this month's account yield is 33% ($ 1,650 / $ 5,000). It may seem very high, and it's a very good return. See Improvements below to see how this feedback could be affected.

Larger loss than expected

It will not always be possible to find five good morning trades every day, especially when the market moves very slowly for long periods.

Slippage is an inevitable part of the trade. This results in a larger loss than expected, even when using a stop-loss order. It is common in very fast markets.

To explain the slippage in the calculation of your potential profit, reduce the net profit by 10% (this is a high estimate of slippage, assuming you avoid publishing large amounts of economic data). This would reduce the potential for net earnings generated by its trading capital from $ 5,000 to $ 1,485 per month.

You can adjust the above scenario based on your typical stop loss and goal, capital, slippage, win rate, position size, and commission parameters.

Conclusion

This simple risk control strategy says that with a 55% gain rate and win more winners than losing trades, you can earn returns of up to 20% per month with Forex Day Trading. Most traders should not expect to earn much; Although it sounds simple, it's actually harder.

Still, with a decent win rate and a risk / reward ratio, a dedicated day trader with a decent strategy can earn between 5% and 15% per month through leverage. Remember that you do not need a lot of capital to start with; Usually $ 500 to $ 1,000.

WHAT WILL IT TAKE TO MAKE $15,000 PER MONTH CURRENCY TRADING?

To make such a large profit per month, you must have an initial account of at least $ **33,000** (Analysis later). Many traders asked if they could earn $ 15,000 a month with a starting $ 10,000 account.

This is a big question. Many novice traders who are trying to make a lot of money exchanging currency fall into the trap of "unrealistic expectations" and I will take this opportunity to show you what I mean.

The foreign exchange trade has received a lot of attention over the years because of all the wonderful benefits it offers, especially accessibility and turnover in particular. You have undoubtedly read (or heard about) people who produce five or even six issues per month in this market.

Well, let's take a glance at what it really means to earn 5 digits in the fx currency market. $ 500 a day equals $ 15,000 a month. So, mostly, what you are really asking is how to double your money at least until the first month.

Let 's analyze again and see if it will work...

ANALYSIS

Let's suppose that you decide to make a trade a day (thus 20 trades for the month) to meet your target of $ 500 per day. Also, with $ 10,000 of starting capital, it is best to start with a mini-account (compared to a standard account). Now, on a mini account, each mini-batch generates $ 1 per pip captured (on average). Of course, it varies with currency pairs, but we'll assume it's $ 1 for that analysis. Now, at $ 1 / pip captured, you will need to capture 500 pips per day.

Ask yourself: is this realistic?

This is, unfortunately, not the case. And if you try to do it, you take too much risk to justify it in the first place. This leaves you with another alternative: increase the number of mini lots traded each day to increase your net gain per pip captured. You will reduce the number of pips you will need to capture daily.

Here are some possibilities:

- 2 mini lots - 250 pips required
- 5 mini lots - 100 pips required
- 7 mini-lots - 70 pips required (approximately)
- 10 mini lots - 50 pips required

Looking at these estimates above, 50 to 70 pips / day seem a better goal. Succinctly put, I think it's possible to capture 50-70 pips / day in this market, realistically, against 500 pip per day.

Now, I'm not saying that it's not possible to get 100 pips / day or even 500 pips (especially on days when there's a key ad). Plus, money changers are constantly coming in and out of this market, taking 1, 2, or 5 to 10 pips at once and doing it all day ... Your daily pips are sure to increase. But still, when you look at the ups and downs of a typical day in the major markets, you will find that even though the markets tend to be quite large, it is still worth keeping. And bear in mind, there will be days when you seek bargaining and simply will not find opportunities. Stupid traders forget it, which is very dangerous because they end up seeing what they want to see, all because they have a daily service goal (like 500 pips / day). Do you see where I'm coming from? Realistic expectations help you negotiate better, which preserves your capital in the long run. Needless to say, preserving capital means being able to make a profit in the future because it keeps you in the game longer. Trust me!

Let's go back to the analysis ...

So, let ' say's we are confident that we can find 70 pips / day of trading of the euro and the pound. We sell 7 mini lots, which means:

$ 7 profit / pip captured if the market favors us

... OR ...

$ 7 loss per pip if the trade turns against us.

Well, now we have to look at the risk. If you work at a ratio of 1: 1.5 (aiming to earn $ 1.50 for every $ 1.00 risky), you risk about $ 330 / swap (or 47 pips). About $ 500 is about 1.5 times the $ 330 (I use round numbers here instead of real numbers for simplicity). In 47 pips at risk (ex: in creating stop losses, which are 47 pips, I feel really comfortable because ' enough room for the market to move before I get stopped prematurely - so that looks good). The next point I should address is the percentage of risk I would take to make such a trade. In other words, if I ended up losing $ 330 in this business (instead of earning $ 500), what% of my business capital would be lost (or written off)? It turns out that $ 330 represents a capital loss of 3.3%, and it's not good. At this rate, my whole account would be exhausted in just 30 operations! It's a bad sign and a red flag that should immediately stop any trade.

Let go back to the original question now ...

You want to earn $ 500 a day with your $ 10,000 capital, but that would be very risky. You would need:

- Increase your capital or
- Try to earn less each day

If you're wondering, a loss of $ 330 represents 2.2% of $ 15,000 and about 1.7% of $ 20,000. In other words, you would need at least $ 20,000 on your account to justify the type of trading you intend to do (to my humble and conservative opinion, I had developed by blowing up my own account when I started). And just to shake your feathers a little more ... 1.7% is way too high for my taste. I would not exceed 1%, which represents an initial account of at least **$ 33,000.**

Yes, you read correctly: you need a good amount of money to really earn decent money in the foreign exchange market.

134

Make the accounts with $ 250 / day of profits or up to $ 350 and see how your risk levels are changing. If you are in the range of 1% to 2% (depending on your own risk tolerance), you'll have a better plan (assuming you're ready to earn $ 350 / day or up to $ 250 / day instead of $ 25). 500 - for now) . I would say that this is not a bad place to start!

CHAPTER TEN – STRATEGIES TO CREATE PASSIVE INCOME WITH CRYPTOCURRENCIES

If you're looking for more ways to potentially improve your cryptocurrency revenue, this chapter is for you. As cryptocurrency proliferates in the digital world, more than ever, there are many ways, aside from mining and currency preservation, to earn passive income from your investments.

So, if you have an interest in more than just hanging on to your chips and want to see your investments grow, read on. There are some options available, so I'm sure you'll find one that meets your encryption needs and fits your investment capacity.

This book examines ways to increase your encryption gains by taking advantage of your current challenges and making smarter investments in hardware that supports the distribution networks in which your currencies operate. Let's be honest; mining is not a possibility conceivable for most of us. However, there are many less capital and time-consuming ways to increase your encryption richness.

Here you will acquire the basic information you require to understand how to increase your stakes. This is the appropriate place to start before you do more research on the right method for you and your investment capabilities.

This chapter follows the following ways to increase your encryption gains passively.

- Run a Lightning Node: for the technical expert

- Foreign currency loan: margin trading and foreign currency lending
- Airdrops, Forks, and Buybacks
- EOS systems
    1.   EOS dApp
    2.   Ethereum dApps
- Staking cryptocurrency and proof of stake
- Masternodes Cryptocurrency

PASSIVE V. SORTA-PASSIVE

This chapter will focus on ways liabilities earn income in the cryptographic world, particularly on ways of your interest in your current issues. Most include participating in strengthening the decentralized network , or wagering their own chips and gaining interest in their current holdings.

Some of these investment strategies definitely need more commitment than others. Whatever your decision, make the decision based on your present comfort level and what fits your budget.

Remember, the higher the risk, the higher your potential rewards. Still, I'm always in favor of doing your homework and knowing what kind of options there are.

Here are 7 viable ways to potentially increase your earnings while you Hodl (hold on to your coins for Dear Life).

RUNNING A LIGHTING NODE

Layer 1 and Layer 2

In Blockchain Basics, Daniel Drescher describes the blockchain as a two-tier software system; *Application* and *implementation*:

- Layer 1 is the application layer. This layer is responsible for all the components intended for the user. These are the things you use when interacting with your crypto-currencies.
- Layer 2 of the deployment layer is the physical technology and design that makes the application work; These are things like the protocols and the code that run the program.

The lightning network refers to the payment protocol "Layer 2". This network runs on a cryptocurrency based on the blockchain (such as Bitcoin). In a way, it is excess to the blockchain. And by using Lightning networks, transactions are done much faster.

Lightning networks allow encryption micropayments to run on a bidirectional payment channel. In contrast, typical transactions are one-way; When Alice sends Bitcoin to Bob, it means that Bob can not use the same channel to send or receive funds from Alice.

But here's the problem: for bidirectional channels to work, our hypothetical users, Alice and Bob, must accept the deal before the transaction can be confirmed. Then, when opening a transaction, both must confirm the number of Bitcoins each will deposit on the same channel.

Join the Lightning Network

Lightning networks use a flexible fork such as Segregated Witness or SegWit. A SegWit flexible fork is used to provide flexible transactions. SegWit is used in the Bitcoin Layer 1 blockchain, which is a smooth modification of the cryptocurrency bitcoin transaction format.

A smooth range divides the transaction into two segments; This deletes the signature or, more specifically, the unlocking signature (or "cookie data"). This actually does two separate transactions, where the original part is separated from the end of the script structure.

In doing so, the original section contains the sender and recipient data, and the new "witness" structure contains scripts and signatures. The "control" segment is counted as one-quarter of its actual size, while the original data segment is counted typically. And so, the trading can move faster because it is actually moved to pieces.

Lower Fees using Lightning

So why is this a great way to generate passive income? Because it is a partial answer to the problems of scalability and fluctuation of transaction rates. The lightning rod makes money by processing transactions; many transactions, quickly.

This not only speeds up the transactions but over time, the Lightning network charges should also reduce Bitcoin transaction fees. Indeed, when transactions are faster, easier, and cheaper, this solves some of the current scalability issues facing distributed networks.

Transaction costs are proportional to the time the funds are retained and how long they take to process a specific route í is the network. The rate also affected by high traffic on the network. But lightning technology allows for many transactions to be treated on one single blockchain transaction.

Moreover, as it is now, it is not financially viable to send Bitcoin micropayments. However, with cheaper rates and faster transactions, the scalability of micropayments will facilitate most of the system.

Because lightning networks act as a soft fork, they create more malleability than a Bitcoin transaction. The Bitcoin script was intentionally designed with the original limitations in place. These limitations prevent the involuntary malleability of transactions.

Invest in lightning

Although Lightning Networks nodes do not offer significant immediate returns, they offer transaction fees. And, of course, the market will need them more in the very near future.

Here is a conclusion of some of the challenges that Lightning Networks is helping to improve, described by Poon and Dryja:

- Almost instant transactions make the payment of small purchases via Bitcoin feasible and not revocable.
- Reduce the need for cold storage portfolios (offline storage), allowing you to make large payments in and out of business quickly. It could also potentially reduce the risk of theft and third-party intervention.
- Third-party custodians would no longer be required for micropayments. Bitcoin blockchain rates are currently too high to accept micropayments.
- Move oversize and time-sensitive channel calculations to improve the rate of smart financial and escrow deals.

COIN LENDING

Coin lending is a totally passive way to obtain cryptographic funds and increase your investments. The best way to participate in foreign currency loans is probably to set up automated loans on an exchange platform. Coinlend offers a fully automated system in which the IA manages and coordinates loans of all currencies in this exchange.

Letting the system manage the loans for you is easily the most effective and efficient way to lend. The more funds you have for loan swaps, the more your automated system will work for you, and the more you will earn passive income. But it also means keeping a large amount of stock market encryption, which you should also consider when evaluating your risk appetite.

While bots do most of the work, the user controls the loan settings. Thus, you can define the duration and value of your loans. Loans can range from a few days to several months and also their size; It all depends on your passive income.

Bots for rent

How do your coins earn money?

Automated encryption exchanges allow you to optimize margin trading. Margin trading means using funds borrowed from a broker (or stock exchange) to exchange your cryptocurrency. The funds are used as a guaranteed wallet. The pieces are ã the BORROWED made profits for traders by changes to interfaces like Bitfinex and Poloniex.

Although there are several variables to take into account, including which coins to lend, the amount of the loan, and the duration, it is possible to earn 2% per day lending coins. Higher loan rates occur during parachuting or forks, as an unusually large number of traders want to reduce assets.

Airdrops, Forks, Burns, and Buybacks:

Taking advantage of airdrops, forks, burns, and redemptions is probably the most passive way to earn on your investments.

While these opportunities offer real benefits, they require a little more chance from the investor than from actual experience. But you can increase the chances of benefiting from it. To do this, you must absolutely follow the activity in the world of cryptocurrencies and monitor your stocks. If you know an air launch, it's a good way to increase your income in a very short time.

If you're ready to do your homework, it's an easy way to enjoy being in the right place at the right time. Here's how they work; Projects that create protocol-level (second) applications are more likely to offer drops. In this case, you will find more parachutes from protocol-level cryptocurrencies like Ethereum, EOS, and Stellar.

What exactly is this? And how can you make most of these opportunities?

Air Drops

An air stream is a widespread distribution of a token or coin of cryptocurrency, which usually gives current coin holders a direct blow to the wallet. Those - are used primarily to draw attention to them and new followers. The amount you can potentially receive is usually directly proportional to your current issues.

But if you realize that the fall is early, you may have a chance to take advantage of the fall. This is part of the interest of an air-launch, to attract attention and encourage others to adopt a native token. These purchases are free as long as you already have the currency.

143

However, parachuting is not something you can rely on regularly to increase your income.

The Bitcoin cash, which is a fork of Bitcoin blockchain of origin, held one of the most remarkable scenes of all time. This took place in August 2017 and has resulted in owners' will be rivers of the original Bitcoin has the same amount of Bitcoins Bitcoin and Cash. Both have lasted, and Bitcoin Cash is among the most traded currencies on stock exchanges.

forks

Although forks can be lucrative, bands are also a much less reliable way to earn passive income than lending coins or running Lightning networks. Forks can be considered a bank error in your favor . Here is what happens; If a blockchain is detached from the main chain, sometimes this new fork creates an opportunity for a holder to obtain a proportionality (or comparable) to his assets in the new blockchain fork.

Again, the forks are excellent when they work for you, but you can not count on them as a stable way to passively develop an investment portfolio.

Burns and Buybacks

Burns and buybacks, like airdrops, are quite variable. But again, you may be lucky and miss to admit that in any investment, hopefully, do never wrong. Sometimes burns and redemptions can mean that the creator of a cryptocurrency buys his native token.

Redemptions are usually organized to burn part of the room. This is when a firm takes a certain amount of its currency. Creators send this currency to an address without a private key, which means that no one can access the currency. It is metaphorically called "burning" because money is artificially eliminated in an effort to control inflation.

Engraving is done to create a shortage because it eliminates part of the circulating currency in order to increase the value of the remaining currency. This can be a successful measure as it eliminates the problems of over-circulation and deflation. And in general, the value of the cryptocurrency you own should increase.

Again, you will need to keep cryptocurrency in your own personal or cold storage portfolio to be the complete recipient of the fork and parachute benefit. If your funds are held in a purse, she will likely receive the funds. So make sure to read the fine print.

As said earlier, these are not the best ways to earn a passive income simply because they look more like unexpected profits than a very complex strategy. But what you can do is keep the pair from advancing their investments, which, frankly, is good advice for all of us. And if you can enjoy a fall or a redemption, why not hit while the iron is hot!

Participate in EOS dApps

You can also get passive income on the Ethereum platform simply by betting your own chips. This allows other users to use the different Ethernet applications. And with you betting your own chips, you can earn some interest.

What exactly is happening here, you may be wondering. Let's take a look at the functioning of decentralized applications taken in load by EOS Dapps or Ethereum, and why you can bet your chips on EOS Dapps .

What is EOS dApps

EOS is an abbreviation for Ethereum operating applications or Ethereum operating systems. These dApps are created on the Ethereum blockchain and work on the decentralized network. They are more flexible applications and therefore do not suffer from the same transaction scalability that other blocks of channels and platforms - forms of decentralized networks such as Bitcoin.

Ethereum is best known for its decentralized applications rather than for the value of its native token. Ethereum is still the second major valuable cryptocurrency on the market today. And Ethereum's original coin offer is the most successful ICO so far. More than $ 4.1 billion was raised between June 2017 and June 2018.

To launch dApps on the EOS platform, you need your native token, Ether. Using the open platform of EOS, technology developers can create their own decentralized applications, called dApps. These dApps are executed using intelligent contracts, which are simply automated contracts that have been written in a compatible programming language.

EOSDivdends displays dApps with which you can earn dividends in EOS.

EOS and passive gains

This passive income method requires an investment in your equipment because you will not necessarily be able to use your personal computer. To participate in the splitting of your chips into EOS dApps, you will need a CPU and a RAM.

You must also have EOS tokens to run the programs. Betting your chips is a great way to earn a passive income because it allows you to earn interest. Indeed, the placement of your chips allows other people to use dApps. The DAPPS popular have to need Paris are for players like poker and play.

Once again, the interest you earn will depend on the number of chips you have and the scope of your loan. However, you can earn a daily interest in your chips.

But to make the most of the interest, you will need to buy the native App token, as not all of them necessarily work on Aether alone. Investing in new native chips is always a risk, so it's best to research and see which chips have been able to maintain their value for a reasonable period of time.

Participating in Ethereum dApps

The Dapps Ethereum as Golem, MakerDao, and Augur allow investors to get chips supporting the network. Ethereum dApps specifically has fewer active users. However, these dAs are a growing concern and can, therefore, become even more lucrative in the future.

In addition, if you already have Ether, participation in these lower performance dApps is only one set. Most importantly, the system relies on Ether to run dApps.

MakerDao provides an exceptional incentive to act as the necessary guardian to maintain the DAI token counter. The process can be fully automated for you. The bots then look for opportunities to arbitration encryption, which keeps the anchoring of DAI and accelerates the settlement when the ETH prices drop.

STAKING AND POS

Bets can be the most direct and passive way to make money on your encryption investments. Unlike the expectation of an unexpected crop of a jet of air or a buy-back, this method gives a much more predictable return on income potential. In addition, you do not have to invest in special equipment; you just need the parts you bet on to help manage the network.

What is staking?

Staking is part of what is known as PoS or "proof of implantation." PoS is a consensus algorithm; the Buterin Ethereum is a big fan of this method.

Therefore, "bet" means that you bet your coins as part of the network consensus to add new blocks to the blockchain in which you are trading.

Here is how it works. You can only bet up to the total amount of coins you have. Your currencies are used to validate new transactions on the platform. And although you can only bet as many coins as you have, the more coins you bet, the more power you have to validate transactions.

How does PoS work ?

PoS is essentially the opposite of PoW or Bitcoin mining. One of the problems of mining is that it is a kind of bet on the node that will succeed. With mining, the first node to resolve the complex algorithm and achieve the hash goal is the one that will be rewarded by the new Bitcoins. As a result, not only is mining extremely expensive, both informally and energetically, but real money investors do not necessarily have a role to play in mining.

But with the PoS protocol, the miners are the ones who have assets in digital currency. Therefore, betting your coins means participating in mining and consensus. The knot simply bets a number of coins in his wallet, creating a new block. The minor is randomly selected in the selection by other coin holders.

The amount you can bet and mine is directly proportional to your bets. As a result, if you have 10% of the total currency in circulation, your node can extract up to 10% of new block trades. This will earn you interest in the coins you bet. In general, there is also a period of maturity. Which means you have to bet your chips for a while before you can start winning rewards.

Benefits of Staking Coins

Placement of parts has several advantages for mining operators compared to PoW. Here are a few:

> • You do not need mining equipment to participate in the setting; The betting application is made from an electronic wallet.
> • Those who hold stakes are responsible for the validation of transactions. This has the potential to encourage good behavior because you what interested in maintaining the validity of blockchain and the currency in which it invests.

- PoS does not suffer the same type of depreciation as the ASIC hardware, which is the current standard for mining with PoW. The investment is in foreign currency and is not wasted on equipment expenses.
- In short, PoW is less expensive in terms of calculation and therefore does not require the same amount of energy that Bitcoin PoW requires from its pools, which is a huge hurdle that the Bitcoin blockchain must handle.
- Many PoS supporters, including Ethereum creator Vitalik Buterin, believe that betting is the solution to one of the cryptocurrency use and scalability problems.

But most importantly, for this chapter, bet chips is a great way to get a potential passive income from your crypto-investment. Essentially, by betting, the holder earns interest in everything he holds and is willing to bet. This amounts to earning interest on your savings account. Fortunately, it will be more profitable, and you will be paid in the same currency as the one you are betting on.

The use of PoS and coin issues is becoming more and more popular in the world of encryption. PoS is increasingly integrated with new currency consensus models. Again, the interest you earn will not be consistent across each currency or electronic wallet.

Winnings are based on a number of factors, including the value of the coin, the amount you own, and the duration of your bets.

Here are some crypto-currencies on which you can bet currencies, and you should spend time looking for if you are interested in betting:

- **DASH**: or digital money. This was the first coin to introduce bets on coins. It was created at the heart of Bitcoin but has made some improvements by adding PrivateSend and InstantSend resources.

- **NEO:** Platform participants can bet their currencies by linking currencies to a NEON wallet.
- **OkCash:** OkCash was founded in 2014 and is suitable for microtransactions.

MASTERNODES: MEDIUM PASSIVE INCOME

It is a little exaggerated to add masternodes to the list of "passive income." But you can say that after the initial masternode creation work, there is a lot more passive work to do.

The masternodes are expensive and take the time. However, if you can manage the capital to start your own, there is a significant return on investment potential.

Masternodes are complete nodes and encourage node operators to perform the basic consensus functions required to execute a blockchain. Masternodes exist to try to solve some of the problems of running complete nodes, mainly the cost of the equipment and the high energy demand.

Today, blockchain network management faces the challenges of rising costs, as well as the technical complexities of running a full-node computer. The result of these problems has been a reduction in computers with complete nodes.

With fewer complete nodes, the blockchain can not operate with maximum efficiency. This is a constant problem faced by crypto-currencies and blockchains in general, scalability and energy efficiency still need to be fully optimized.

The bottom line, though, is that running your typical complete node and blockchain consensus participation is not very profitable at the moment.

In addition, mining basins alone require a significant amount of energy. The cost of mining has resulted in a decrease in the total number of nodes and in the same way to the efficiency of the blockchain.

Running a masternode

Master nodes operate on a work - tested system because they act as complete nodes. It is also a warranty-based system designed to encourage the maintenance of the blockchain network base. However, running a master node is not a passive activity.

Masternodes are composed of servers that maintain the network of a blockchain. These nodes are responsible for specific services that allow minors can not do. Masternodes participate in the test of the consensus mechanism at work. The first crypto to make use of a masternode as part of its blockchain consensus mechanism was Darkcoin, which was later renamed DASH.

As a result, Masternodes also participate in betting. This means that a masternode uses similar protocols to implement protocol evidence. When staking tokens, a certain amount of chips is stuck in your network.

Risks and rewards

Again, running a masternode can be very lucrative. You can earn up to 10% interest per year by running a masternode. However, some warnings and costs must be taken seriously. In the meantime, we can probably label the masternode as a *mean passive* gain. But although they are much more expensive, masternodes can be a much more lucrative investment than direct bets.

Masternodes v. Staking

As expected, the potential for higher rewards also requires greater risk. Although masternodes are a very lucrative investment, and once you have them as a passive form of income, there are still several essential factors to consider.

If you are seriously considering increasing your investments in masternode or staking, here are some things to consider:

- If you want to take part effectively, you will need to maintain a diversified portfolio of currencies. Having holdings in various currencies can be a very good thing, but it also opens up more risks. The fact is that not all currencies on the market have power, so it's a bit of a gamble for everyone.

- To take part effectively in a masternode, you will need to have bigger stakes in the currencies you are betting on. Implementation tokens require only modest maintenance, although this is not the case with masternodes.

- Again, the bet has a very low cost and a modest return on investment. However, masternodes need a little more capital to make them work. You must have access to a dedicated server and cover the expenses associated with it.

- Staking is much less difficult technically and does not require any specific equipment. Alternatively, master nodes have a steeper learning curve and require much more technical knowledge.

- In short, gambling is a much more passive form of income than a masternode. Masternodes must be actively maintained and therefore require much more attention.

REVIEW

Now, I hope you understand that there are many ways to participate in the growing world of cryptocurrencies and many ways to increase your investments. As might be expected, some methods require more work than others.

Let's glance at some of the passive strategies we talked about:

Run a Lightning Node

- Lightning networks are a Layer 2 solution. They work as a complete node and make transactions faster and easier, as well as micropayment on the Bitcoin network.
- Lightning Networks offer cheaper rates and faster transactions. However, the scalability of micropayments will ease most of the system.
- Although Lightning Networks nodes do not offer significant immediate returns given the value they add to cryptocurrency networks; it makes sense that they will need more of them in the market as they become more valuable. popular. As such, network owners should see their yields increase as their use increases.

Coin Lending: margin trading and coin lending

- This is the easiest way to get passive income. All that is needed is to put your current reserves in service for trading and margin loans.

- The easiest way to take part is to set up automated loans on a trading platform like Coinlend. These systems are fully automated, and the AI manages and coordinates the loans of all currencies in this exchange.
- Using the automated system is the most effective and efficient way to lend, because of the more funds you have available for loan swaps, the more your automated system will work for you.
- So, let the bots run and make money!

Airdrops, Forks, and Buybacks

- Airdrops, forks, and buybacks require a bit of luck and a little knowledge. These unexpected gains have obvious benefits, but they require a little more luck for the investor.
- To benefit, follow the steps of your tokens and current commercial developments.
- It's a great way to potentially increase revenue in a very short time, which is very easy.
- Second-level / protocol applications have more frequent airdrops than others. This means that protocol-level crypto-currencies such as Ethereum, EOS, and Stellar tend to offer parachutes and forks more often than others.

EOS systems

- This passive income method requires investment and upgrading of your equipment. To participate in the splitting of your chips in EOS of APPs, you will need a computer with CPU and RAM.
- You must also have good EOS tokens to run programs, not just Ether, but also other native tokens.
- Placement of the chips allows you to gain interest by using your chips to perform other dApps. The DAPPS are typical for players like poker and play.
- The interest you get depends on the number of chips you have and the scope of your loan. However, you can earn a daily interest in your chips.
- To get the most out of your interest gain, you will need the native App token, which means some will inevitably work better than others.

Staking cryptocurrencies and Proof of Stake

- By betting, the holder earns interest in everything he holds and is willing to bet. This is like earning interest on your savings account. Hopefully, it will be more profitable, and you will be paid in the same currency as the one you are betting on.
- Betting can be the most direct and passive way to win your encryption investments actively; This method offers a much more predictable return. To

bet, you must only have the coins you are betting on.

• The owner can bet the number of coins he owns; these coins are used to validate new transactions on the platform. You can only bet as many coins as you need. But the more coins you bet, the more power you have to validate transactions.

• Real gains are based on several factors; who understands the value of the coin, how much you hold, and how long you bet.

Masternodes and staking

• Master nodes operate on a work - tested system because they act as complete nodes. It's also a guarantee-based system, so the more you can invest, the more you can earn.

• The masternodes are responsible for enabling the Service ç specific e phage that miners n ã can it do and can participate in the consensus mechanism for the trial work.

• The first crypto to make use of a masternode as part of its blockchain consensus mechanism was Darkcoin, which was later renamed DASH.

• Masternodes participate in staking. Staking tokens mean that a certain amount of chips is stuck in your network.

• You can earn up to 10% interest per year by running a masternode. Masternodes are a much more lucrative investment than direct bets.

MANY WAYS OF EARNING

The bottom line is that if you wish to see your investments grow, you need to take a more practical approach to manage them. However, this is not necessarily bad news for cryptography enthusiasts. And there are easy ways that are much more passive than active.

Lightning Networks nodes and Masternodes may require a bit more investment. But if you already have a coin in a purse or platform, there is no reason not to gain interest in wagering your coins as soon as possible.

The decision you make is how much time you want to invest in increasing your cryptographic wealth and what level of risk is right for you.

If you want to dive and take passive encryption revenue seriously, we encourage you to take a closer look at masternodes and lightning networks. As I mentioned, none of these are proving to have very high returns in a short time. However, both offer secondary passive income.

More importantly, for now, both contribute to better encryption systems. So, if you have capital and knowledge, running a Lightning network or buying a master node will earn you more revenue over time and help improve the system.

Now, if you have lots of quality coins, it may be in your interest to lend coins, and if you are investing in EOS or Ethereum systems, bet your chips. This is by far the easiest method to use your assets. To take part, all you do is set up automated loans on a purse like Coinlend , and the bots will work to make money.

Finally, we have the unexpected gains of parachuting, burns, and buybacks. To make the most of these incredible lotteries that can increase your wealth, you need to have a diversified portfolio of crypto-currencies, a wallet, and keep control of your investments.

Conclusion

We've looked at ways to increase your encryption wealth from the most intelligent to the most passive. The methods we have discussed range from low-interest income to higher interest income.

Here is an examination of the passive income investing methods we discussed:

- **Run Lightning Node; Foreign currency loans: margin operations and foreign currency loans; Airdrops, Forks, and Buybacks; EOS systems; Currency Encryption and Proof of Participation; Cryptocurrency Masternodes**

- Remember, this is not investment advice. These are examples of ways you can increase your wealth. But, as I mentioned, it is essential to do your homework. Before investing in ICO or IEO, check what's going on under the hood. What works for one investor does not work for another.

All of these passive income approaches are in their infancy. This means that there is probably a lot to gain from being one of the first to adopt. However, it also means that we really do not know what will remain. All this to say that before you go to town to build your own mining area, see what a reasonable and achievable project for you is.

Finally, your income varies proportionally depending on what you are willing and able to invest, the methods and currencies you choose, and your business knowledge. I have omitted any solid prediction about the real gain potential for many of these passive methods simply because it will depend on a confluence of factors.

One of the key factors for successful passive income will be how you stay informed and stay calm in the face of the volatile encryption market. It's a gold rush! Some will get richer, and others will find nuggets in the sand. But you can not win if you do not play!

SWING AND DAY TRADING 2021

Introduction

Is it true that you are an ingenious and decided individual, yet at the same time think that its difficult to make enough money to improve your way of life? Is it true that you are keen on knowing how a regular person like you can make 5 figures each month day or swing trading, yet uncertain how to begin?

Swing and Day trading is a growing industry that develops at a rapid rate, yet many individuals that plunge into it without the correct mentality and aptitudes wind up squandering their money and lamenting their activities.

However, regardless of the talk about how troublesome and costly it very well maybe, do you know that there is a straightforward method to begin a swing and day trading business and develop it into six figures regardless of whether you have no past trading experience?

This book was written to tell you the best way to win your day by day market fights and shield yourself from misinformed

164

trading positions, whether you are a specialist trader or a novice with zero trading experience. By utilizing the instruments, trading strategies and systems uncovered in this book; you'll figure out how to trade in high likelihood markets with laser exactness and make reliable fortunes even in troublesome conditions.

Inside this book, you'll see how swing and day trading functions in clear terms. It uncovers productive trading ideas that depend on demonstrated standards without confused pointers or complex science.

With clear information for non-specialized readers and direct depictions that streamline trading and kill mystery, this book is the quickest and simplest approach to see how to manage risks, cut losses and let the champs run without steady battles.

Within the pages of this book, you'll see:

- What swing and day trading is and how you can benefit from it regardless of whether you are a non-specialized individual

- The trading procedures that can help you earn up to $15,000 in a month and get a profit of over $150,000 every year

- The systems that you can use to manage risks and cut losses definitely

- Step by step instructions to keep away from the regular traps that can demolish your swing and day trading

- Step by step instructions to build up a beneficial swing and day trading framework in 2020 regardless of whether you are a newbie at this.

By

Chapter One

Understanding Swing Trading

Swing trading is a trading approach that tries to catch a swing (or "one move").

The thought is to suffer as "little torment" as conceivable by leaving your trades before the restricting weight comes in.

This implies you'll book your benefits before the market switch and crash your benefits.

Let us take a super quick look at the pros and cons of swing trading. They would be discussed fully in a later chapter.

Pros

1. You need not go through hours before your screen in light of the fact that your trades keep going for a considerable length of time or even weeks

2. It's appropriate for those with an all-day work

3. Less pressure contrasted with day exchanging

Cons

1. You won't have the option to ride patterns

2. You have medium-term chance

Everything looks OK?

At this point, we should proceed onward.

Swing Exchanging Techniques

#1 Stuck in a crate

I will be unique and fascinating names to refer to the swing trading techniques I am about to show you in this section.

This causes you to comprehend the trading technique better, so you realize how to apply it to your trading.

Presently, let me acquaint with you the primary swing trading technique for now.

Stuck in a crate is swing trading within a range market in light of the fact that the market is "trapped" between Support and Resistance (to some degree like a container).

Here's the way it works:

Distinguish a range market

Wait patiently for the price to break beneath Support

In the event that the price breaks underneath Support, at that point sit tight and wait for a solid price dismissal (a nearby above Support)

On the off chance that there's a solid value dismissal, at that point go long on the following candle open

Set your stop loss 1 ATR beneath the candle low and take benefits before Resistance

Presently you may be pondering:

"For what reason would it be a good idea for me to take benefits before Resistance?"

The truth is that as a swing trader, you're searching for "one move" in the market.

So to guarantee a high likelihood of achievement, you need to leave your trades before the selling pressure steps in (which is at Resistance).

Bode well?

Great since we'll be applying this idea to the rest of the swing trading techniques.

#2: Catch the wave

This swing trading technique centers around getting "one move" in an inclining market (like a surfer attempting to get the wave).

The thought here is to enter after the pullback has finished when the pattern is probably going to proceed.

Nonetheless, this doesn't work for a wide range of patterns.

Rather, you need to trade trends that have a more profound pullback on the grounds that there's more "meat" towards the upside.

As a rule, you need to see a pullback in any event towards the 50-period frame moving average (MA) or more profound.

Now, let us figure out how to get the wave with this swing trading technique:

Distinguish a pattern that regards the 50MA

In the event that the market moves toward the moving normal, at that point hang tight at a bullish cost dismissal

In the event that there's a bullish value dismissal, at that point go long on next flame

Set your stop loss 1 ATR beneath the low and take benefits just before the swing high

Presently you may be pondering:

"In any case, why the 50-period frame moving average?"

Going with the 50MA is advisable on the grounds that it's viewed by dealers around the globe so that it could prompt an inevitable outcome.

What's more, as a rule, the 50MA agrees with past Resistance turned Support, which makes it progressively noteworthy.

Presently, it doesn't mean you can't utilize 55, 67, 89, or whatever moving average you pick on the grounds that the idea is what makes a difference.

#3: Fade the move

Presently you're most likely reasoning:

"What's the significance of fade?"

It implies to conflict with.

Fundamentally, you're trading against the momentum (otherwise called counter-trend).

Along these lines, if you're the broker that likes to "conflict with the group," at that point, this trading procedure is for you.

Below are the means by which it works.

Recognize a solid momentum move into Resistance that takes out the past high

Search for a solid cost dismissal as the candle structures a solid bearish close

Go short on the following candle and set your stop loss 1 ATR over the highs

173

Take benefits before the closest swing low

Presently, you have learned 3 sorts of swing trading systems that work.

Be that as it may, there's one extra important thing that is not secured. This thing is your trade management.

For instance:

Consider the possibility that you enter a trade, and the market didn't hit your stop loss.

Be that as it may, neither has it arrived at your objective profit.

So what would it be a good idea for you to do?

Do you hold the trade?

Do you leave the trade?

Or, on the other hand, do you say some prayers?

All things considered, I'll spread all these and more in the following segment

Step By Step Instructions To Properly Handle Your Trades So You Can Trade With Certainty And Conviction

Presently, with trade management, there are 2 different ways you can go about it. These are passive trade management and dynamic or active management.

I'll clarify.

1. Passive trade management

For this technique, you'll either let the market either hit your stop loss or target benefit — anything between, you'll sit idle.

Preferably, you need to set your stop loss away from the "clamor" of the business sectors and have an objective benefit inside a sensible reach (before key market structure).

175

Below, ypu will find the pros and cons of it.

Pros:

- Trading is progressively loose as your choices become increasingly "digitized."

Cons:

- You can't leave your trade early despite the fact that the market is giving indications of inversion.

It is conceivable to see a triumphant trade become a full 1R misfortune.

2. Dynamic (active) trading

For this, you'll observe how the market responds and afterward choose whether you need to hold or leave the trade.

Presently, this is significant.

For a functioning way to deal with work, you should deal with your trades on your entrance time period (or higher).

Try not to wrongly manage it on a lower time period since you'll terrify yourself out of a trade on each pullback that happens.

Beneath, you will see the pros and cons of it.

Pros

You can limit your losses as opposed to getting a full 1R loss.

Cons

- Progressively stressful

You may leave your trade too early without giving it enough space to run

In the event that dynamic trade management is for you, at that point, below are two methods you can consider.

Moving Average

This method includes utilizing a moving average marker to trail your stops.

You'll clutch the trade if the cost doesn't break past the moving average.

In the event that it does, at that point, you'll leave the trade.

This system is valuable for swing trading methodologies like Catch the Wave in light of the fact that the moving average will, in general, go about as a unique Support and Resistance in slanting markets.

Past bar high/low

This strategy depends on the past bar high/low to trail your stop loss.

This implies on the off chance that you're short, at that point you'll trail your stop loss utilizing the past bar high.

In the event that the market breaks and closes above it, at that point, you'll leave the trade (and the other way around).

This is what I mean:

This method is helpful for swing trading techniques like Fade the Move on the grounds that the market can rapidly turn around against you.

In this way, you would prefer not to give your trade an excessive amount of space to move around and immediately cut your misfortunes when the market gives indications of inversion.

Scalping

Scalping is one of the most well-known systems. It includes selling very quickly after a trade gets gainful. The value target is whatever consider that interprets along with "you've profited on this arrangement."

Fading

Fading includes shorting stocks after fast moves upward. This depends on the presumption that first, they are overpurchased, second, early buyers are prepared to start taking profits, and third existing buyers might be scared off. Albeit unsafe, this procedure can be amazingly fulfilling. Here, the value target is when purchasers start stepping in once more.

Every day Pivots

This system includes benefitting from a stock's day by day instability. This is finished by endeavoring to purchase at the low of the day and sell at the high of the day. Here, the value target is essentially at the following indication of an inversion.

Momentum

This technique normally includes exchanging on news discharges or finding solid slanting moves bolstered by high volume. One sort of force dealer will purchase on news discharges and ride a pattern until it shows indications of inversion. The other kind will blur the value flood. Here, the value target is when volume starts to diminish.

Much of the time, you'll need to leave an advantage when there is diminished enthusiasm for the stock, as shown by the

Level 2/ECN and volume. The benefit target ought to likewise take into consideration more benefits to be made on winning trades than is lost on losing trades. On the off chance that your stop loss is $0.05 away from your entrance value, your objective ought to be more than $0.05 away.

Much the same as your entrance point, characterize precisely how you will leave your trades before entering them. The leave criteria must be sufficiently explicit to be repeatable and testable.

Chapter Two

Understanding Day Trading

Day trading is the demonstration of purchasing and selling a money related instrument around the same time or even on various occasions through the span of a day. Exploiting little value moves can be a rewarding game—on the off chance that it is played accurately. However, it very well may be a risky game for amateurs or any individual who doesn't stick to a well-considered system. In addition, not all merchants are appropriate for the high volume of trades made by day traders. A few traders, be that as it may, are planned in view of the day trader.

How about we investigate some broad day trading standards and afterward proceed onward to choosing when to purchase and sell, regular day trading procedures, fundamental diagrams, and examples, and how to restrict misfortunes.

1. Information Is Power

Notwithstanding information on essential exchanging systems, day traders need to keep up on the most recent securities exchange news and occasions that influence stocks—the Fed's financing cost designs, the monetary standpoint, and so on. So get your work done. Make a list of things to get an idea of stocks you'd prefer to trade and keep yourself educated about the chose organizations and general markets. Output business news and visit dependable money related sites.

2. Put Aside Funds

Do a proper evaluation of how much capital you're willing to hazard on each trade. Numerous fruitful day traders chance under 1% to 2% of their record per trade. In the event that you have a $40,000 trading account and are eager to chance 0.5%

of your capital on each trade, your most extreme loss per trade is $200 (0.005 x $40,000). Put aside a surplus measure of assets you can exchange with, and you're set up to lose. Keep in mind; it could possibly occur.

3. Put Aside Time, Too

Day trading requires your time. That is the reason it's called day trading. You'll have to surrender the vast majority of your day, truth be told. Try not to think of it as in the event that you have restricted time to save. The procedure requires a broker to follow the business sectors and spot openings, which can emerge whenever during trading hours. Moving rapidly is critical.

4. Start Small

As a learner, center around a limit of one to two stocks during a session. Following and discovering openings is simpler, with only a couple of stocks.

As of late, it has gotten progressively normal to have the option to trade fragmentary offers, so you can determine explicitly, littler dollar sums you wish to contribute. That implies if Apple shares are trading at $250 and you just need to purchase $50 worth, numerous representatives will currently let you buy one-fifth of an offer.

5. Stay away from Penny Stocks

You're most likely searching at arrangements and low costs, yet avoid penny stocks. These stocks are regularly illiquid, and the odds of hitting a big stake are frequently somber. Numerous stocks trading under $5 an offer become de-recorded from significant stock trades and are just tradable over-the-counter (OTC). Except if you see a genuine chance and have done your examination, avoid these.

6. Time Those Trades

Numerous requests set by investors and brokers start to execute when the business sectors open in the first part of the day, which adds to value instability. A prepared player might have the option to perceive examples and pick fittingly to make benefits. Be that as it may, for beginners, it might be better just to peruse the market without making any moves for the initial 15 to 20 minutes. The center hours are typically less unpredictable, and afterward, development starts to get again toward the end ringer. Despite the fact that the times of heavy traffic offer chances, it's more secure for amateurs to maintain a strategic distance from them from the start.

7. Cut Losses With Limit Orders

Choose what kind of orders you'll use to enter and leave trades. Will you use showcase requests or farthest point orders? At the point when you put in a market request, it's executed at the best value accessible at the time—hence, no value ensures.

A cutoff request, then, ensures the cost, however, not the execution. Farthest point orders assist you with trading with more accuracy, wherein you set your cost (not ridiculous but rather executable) for purchasing just like selling. Progressively advanced and experienced informal investors may utilize the utilization of alternatives methodologies to support their situations also.

8. Be Realistic About Profits

A system doesn't have to win constantly to be productive. Plenty traders just win half to 60% of their trades. In any case, they make more on their victors than they lose on their washouts. Ensure the hazard on each trade is constrained to a particular level of the record, and that section and leave techniques are unmistakably characterized and recorded.

9. Remain Cool

There are times when the securities trades test your nerves. As a day trader, you have to figure out how to keep ravenousness, expectation, and dread under control. Choices ought to be represented by rationale and not feeling.

10. Stay on track

Effective brokers need to move quickly, yet they don't need to think quick. Why? Since they've built up a trading procedure advance, alongside the control to adhere to that system. It is critical to pursue your recipe intently as opposed to attempt to pursue benefits. Try not to let your feelings defeat you and relinquish your methodology. There's a mantra among day traders: "Plan your trade and trade your plan."

Before we go into a portion of the intricate details of day trading, how about, we take a look at a portion of the reasons why day trading can be so troublesome.

What Makes Day Trading Difficult?

Day trading takes a ton of training and ability, and there are a few factors that can make the procedure testing.

To start with, realize that you're going toward experts whose vocations rotate around trading. These individuals approach the best innovation and associations in the business, so regardless of whether they come up short, they're set up to prevail at last. In the event that you get on board with the temporary fad, it implies more benefits for them.

Uncle Sam will likewise need a cut of your benefits, regardless of how thin. Recollect that you'll need to pay assesses on any transient additions—or any ventures you hold for one year or less—at the negligible rate. The one admonition is that your misfortunes will balance any additions.

As an individual financial specialist, you might be inclined to enthusiastic and mental inclinations. Proficient brokers are typically ready to remove these of their exchanging methodologies, yet when it's your own capital Included, it will, in general, be an alternate story.

Choosing What and When to Buy

Day traders attempt to make cash by abusing minute value developments in singular resources (stocks, monetary standards, prospects, and alternatives), typically utilizing a lot of money to do as such. In choosing what to concentrate on— in a stock, say—a run of the mill day trader searches for three things:

Liquidity: Liquidity enables you to enter and leave a stock at a decent cost. For example, tight spreads or the contrast between the offer and solicit cost from stock, and low slippage or the distinction between the normal cost of exchange and the real cost.

Unpredictability: Volatility is essentially a proportion of the normal everyday value extend—the range wherein an informal investor works. Greater unpredictability implies more prominent benefit or misfortune.

Trading volume: This is a proportion of how often stock is purchased and sold in a given time span—most ordinarily known as the normal day by day exchanging volume. A high level of volume demonstrates a great deal of enthusiasm for a stock. Expansion in a stock's volume is frequently a harbinger of a value bounce, either up or down.

When you recognize what sort of stocks (or different resources) you're searching for, you have to figure out how to distinguish section focuses—that is, at what exact minute you will contribute. Devices that can assist you in doing this include:

Constant news administrations: News moves stocks, so it's critical to buy into administrations that disclose to you when possibly showcase moving news turns out.

ECN/Level 2 statements: ECNs, or electronic correspondence systems, are PC based frameworks that show the best accessible offer and ask cites from various market members and afterward naturally coordinate and execute orders. Level 2 is a membership-based help that gives ongoing access to the Nasdaq request book made out of value cites from market producers enlisting each Nasdaq-recorded and OTC Bulletin Board security. Together, they can give you a feeling of requests being executed continuously.

Intraday candle outlines: Candlesticks give a crude examination of value activity. More on these later.

Characterize and record the conditions under which you'll enter a position. "Purchase during upturn" isn't sufficiently explicit. Something like this is considerably more explicit and furthermore testable: "Purchase when value breaks over the upper trendline of a triangle design, where the triangle was gone before by an upturn (in any event one higher swing highs and higher swing low before the triangle framed) on the two-minute diagram in the initial two hours of the exchanging day."

When you have a particular arrangement of section rules, filter through more graphs to check whether those conditions are created every day (accepting you need to day trade each day) and, as a rule, produce a value move the foreseen way. Assuming this is the case, you have a potential passage point for a system. You'll at that point need to evaluate how to exit, or sell, those trades.

Choosing When to Sell

There are different approaches to leave a triumphant position, including trailing stops and benefit targets. Benefit targets are the most widely recognized leave technique, taking a benefit at a pre-decided level.

Day Trading Charts and Patterns

To help decide the perfect minute to purchase a stock (or anything that benefit you're exchanging), numerous merchants use:

- Candle designs, including inundating candles and dojis

- Specialized analysis, including pattern lines and triangles

Volume—expanding or diminishing

There are numerous candle arrangements a day trader can search for to discover a section point. Whenever utilized appropriately, the doji inversion design (featured in yellow in the graph underneath) is one of the most solid ones.

Day Trading Patterns

Commonly, search for an example like this with a few affirmations:

To begin with, search for a volume spike, which will give you whether traders are supporting the cost at this level. Note: this can be either on the doji light or on the candles promptly tailing it.

Second, search for earlier help at this value level — for instance, the earlier low of day (LOD) or high of day (HOD).

At long last, take a look at the Level 2 circumstance, which will show all the open requests and request sizes.

In the event that you pursue these three stages, you can decide if the doji is probably going to deliver a genuine turnaround and can take a position if the conditions are good.

Conventional examination of graph designs additionally gives benefit focuses to exits. For instance, the stature of a triangle at the most extensive part is added to the breakout purpose of the triangle (for an upside breakout), giving a cost at which to take benefits.

The Most Effective Method To Limit Losses When Day Trading

A stop-loss request is intended to confine losses on a situation in a security. For long positions, a stop loss can be put beneath an ongoing low, or for short positions, over an ongoing high. It can likewise be founded on unpredictability. For instance, on the off chance that stock value is moving about $0.05 per minute, at that point, you may put a prevent loss $0.15 away from your entrance to give the value some space to change before it moves your foreseen way.

Characterize precisely how you'll control the risk on the trades. On account of a triangle design, for example, a stop loss can be set $0.02 beneath an ongoing swing low if purchasing a breakout, or $0.02 underneath the example. (The $0.02 is subjective; the fact is just to be explicit.)

One procedure is to set two stop loss:

A physical stop-loss request put at a specific value level that suits your hazard resilience. Basically, this is the most cash you can remain to lose.

A psychological stop-loss set at where your entrance criteria are abused. This implies if the trade makes a surprising turn, you'll quickly leave your position.

Any way you choose to leave your trades, the leave criteria must be sufficiently explicit to be testable and repeatable. Likewise, it's critical to set a most extreme misfortune for every day you can stand to withstand—both monetarily and rationally. At whatever point you hit this point, take the remainder of a vacation day.

Adhere to your arrangement and your borders. All things considered, tomorrow is another (trading) day.

When you've characterized how you enter trades and where you'll put a stop misfortune, you can survey whether the potential system fits inside your hazard limit. On the off chance that the procedure uncovered you an excessive amount of hazard, you have to change the system here and there to decrease the hazard.

In the event that the procedure is inside your hazard limit, at that point, testing starts. Physically experience verifiable outlines to discover your entrances, taking note of whether your stop loss or target would have been hit. Paper trade along these lines for at any rate 50 to 100 trades, taking note of whether the procedure was gainful and on the off chance that it lives up to your desires. On the off chance that it does, continue to trading the system of a demo account progressively. On the off chance that it's beneficial through the span of two months or more in a mimicked domain, continue with day exchanging the methodology with genuine capital. In the event that the procedure isn't productive, begin once again.

At long last, remember that if trading on margin—which means you're getting your venture assets from a financier firm (and remember that margin prerequisite for day trading are high)—you're unquestionably progressively defenseless against sharp value developments. Margin enhances the trading results of benefits, yet of losses also if trade conflicts with you. Thusly, utilizing stop losses is pivotal when day trading on margin.

Chapter Three

Contrasts Between Day Trading and Swing Trading

The time span on which a trader selects to trade can significantly affect the trading system and benefit. Day traders open and close numerous positions inside a solitary day, while swing merchants take trades that last several days, weeks, or even months. These two diverse trading styles can suit different brokers relying upon the measure of capital accessible, time accessibility, brain science, and the market being traded.

One trading style isn't superior to the other, and it truly comes down to which style suits a trader's close to home conditions. A few brokers select to do either, while others might be day traders, swing traders and purchase and-hold investors at the same time.

Day Trading Versus Swing Trading

Potential Returns

Day trading pulls in traders searching for a fast exacerbating of profits. Assume a broker risks 0.5% of their capital on each exchange. In the event that they lose, they shall lose 0.5%, yet in the event that they win, they'll make 1% (2:1 reward to risk proportion).

Additionally, assume they win half of their trades. On the off chance that they make six trades for every day, by and large, they will add about 1.5% to their record balance every day, minus trading expenses. Earning at least 1% a day would grow a trading account by over 200% throughout the year, uncompounded.

On the other side, while the numbers appear to be anything but difficult to repeat for enormous returns, nothing's ever that simple. Making twice as much on wins as you lost on failures, while additionally winning half of the considerable number of trades you take, doesn't come easily. You can make brisk increases, yet you can likewise quickly drain your trading account through day trading.

Swing trading gathers additions and misfortunes more gradually than day trading. However you can, in any case, have certain swing trades that rapidly bring about large gains or losses. Assume a swing trader utilizes a similar risk management rule and risks 0.5% of their capital on each trade with the objective of attempting to make 1% to 2% on their triumphant trades.

Assume they acquire 1.5% by and large for winning exchanges, losing 0.5% on losing exchanges. They make six exchanges for every month and win half of those exchanges. In a common month, the swing trader could add 3% to their account balance, minus expenses. Through the span of the year, that turns out to about 36%, which sounds great;

however, offers less potential than a day trader's conceivable profit.

These model situations serve to outline the difference between the two trading styles. Adjusting the level of trades won, the normal win contrasted with normal loss, or the number of trades, will definitely influence a procedure's procuring potential.

When in doubt, day trading has more benefit potential, in any event on littler accounts. As the size of the account develops, it gets increasingly hard to use all the capital on exceptionally transient day trades viably.

Day traders may discover their rate returns decrease the more capital they have. Their dollar returns may, in any case, go up, since making 5% on $1 million compares to significantly more than 20% on $100,000. Swing traders have less possibility of this occurrence.

Fluctuating Capital Necessities

Capital necessities fluctuate as per the market being traded. Day traders and swing traders can begin with varying measures of capital relying upon whether they trade in the stock, forex, or futures markets .

In places like the United States of America, Day trading stocks requires an account balance of at any rate $25,000. No lawful minimum exists to swing trade stocks, albeit a swing trader will probably need to have at any rate $10,000 in their account, and ideally $20,000 if hoping to draw a salary from trading.

To day trade the forex market, no lawful minimum exists, yet it is prescribed that traders start with at least $500, yet ideally $1,000 or more. To swing trade forex, the base suggested is about $1,500, however ideally more. This measure of capital will enable you to enter at any rate a couple of trades one after another.

To day trade futures, start with at any rate $5,000 to $7,500, and increasing capital would be far and more superior. These sums rely upon the prospects contract being exchanged. With day trading, a few agreements could require substantially more capital, while a couple of agreements, for example, miniaturized scale contracts, may require less.

To swing trade an assortment of futures contracts, you need at any rate $10,000, and likely $20,000 or more. The sum required relies upon the margin prerequisites of the particular contract being traded.

Time for Trading Differs

Both types of trading need a measure of time investment, yet day trading commonly occupies significantly more time. Day traders as a rule trade for in any event two hours out of each day. Including planning time and chart/trading audit implies spending at any rate three to four hours at the PC, at any rate. In the event that a day trader selects to trade for in excess of several hours per day, the time venture goes up impressively, and it turns into an all-day work.

Swing trading, then again, can take considerably less time. For instance, in case you're swing trading off a day by day chart, you could discover new trades and update orders on current situations in around 45 minutes every night. These exercises may not be required on a daily premise.

Some traders who engage in swing trading, taking trades that last weeks or months, may just need to search for trades and update orders once every week, bringing the time responsibility down to about an hour out of every week rather than every night, or refreshing orders may not be required on a daily premise.

You should likewise do day trading while a market is open and dynamic. The best hours for day trading are constrained to specific times of the day. In the event that you can't day trade during those hours, at that point, pick swing trading as a superior alternative. Swing traders can search for trades or spot orders whenever in the day, significantly after the market has shut.

Swing traders are less influenced continuously to-second changes in the cost of an advantage. They center around the master plan, normally seeing day by day charts, so setting trades after the market closes on a specific day works fine and dandy. Day traders make cash off second-by-second developments, so they should be included while the activity is going on.

Focus, Time, and Practice

Day trading and Swing trading both require a decent arrangement of work and information to create benefits reliably, despite the fact that the information required isn't really "book smarts." Successful trading comes about because of finding a methodology that delivers an edge, or a benefit over a noteworthy number of trades, and afterward executing that technique again and again.

Some information available being traded and one beneficial procedure can begin creating pay, alongside parts and bunches of training. Everyday costs move uniquely in contrast to they did on the last, which implies the broker should have the option to actualize their procedure under different conditions and adjust as conditions change.

This shows a troublesome test, and predictable outcomes just originate from rehearsing a methodology under heaps of various market situations. That requires some serious energy and ought to include making many trades a demo account before gambling real capital.

Picking day trading or swing trading likewise comes down to character. Day trading ordinarily includes more pressure, requires continued concentration for expanded timeframes, and takes mind-boggling discipline. Individuals that like activity, have quick reflexes, and additionally like computer games and poker will in general incline toward day trading.

Swing trading occurs at a more slow pace, with any longer slips between activities like entering or leaving trades. It can even now be high pressure, and furthermore requires tremendous order and tolerance.

It doesn't require as much focus, so on the off chance that you experience issues remaining focused, swing trading might be the better alternative. Quick reflexes don't make a difference in swing trading as trades can be taken after the market closes, and prices have quit moving.

Swing trading and day trading both offer freedom in the sense that a broker works for themselves. Brokers commonly take a shot at their own, and they are liable for subsidizing their accounts and for all losses and benefits created. One can contend that swing traders have more opportunity as far as time since swing trading occupies less time than day exchanging.

A Final Comparison

One trading style isn't superior to the next; they simply suit varying needs. Day trading has more benefit potential, in any event in rate terms on littler estimated trading accounts. Swing traders have a superior possibility of keeping up their rate returns even as their account develops, in a specific way.

Capital prerequisites fluctuate a considerable amount over the various markets and trading styles. Day trading requires additional time than swing trading, while both take a lot of training to pick up consistency. Day training makes the best alternative for activity lovers. Those looking for a lower-push and less time-escalated choice can grasp swing trading.

Chapter Four

The Upsides and Downsides of Day Trading and Swing Trading

As already stated in multiple places in this book, dynamic traders frequently bunch themselves into two camps: the swing traders and the day traders. Both look to benefit from momentary stock developments (versus long haul speculations), yet which trading technique is the better one? Beneath, we investigate the upsides and downsides of day trading as opposed to swing trading.

Day trading, as the name proposes, includes making many trades in a solitary day, in view of specialized examination and modern outlining frameworks. The day trader's goal is to bring home the bacon from trading stocks, products or monetary forms, by making little benefits on various trades and topping loses on unfruitful trades. Day traders commonly don't keep any positions or possess any securities longer than one day.

213

Swing trading depends on distinguishing swings in stocks, products, or monetary forms (currencies) that occur over a period of days. A swing trade may take a couple of days to half a month to work out. In contrast to a day trader, a swing trader probably isn't going to make such trading a full-time profession.

Day Trading Upsides and Downsides

Upsides

1. Potential to make considerable benefits: The greatest bait of day trading is the potential for terrific benefits. Be that as it may, this may just be a likelihood for the uncommon person who has every one of the qualities – definitiveness, discipline, and perseverance – required to turn into a fruitful day trader.

2. Work for yourself: The day trader works alone, autonomous from the impulses of corporate fat cats. He can have an adaptable working timetable, get some much-needed rest at whatever point required, and work at his own pace, in contrast to somebody on the corporate treadmill.

3. A constant flood of excitement: Long-time day traders love the rush of setting their brains in opposition to the market and different experts throughout each and every day. The adrenaline surge from fast fire trading is something that relatively few brokers will admit to, yet is a major factor in their choice to bring home the bacon from trading, contrasted, and going through their days selling gadgets or poring over numbers in an office work area.

4. Costly training not required: For some occupations in finances, having the correct degree from the correct college is essential only for a meeting. Day trading, interestingly, doesn't require costly instruction from an Ivy League school. While there are no formal instructive necessities for turning into a day trader, courses in specialized analysis and digital trading might be useful.

5. Independent work benefits: As an independently employed individual, a day trader can discount certain costs for tax purposes, which can't be guaranteed by an employed person.

Downsides

1. The danger of considerable loses: One major truth about day trading is that day traders regularly endure monetary losses in their first long stretches of trading, and numerous never graduate to benefit making status. While the many investment and stockbroking platforms advice that day traders should just hazard cash they can bear to lose. Actually, numerous day traders incur immense losses on monies they borrowed, either through margined trades or capital acquired from family or different sources. These losses may reduce their day trading profession, and additionally put them in considerable debt.

2. Huge beginning and progressing costs: Day traders need to contend with high-recurrence brokers, hedge funds, and other market experts who burn through millions to pick up trading points of interest. In this condition, a day trader has a minimal decision but to spend intensely on a charting software, trading platform, best model PCs, and so forth. Continuous costs incorporate expenses for getting live cost statements and commission costs that can accrue due to the volume of trades.

3. Work for yourself: To truly make a to go at it, a trader must stop his normal everyday employment and surrender his consistent, regularly scheduled salary. From that point on, the informal investor must depend altogether alone on expertise and endeavors to produce enough benefit to take care of the tabs and appreciate an okay way of life.

4. High pressure and danger of burnout: Day trading is stressful as a direct result of the need to watch numerous screens to spot trading openings and afterward act rapidly to make optimal use of them. This has to be done daily without missing a single day, and the prerequisite for such a high level of concentration and fixation can frequently prompt burnout.

Swing Trading Upsides and Downsides

Upsides

1. Doesn't need to be your all-day work: Anyone with the information and investment capital can have a go at swing trading. Due to the more drawn out time period (from days to weeks instead of minutes and hours), trades don't need to be continually observed. A swing trader can even keep up a different all-day work (as long as the person isn't checking trading screens constantly at work).

2. Potential for critical benefits: Trades, for the most part, need time to work out, and keeping a trade open for a couple of days or weeks may bring about higher benefits than trading in and out of the same security on various occasions a day.

3. Steady observing not required: The swing trader can ensure those stop losses are set up. While there is a danger of a stop being executed at a horrible value, it beats the steady checking of every vacant position that is an element of day trading.

4. Less pressure and danger of burnout: Since swing trading is only here and there an all-day work, there is substantially less possibility of burnout through pressure. Swing traders, for the most part, have a standard activity or another wellspring of salary from which they can balance or alleviate trading misfortunes.

5. Costly investment not required: Swing trading should be possible with only one PC and traditional trading instruments. It doesn't require the cutting edge innovation of day trading.

Downsides

1. Higher edge prerequisites: Since swing trading, for the most part, includes positions held at any rate medium-term, edge necessities are higher. Most extreme influence is generally multiple times one's capital. Contrast this and day trading where edges are multiple times one's capital.

2. The danger of generous losses: As with any style of trading, swing trading can likewise bring about significant losses. Since swing brokers hold their situations for longer than day traders, they likewise risk bigger losses.

Day Trading or Swing Trading?

Day trading and swing trading each have points of interest and disadvantages. Neither one of the strategies is superior to the next, and traders ought to pick the methodology that works best for their abilities, inclinations, and way of life. Day trading is more qualified for people who are enthusiastic about exchanging full-time and have the three Ds - decisiveness, discipline, and determination(essentials for fruitful day trading). Day trading achievement likewise requires a propelled comprehension of specialized trading and charting. Since day trading is exceptional and stressful, merchants ought to have the option to remain quiet and control their feelings enduring an onslaught. Day trading includes risk and traders ought to be set up to some of the time leave with 100 percent losses.

Swing trading, then again, doesn't require such an imposing arrangement of attributes. Since swing trading can be embraced by anybody with some venture capital and doesn't require full-time consideration, it is a reasonable alternative for brokers who need to keep their all day occupations, yet in addition, fiddle with the business sectors. Swing trading ought to likewise have the option to apply a blend of key and specialized analysis as opposed to specialized analysis alone.

Chapter Five

Day Trading Strategies the Pros Don't Want You to Know

Day trading is quick-paced. It requires an order and exceptionally quick reflexes to pull the trigger once a promising trading opportunity uncovers. It very well may be a lucrative and energizing exchanging style in the event that you get the establishments right.

That is the reason we've made a rundown of multi-day trading tips to stay by. From risk management to trend following, pursue these focuses and see your main concern developing.

1. Get ready for your trading day

As a day trader, readiness is one of the most significant undertakings you should begin your day with. This incorporates not just examining the market for potential trade

223

arrangements yet additionally mental and physical readiness and exercise.

Set your alert promptly toward the beginning of the day, so you can have the opportunity to do some short extending activities and prepare for the exchanging day. Before the financial trade opening ringer or the start of the Forex session, look through your outlines and see whether there are some potential exchange arrangements that are in accordance with your trading procedure.

Numerous day traders check the market late at night to plan for the accompanying trading day, which can likewise be a compelling methodology in case you're a night owl.

2. Investigate the principal trading hour

The main trading hour of any monetary market uncovers a ton about the present trading day. Pending requests that were put by traders the day preceding get executed in the initial couple of moments of the new trading day, which can give important knowledge into where the market is going.

Forex traders frequently pursue the value activity of the early trading session to get a feel of the market beat. In the event that there're huge breakout candles, this frequently establishes the pace for the rest of the day. Similar remains constant for stock dealers – feel the market notion by hanging tight for the initial 1-hour flame of the stock you need to trade.

3. Check a financial schedule

Financial schedules incorporate significant market occasions and reports that can make outrageous unpredictability in the market – and instability is fundamental for day trading. Most of the monetary schedules incorporate the stock or cash that is likely affected by the discharge, the anticipated number (additionally called Street desire), the past number, and the real discharge.

Checking a financial schedule for the most significant market reports planned for the day ought to be a customary piece of your morning readiness schedule. Record or recollect the specific occasions of the discharges to stay away from any horrendous astonishments not far off.

Markets will, in general, be unstable if the genuine number varies from the normal number to a huge degree. Contingent upon your market sees this unpredictability can work either possibly in support of you.

4. Peruse significant market news

While most day traders utilize specialized investigation in their trading, its a well-known fact that basics have a vital impact in monetary markets. Essentials can frame new patterns, invert them, and cause significant help and obstruction levels to break, which makes it critical to pursue market news when day trading.

226

Numerous brokers go through famous budgetary entryways to remain to-date on showcase news, for example, Bloomberg or Reuters. While you don't need to peruse any news that runs over, realizing what is happening in the market will assist you with your market investigation and produce new trading thoughts.

5. Find oversold and overbought budgetary instruments

The trading techniques of day traders can, as a rule, be gathered into three classes: trend following, breakout trading, and counter-trend trading. Whichever procedure you use, finding and trading overbought and oversold budgetary instruments can have a huge effect on your main concern.

Overbought securities will, in general, tumble to their normal trading range, while oversold securities will in general, ascent to their normal trading range after some time. A well-known device to distinguish protections that trade at those extraordinary levels is the Relative Strength Index, which comes worked in with most mainstream trading stages.

Just apply the RSI to your graph and read its worth – an estimation of beneath 30 shows an oversold economic situation, while an estimation of over 70 flag an overbought economic situation. Abstain from purchasing securities that are overbought and selling securities that are oversold.

6. Take trades in the course of the trend

Trend following is one of the most famous trading systems among day traders for an explanation – it works. Trend following alludes to taking trades only the course of the setup trend. In the event that the present trend is up, search for purchasing openings, and if the momentum trend is down, search for selling openings.

To recognize the present trend, you can utilize a simple peak and trough examination or a specialized marker, for example, the ADX (Average Directional Index). A market in an uptrend shapes back to back higher highs and higher lows, while a downtrend market frames continuous lower lows and lower highs. You'll regularly find that, during an upswing, securities become oversold precisely at the purpose of a crisp higher low, which is the value level at which you ought to consider purchasing the security or money pair.

Essentially, during a downtrend, securities typically get overbought directly at where a new lower high is framing, which flag a potential selling opportunity.

In the event that you have to employ the use of the ADX pointer to recognize and exchange patterns, at that point, follow the estimation of the ADX line. A value beneath 25 shows that the market isn't inclining, a value somewhere in the range of 25 and 50 flag a drifting business sector, while values over 50 sign an extremely solid pattern. Utilize the – DI and

229

+DI lines to recognize the bearing of the pattern – if the – DI line is over the +DI line, you're managing a downtrend, and if the +DI line is over the – DI line, you're managing an upswing.

7. Counter-trend trades can be unsafe

The contrary way to deal with trend following, counter-trend trading alludes to taking trades the other way of a built uptrend. Counter-trend traders expect to benefit on transient value remedies; for example, they attempt to sell at the highest point of higher highs during an upturn, and to purchase at the base of lower lows during downtrends.

At the point when joined with trend following methodologies, counter-trend trading can make all the more trading open doors for traders. Be that as it may, remember that counter-trend trades are commonly less secure than trades that are taken toward the basic pattern.

8. Have severe risk management systems set up

Without sound risk management rules, even the best trading procedure will, at last, lead to huge losses. Risk management encourages you to assume responsibility for your trades, position sizes, losses and benefits. No single trade ought to be permitted to clear out an enormous bit of your trading account, or you'll make some hard memories attempting to return to earn back the original investment.

For instance, in the event that you lose half of your trading account on a solitary trade or two or three trades , it will take you 100% of profits just to come back to breakeven. That is the reason you ought to break down the potential danger of any trade arrangement, utilize a foreordained risk for every trade, take trades with a sufficiently high reward-to-risk proportion, and adhere to the 6% rule.

9. Continuously risk a fixed level of your trading account on any trade

To avoid losses to gain out of power, you should only risk a fixed level of your trading account on any single trade. The brilliant guideline is to never chance over 2% of your trading account on a trade. Here is an example: in the event that you have a $10,000 account, at that point, you shouldn't risk more than $200 on any single trade. Spot your stop-loss precisely at the value level where your all-out loss for that trade would rise to $200.

While 2% is the most extreme risk you ought to be taking on any single trade, you can lessen this rate if you need to. For traders with bigger trading accounts, it's entirely expected to risk just 1% or even 0.5% of their accounts.

10. Break down the reward-to-risk proportion of potential arrangements

232

The reward-to-risk proportion of a trade alludes to the potential benefit of the trade divided by its potential loss. For instance, in case you're taking a trade that has a benefit capability of $50, however, you're gambling $100, the prize to-chance proportion of that trade would be 0.5. As it were, you're gambling $2 to pick up $1.

This is a case of an ominous reward-to-risk proportion. You ought to never chance beyond what you can conceivably pick up. The best trade arrangements have a prize to-hazard proportion of in any event 2:1 or significantly more; for example, you're gambling $1 to pick up 2$ or more.

11. Adhere to the 6% rule

While the risk per-trade rule of 2% is intended to secure you against an enormous solitary loss that can cause hopeless harm to your trading account, the 6% rule is intended to ensure you against countless littler losses.

233

This standard says that the most extreme sum you should risk on the entirety of your open trades shouldn't surpass 6% of your trading account size. As an example, on the off chance that you stay by risk for each trade of 2%, the all out number of trades you can have at the same time open would be (3 x 2% = 6%). Be that as it may, in the event that you lessen the risk per-trade to 0.5%, at that point the greatest number of trades you can have at the same time running trips to (12 x 0.5% = 6%).

The 6% rule is an incredible defensive measure against a terrible trading day. Envision the entirety of your open trades betray you and hit stop loss, with the 6% rule you would lose just 6% of your trading account.

12. Utilize pending requests where conceivable

Pending requests incorporate stop and breaking point arranges that become market orders when certain conditions are met. Pending requests are amazingly well known among breakout informal investors.

Essentially put in a pending request above or underneath a potential breakout point, and the pending request will naturally execute a market request once the value comes to the predetermined value level. Along these lines, traders don't need to hold up before their exchanging stages throughout the day to get a breakout trade.

Pending requests can likewise lessen slippage, as they get filled just when the market comes to the pre-indicated cost or don't get filled by any means.

13. Keep a trading diary

Trading diaries are an extraordinary method to improve your day trading abilities whenever utilized the right way. By and large, trading diaries ought to incorporate every one of the trades you've taken before, with their individual section levels, stop-loss, and take-profit levels, purposes behind taking the trade, position sizes and other data you may discover pertinent.

14. Make standard reviews of your trade history

In the event that you're normally keeping a trading diary, at that point, remember to perform reviews of your diary passages now and again. This should be possible once every week or once per month, for instance.

These diary reviews will assist you with recognizing repeating trading botches that have prompted losing trades. Is it a specific chart design that just doesn't work for you? Or, on the other hand, do you place your take-benefits excessively wide and stop-losses excessively tight? A trading diary review will give answers to those and different inquiries.

15. Hang tight for affirmation before entering a trade

Did you discover a trade arrangement worth trading? Everything is in accordance with your trading system, and you've distinguished levels to put your stop-loss and take-profit orders? Fantastic! Be that as it may, before you pull the trigger, hanging tight for affirmation can build your prosperity rate fundamentally.

A trade affirmation alludes to market conduct that affirms your analysis; for example, the value begins to move toward you and demonstrates that your analysis looks right.

Candle patterns are an extraordinary device to affirm a trade. Examples, for example, inundating examples, morning and night stars, dojis, sleds, and pin bars are regularly utilized by day traders to affirm a trade arrangement; lastly, open the exchange.

237

In case you're trading breakouts, you can likewise hang tight for the end of the breakout candle before going into a trade. This is done to forestall counterfeit breakouts and limit potential losses.

16. Try not to let feelings meddle with your trading choices

Trading dependent on feelings is one of the most well-known slip-ups made by day traders that immensely influence their trading execution. Feelings, for example, dread and ravenousness, cause merchants to allow their misfortunes to run and stop their benefits – the two activities that can do critical harm to your trading account.

How to avoid feelings to meddle with your trading and keep a composed mind? The best arrangement is to have a well-characterized trading plan and just to take trades that line up with your methodology. A total trading plan ought to likewise depict your risk management and section and leave focuses.

It makes an orderly way to deal with trading– one which has a lot bigger pace of achievement than trading dependent on feelings.

17. Continuously use stop-losses

Regardless of whether you are day trading, swing trading or scalping, you should utilize stop-losses arranged trading in the entirety of your trades. Stop-losses counteract huge and erratic losses and have a significant impact on risk management. Without stop-losses, you won't have the option to have an exact risk for every trade or apply the 6% rule.

There are four fundamental kinds of stop-losses: volatility stops, chart stops, percentage stops, and time stops. Out of these four sorts, the chart stops return the best outcomes. Chart stops utilize significant specialized levels in an outline, for example, backing and obstruction zones, to locate the best puts in for stop-misfortune requests.

18. Secure your profits

Perhaps the greatest misstep of day traders is that they don't secure their unrealized profits. At the point when you open a trade and it moves into a productive domain, those profits are as yet not your own. They're unrealized until you close the position either altogether or move your stop-losses over your break-even level. When you do that, unrealized profits become acknowledged and secured.

As a dependable guideline, you ought to secure your profits as your trade arrives at nearer to TP. At the point when the trade arrives at 1/3 of your TP, move the SL to breakeven, and when it arrives at 2/3 of your TP, move the SL to 1/3 of TP.

19. Use trailing stops where conceivable

Another effective method to secure your unrealized profits is by utilizing trailing stops. As their name recommends, trailing stops "trail" the value – with each new value tick in support of you, a trailing stop moves your stop-loss one tick in support of you. Be that as it may, if the new value tick isn't in support of you, your stop-loss will remain at its latest level.

Trailing stops are particularly famous among patterns following day traders. By utilizing trailing stops, they're ready to remain inside a pattern as long as it keeps going and press the most benefits out of it.

20. Try not to trade during significant market reports

Day traders live on instability, and market reports frequently give the vital unpredictability to gainful trades. Without unpredictability, there's no risk and no profits to be made.

Nonetheless, trading during significant market reports can make a situation of pointless risk as business sectors are infamous to make enormous spikes in the seconds following a market release. These spikes frequently lead to a huge broadening of spreads, slippage, and the activating of stop-loss orders.

21. Holding trades medium-term can be unsafe

Day traders are day traders since they hold their exchanges for a solitary day typically– that is it. Most day traders open their trades in the morning and let them run until either their stop-loss or take-profit gets activated.

In the event that an exchange is as yet open before the finish of the trading day, close it and assume the loss of profit. Holding trades medium-term puts you helpless before market developments that may not be in support of you.

22. Make an arrangement of trades

242

To wrap things up, consider making an arrangement of trades to decrease your risk. The portfolio takes a shot at any time allotment, in any event, for day trading. For instance, in the event that you've just taken three trades that are done in the US dollar, consider including a fourth trade that is contrarily connected to the initial three trades that you've taken (for instance, gold). This will counteract that solitary trades or a few trades do huge harm to your trading account.

Chapter Six

Top 7 Mistakes New Day Traders Make

Entering the universe of stock trading is unquestionably an extremely energizing time for some individuals. Most new traders are appealed by the possibility of profit in the financial trade. This sort of fervor can be an extraordinary help for new traders, be that as it may, it can likewise make them make some rushed, silly choices. At the point when individuals get occupied by the potential for enormous gains, they start treating day trading like a lottery. Trading isn't a lottery and stocks are not lottery tickets. You should never wager on a "hot stock pick" or go "all in" on a play. Trading is a craftsmanship that requires preparing and discipline. Achievement is conceivable. However, it is a procedure, not a moment of delight. In the event that you need to turn into a fruitful day trader, you have to place in the hours and work for it.

Here are the most well-known errors new brokers are typical wont to make:

1. Going in Unprepared

As referenced above, trading stocks ought not to reflect betting. You won't get rich by karma. Of course, a tad of karma can be useful. However, you ought to never rely upon it. You should be set up for the business sectors. The initial phase in readiness is training. You have to teach yourself about trading so you are appropriately prepared to ace the securities trade. You have to know how the market functions, what sorts of arrangements you are searching for and why, and how you will respond in a trade.

Going into the market, ill-equipped is hazardous and numerous brokers explode their records because of their hurriedness. Try not to get removed from the game that quick. Plan yourself so you can have the most noteworthy odds of accomplishment.

245

2. Absence of Proper Tools

Trading is a workmanship, and simply like any specialty, it requires the best possible instruments and assets. Take a stab at building a house without a sled and nails; it's not going to occur. In the event that you need to set yourself up for achievement in the securities trade, you have to ensure you approach the correct instruments. These instruments may incorporate intermediaries, exchanging programming, instructive assets, and that's only the tip of the iceberg. Ensure your tool stash is enough provided before you set out on your trading venture. You'd be astonished at how significant a solitary device, for example, a representative or stage can be. Do your analysis and ensure you have what you have to execute your trading plan appropriately.

3. Going in Too Big

You will regularly observe numerous parallels between new traders and players on the grounds that the financial trade and the gambling club both have a comparable intrigue. They offer you the chance to transform a little entirety of cash into a lot bigger one. The vast majority realize that they have low chances in the gambling club, in any case, very few individuals understand that they have comparative chances in the securities trade in the event that they adopt an inappropriate strategy. We've just referenced the centrality of readiness - this is the initial step to achievement in the business sectors. The following stage is legitimate money management.

Cash management is similarly as significant as trading methodology since it helps you secure your capital. It additionally gives you more pad for losing trades. On the off chance that you just utilize 10% of your capital for any trade, you can never explode your record from a solitary trade. 10% is a discretionary number, yet you ought to get the point. On the off chance that you go in too huge on plays, you open yourself to pointless hazard. Indeed, even a dealer with a 90% success rate has a possibility of exploding their record on the off chance that they bet everything. You wouldn't go into a gambling club and put your life investment funds on red at the roulette table (ideally), so for what reason would you go for broke in your trades? Ensure you are never betting and center around dealing with your cash appropriately. Of course, it's anything but difficult to consider the potential profits. However, you can't disregard the potential losses. It might sting a piece to feel like you could have made more on trade; however, it will sting altogether harder in the event that you explode your trading record and remove yourself from the game.

4. Following versus Learning

At the point when individuals begin trading, they regularly search for a tutor to gain from. There's nothing amiss with that. Truth be told, it's incredible to gain from the victories and disappointments of an accomplished dealer. The issue comes in when you attempt to imitate their prosperity through mimicry. That is the issue with a great deal of alarms administrations. They pull in brokers who just need to duplicate the careful trades of a fruitful trader. You ought to be centered around getting independent. When was the last time you heard somebody ascribe their prosperity to replicating a "guru's" trades? It simply doesn't work that way.

Gain from others, yet don't tail them.

5. Averaging Down

One of the most noticeably awful missteps new trades make is averaging down. This is an extraordinary method to transform a little loss into a record ruiner. We've all been there previously. You've just dedicated to trade so now you have a feeling that you need to finish. "The stock was modest when I got it at $5, so $4 is a take!" This rationale is imperfect and it will push you into difficulty. At the point when you normal down, you're adding to a losing position, in this manner delving yourself more profound in a gap. You're in an ideal situation cutting losses early. Nobody likes to take losses, however, assuming a little loss is far superior to getting yourself in a position where you can be removed from the trading game. There will be a lot of other trading openings in the event that you protect your capital. Have a trading plan and stick to it.

6. Not Cutting Losses

Not cutting losses is like averaging down. It will keep you down and possibly ruin your record. As referenced previously, nobody likes taking losses, yet it is a significant piece of the game. Simply think of it as the expense of working together. In the event that you clutch a failure, you open yourself to superfluous risk. That $100 loss can without much of a stretch go to $200, $400, $1000 and past. You have to know how a lot of cash you are happy to chance on a play and afterward finish it. It's critical to have the most extreme dollar sum that you are eager to risk. On the off chance that you ever lose more than that, you disrupted your trading norms. Be savvy about cutting losses early and you will have a lot more grounded possibility of prevailing in the markets.

7. Retribution Trading

251

There's nothing more terrible than attempting to compensate for an awful trade by setting more trade. "I simply lost $500, so now I have to discover a $500 trade to make it back." When you do this, you are trading wrongly and that is a catastrophe waiting to happen. You ought to never trade to compensate for losses. You should possibly trade when you have a prime arrangement and a strong trading plan. On the off chance that you start feeling like you are trading inwardly, step back and calmly inhale. You don't need to continue trading. This can help keep you from making a poor trade that you will lament over the long haul. Keep in mind; there will consistently be more chances to profit on the off chance that you safeguard your capital. Try not to get excessively on edge.

Chapter Seven

Normal Investor and Trader Blunders

Committing errors is a core piece of the learning procedure with regards to exchanging or contributing. Speculators are commonly engaged with longer-term possessions and will trade stocks; exchange traded assets, and different securities. Traders for the most part, purchase and sell fates and choices, hold those situations for shorter periods, and are associated with a more prominent number of trades.

While traders and traders utilize two unique kinds of trading transactions , they frequently are blameworthy of committing similar sorts of errors. A few mix-ups are progressively destructive to the investor, and others cause more damage to the trader. Both would do well to recall these basic bungles and attempt to avoid them.

1. Lack of a Trading Plan

Seasoned traders get into a trade with a well-characterized plan. They know their accurate passage and leave focuses, the measure of money to put resources into the trade and the greatest loss they are eager to take.

Novice traders might not have a trading plan in place before they initiate trading . Regardless of whether they have an arrangement, they might be progressively inclined to stray from the characterized arrangement than would prepared merchants. Fledgling traders may turn around the course through and through. For instance, going short after first purchasing securities in light of the fact that the offer value is declining—just to wind up getting whipsawed.

2. Pursuing Performance

Numerous investors or traders will choose resource classes, techniques, supervisors, and assets dependent on a current solid exhibition. The inclination that "I'm passing up incredible returns" has most likely prompted more awful investment choices than some other single factor.

In the event that a specific resource class, system, or stock has done amazingly well for three or four years, we know one thing with assurance: We ought to have contributed three or four years prior. Presently, notwithstanding, the specific cycle that prompted this extraordinary presentation might be approaching its end. The savvy cash is moving out, and the moronic cash is pouring in.

3. Not Regaining Balance

Rebalancing is the way toward restoring your portfolio to its objective resource designation, as sketched out in your investment plan. Rebalancing is troublesome in light of the fact that it might constrain you to sell the advantage class that is performing admirably and purchases a greater amount of your most exceedingly terrible performing resource class. This contrarian activity is hard for some tenderfoot investors.

Nonetheless, a portfolio permitted to float with market returns ensures that advantage classes will be overweighted at market tops and underweighted at advertise lows—an equation for horrible showing. Rebalance strictly and receive the long haul benefits.

4. Overlooking Risk Aversion

Try not to dismiss your risk resilience or your ability to go out on a limb. A few investors can't stomach unpredictability and the good and bad times related to the securities trade or increasingly theoretical traders. Different investors may require secure, normal intrigue pay. These generally safe resistance financial specialists would be in an ideal situation putting resources into the blue-chip supplies of built-up firms and should avoid progressively unpredictable development and new business shares.

Recollect that any venture return accompanies a risk. The most minimal risk speculation accessible is U.S. Treasury bonds, bills, and notes. From that point, different sorts of ventures climb in the risk stepping stool, and will likewise offer bigger returns to make up for the higher risk attempted. In the event that a venture offers extremely alluring returns, additionally, see its risk profile and perceive how a lot of cash you could lose if things turn out badly. Never contribute beyond what you can bear to lose.

5. Overlooking Your Time Horizon

Try not to put without a period skyline as a top priority. Consider in the event that you will require the assets you are securing up in a venture before entering the trade. Additionally, decide to what extent—the time skyline—you need to put something aside for your retirement, a downpayment on a home, or an advanced degree for your youngster.

If you intend to aggregate cash to purchase a house, that could be all the more a medium-term time span. Notwithstanding, in the event that you are contributing to back a small kid's advanced degree, that is all the more a long haul venture. On the off chance that you are putting something aside for retirement 30 years, consequently, what the financial

258

exchange does this year or next shouldn't be the greatest concern.

When you comprehend your frame of reference, you can discover ventures that match that profile.

6. Not Using Stop-Loss Orders

A major sign that you don't have a trading plan isn't utilizing stop-loss orders. Stop orders come in a few assortments and can restrict losses because of antagonistic development in a stock or the market overall. These orders will execute consequently once edges you set are met.

Tight stop losses, for the most part, imply that losses are topped before they become sizable. Notwithstanding, there is a risk that a stop request on long positions might be actualized at levels underneath those predetermined should the security all of a sudden hole lower—as happened to numerous investors during the Flash Crash. Indeed, even in view of that idea, the advantages of stop orders far exceed the danger of halting out at an impromptu cost.

An end product to this regular trading botch is the point at which a trader drops a stop order on a losing trade just before it tends to be activated in light of the fact that they accept that the value pattern will invert.

7. Allowing Losses To develop

One of the characterizing attributes of effective investors and traders is their capacity to assume a little loss rapidly if a trade isn't working out and proceed onward to the following trade idea. Ineffective traders, then again, can become incapacitated if a trade conflicts with them. As opposed to making a fast move to top a loss, they may clutch a losing position with the expectation that the exchange will, in the long run, work out. A losing trade can hold up trading capital for quite a while and may bring about mounting losses and extreme consumption of capital.

8. Averaging Up or Down

Averaging down on a lengthy position in a blue-chip stock can be beneficial for a trader who has a long investment skyline, yet it might be loaded with danger for a trader who is trading unpredictable and riskier securities. The absolute greatest trading losses in history had happened in light of the fact that a trader continued adding to a losing position, and was in the end compelled to cut the whole position when the size of the loss got illogical. Traders additionally go short more regularly than preservationist financial specialists and incline toward averaging up, in light of the fact that the security is progressing as opposed to declining. This is a similarly dangerous move that is another normal error made by a fledgling trader.

9. The Importance of Accepting Losses

Awfully frequently, investors neglect to acknowledge the basic reality that they are human and inclined to committing errors similarly as the best investors do. Regardless of whether you made a stock buy-in scramble or one of your large long-term workers has all of a sudden gotten ugly, the best thing you can do is acknowledge it. The most noticeably awful thing you can do is let your pride take need over your wallet and clutch a losing investment. Or then again more awful yet, purchase more portions of the stock. as it is a lot less expensive at this point.

This is an exceptionally regular error, and the individuals who commit it do as such by contrasting the present offer cost and the 52-week high of the stock. Numerous individuals utilizing this check expect that a fallen offer value speaks to a decent purchase. Be that as it may, there was a purpose for that drop and cost, and it is dependent upon you to break down why the value dropped.

10. Trusting False Buy Signals

Breaking down of basics, the resignation of a Chief Executive Officer or expanded challenge are for the most part, potential explanations behind a lower stock cost. These equivalent reasons additionally give great insights to speculate that the stock probably won't increase at any point in the near future. An organization might be worthless now for basic reasons. It is essential to consistently have a basic eye, as a low offer cost may be a bogus purchase signal.

Abstain from purchasing stocks in the scratch and dent section. In numerous examples, there is a solid central explanation behind a value decay. Get your work done and break down a stock's standpoint before you put resources into it. You need to put resources into organizations that will encounter supported development later on. An organization's future working presentation has nothing to do with the cost at which you happened to purchase its offers.

11. Purchasing With Too Much Margin

Margin—utilizing acquired cash from your broker to buy securities, typically futures and options. While margin can assist you with getting more cash, it can likewise misrepresent your losses the same amount. Ensure you see how the margin functions and when your broker could expect you to sell any positions you hold.

The most exceedingly terrible thing you can do as another broker is getting diverted with what appears to free money. In the event that you use margin and your venture doesn't go the manner in which you arranged, at that point, you end up with a huge obligation commitment to no end. Inquire as to whether you would purchase stocks with your Visa. Obviously, you wouldn't. Utilizing margin exorbitantly is basically something very similar, but likely at a lower loan fee.

Further, utilizing margin expects you to screen your positions significantly more intently. Misrepresented increases and misfortunes that go with little developments in cost can spell fiasco. In the event that you lack the opportunity or information to watch out for and settle on choices about your positions and their qualities drop then your business firm will offer your stock to recoup any losses you have gathered.

As another trader use margin sparingly, if by any stretch of the imagination, and just on the off chance that you see the entirety of its viewpoints and risks. It can drive you to sell every one of your situations at the base, where you ought to be in the market for the enormous turnaround.

12. Running With Leverage

As indicated by a notable investment buzzword, influence is a twofold edged sword since it can help returns for gainful trades and intensify loses on losing trades. Similarly, as you shouldn't run with scissors, you shouldn't rush to use them. Novice traders may get stunned by the level of influence they have—particularly in forex (FX) exchanging—however, may before long find that over the top influence can pulverize trading capital. In the event that an influence proportion of 50:1 is utilized—which isn't phenomenal in retail forex exchanging—everything necessary is a 2% unfavorable move to crash one's capital. Forex specialists like IG Group must reveal to traders that more than seventy-five percent of brokers lose cash due to the intricacy of the market and the drawback of influence.

13. Following the Herd

Another regular error made by new traders is that they indiscriminately follow the crowd; in that capacity, they may either wind up paying a lot for hot stocks or may start short positions in securities that have just plunged and might be nearly pivoting. While experienced traders pursue the proclamation of the pattern is your companion, they are acquainted with leaving trades when they become excessively busy. New traders, in any case, may remain in a trade long after the keen cash has moved out of it. Beginner traders may likewise come up short on the certainty to adopt a contrarian strategy when required.

14. Keeping All Your Eggs in One Basket

Broadening is an approach to maintain a strategic distance from overexposure to any one investment. Having a portfolio comprised of numerous investments ensures you on the off chance that one of them loses cash. It additionally secures against unpredictability and extraordinary value developments in any one investment. Additionally, when one resource class is failing to meet expectations, another advantage class might be performing better.

267

Numerous examinations have demonstrated that most chiefs and common assets fail to meet expectations on their benchmarks. Over the long haul, ease record reserves are normally upper second-quartile entertainers or superior to 65%-to-75% of effectively oversaw assets. In spite of the entirety of the proof for ordering, the craving to contribute with dynamic chiefs stays solid.

Index all or an enormous segment (70%-to-80%) of your conventional resource classes. In the event that you can't avoid the energy of seeking after the following incredible performer, at that point, put aside about 20%-to-30% of every benefit class to allot to dynamic supervisors. This may fulfill your craving to seek after outperformance without destroying your portfolio.

15. Evading Your Homework

New traders are frequently liable for not getting their work done or not conducting satisfactory research, or due industriousness, before starting a trade. Doing schoolwork is basic since starting traders don't have the information on occasional patterns, or the planning of information releases, and exchanging designs that accomplished traders have. For another trader, the earnestness to make a trade regularly overpowers the requirement for undertaking some exploration, yet this may at last outcome in a costly exercise.

It is a slip-up not to examine a venture that interests you. Research causes you to comprehend a budgetary instrument and realize what you are getting into. If you are putting resources into stock, for example, inquire about the organization and its marketable strategies. Try not to follow up on the reason that business sectors are proficient and you can't make cash by distinguishing wise ventures. While this isn't a simple undertaking, and each other investor approaches similar data as you do, it is conceivable to recognize wise ventures by doing the examination.

16. Purchasing Unfounded Tips

Everybody presumably commits this error at some point in their contributing profession. You may hear your family members or companions discussing a stock that they heard will get purchased out, have executioner income, or before long discharge a momentous new item. Irrespective of whether these things are valid, they do not necessarily imply that the stock is "the following large thing" and that you should surge onto your online investment fund to submit a purchase request.

Other unwarranted tips originate from investment experts on TV and on the Internet who frequently tout a particular stock just as it's an unquestionable requirement purchase, however, truly is simply the kind of the day. These stock tips regularly don't work out and go straight down after you get them. Keep in mind, purchasing on media tips is frequently established on just a theoretical bet.

It is not necessarily the case that you should shy away from each stock tip. On the off chance that one truly catches your eye, the principal activity is thinking about the source. The following thing is to do your very own schoolwork with the goal that you realize what you are purchasing and why. For instance, purchasing a tech stock with some restrictive innovation ought to be founded on whether it's the correct speculation for you, not exclusively on what a common store director said in a media meet.

Next time you're enticed to purchase dependent on a hot tip, don't do as such until you have every one of the realities and are OK with the organization. In a perfect world, get a second supposition from different speculators or unprejudiced money related consultants.

17. Watching Too Much Financial TV

There is nothing on money-related news shows that can assist you with accomplishing your objectives. There are scarcely any bulletins that can furnish you with anything of significant worth. Regardless of whether there were, how would you distinguish them ahead of time?

On the off chance that anybody truly had productive stock tips, trading guidance, or a mystery recipe to make boatloads of money, would they yak it on TV or offer it to you for $49 every month? No. They'd keep their mouth shut, cash out their millions and not have to offer a bulletin to bring home the bacon. Arrangement? Invest less energy in watching money related shows on TV and understanding bulletins. Invest more energy making—and adhering to—your investment plan.

18. Not Seeing the Big Picture

272

For a long haul investor, one of the most significant yet frequently ignored activities is a subjective investigation, or to take a gander at the master plan. Incredible investor and creator Peter Lynch once expressed that he found the best speculations by seeing his kids' toys and the patterns they would take on. The brand name is likewise entirely important. Take a look at how almost everybody on the planet knows Coke; the budgetary estimation of the name alone is in this manner valued in the billions of dollars. Irrespective of whether it's about iPhones or Big Macs, nobody can contend against reality.

So pouring over budget reports or endeavoring to recognize purchase and sell openings with complex, specialized examination may work a lot of the time, however on the off chance that the world is changing against your organization. Eventually, you will lose. All things considered, an organization in the late 1980s could have outflanked any organization in its industry; however, once PCs began to get normal, an investor in typewriters of that time would have done well to survey the master plan and turn away.

Surveying an organization from a subjective point of view is as significant as taking a gander at its deals and profit. Subjective investigation is a technique that is one of the least demanding and best for assessing potential speculation.

19. Trading Multiple Markets

Starting traders may, in general, flutter from market to market—that is, from stocks to options to currencies to futures, etc. Trading various markets can be a gigantic interruption and may keep the fledgling trader from picking up the experience important to exceed expectations in a single market.

20. Overlooking Uncle Sam

Remember the assessment outcomes before you commit. You will get a tax reduction on certain ventures, for example, city bonds. Before you commit, take a look at what your income will be in the wake of deducting tax, considering the investment, your duty section, and your venture time skyline.

Try not to pay more than you have to on trading and business tax. By clutching your venture and not trading every now and again, you will get a good deal on intermediary taxes. Additionally, look around and locate a facility that doesn't charge exorbitant taxes so you can keep a greater amount of the income you produce from your venture.

21. The Danger of Over-Confidence

Trading is an extremely demanding occupation, yet the "learner's karma" experienced by some amateur traders may persuade that trading is the famous street to fast wealth. Such carelessness is hazardous as it breeds a lack of concern and energizes extreme risk-taking that may come full circle in a trading debacle.

From various investigations, we realize that most traders will fail to meet expectations on their benchmarks. We likewise realize that there's no predictable method to choose, ahead of time, those managers that will outflank. We likewise realize that not very many people can beneficially time the market over the long haul. So for what reason are such huge numbers of investors sure of their capacities to time the market as well as select winning managers?

22. Unpracticed Day Trading

In the event that you want to turn into a functioning broker, reconsider before day trading. Day trading can be a risky game and ought to be endeavored uniquely by the most prepared investors. Notwithstanding investment savviness, an effective day trader may increase a bit of leeway with access to extraordinary gear that is less promptly accessible to the normal broker. Did you realize that the normal day-trading workstation (with programming) can cost a huge number of dollars? You'll likewise require a sizable measure of trading cash to keep up a proficient day-trading methodology.

The requirement for speed is the principal reason you can't successfully begin day trading with the extra $5,000 in your financial balance. Online traders' frameworks are not exactly quick enough to support the genuine day trader; actually, pennies per offer can have the effect between a beneficial and losing trade . Most businesses suggest that investors take day-trading courses before beginning.

Except if you have the ability, a platform, and access to fast order execution, reconsider before day trading. In the event that you aren't truly adept at managing risk and worry, there are greatly improved choices for an investor who's hoping to build riches.

23. Belittling Your Abilities

A few investors will, in general, accept that they can never exceed expectations at contributing on the grounds that financial exchange achievement is held for complex investors as it were. This discernment has no reality by any means. While any commission-based shared reserve sales reps will presumably reveal to you generally, most expert traders and investors don't measure up either, and by far, most fail to meet expectations of the expansive market. With a brief period dedicated to learning and research, financial specialists can turn out to be well-prepared to control their very own portfolios and contributing choices, all while being beneficial. Keep in mind, quite a bit of contributing is adhering to good judgment and discernment.

Other than having the capacity to turn out to be adequately capable, singular investors don't confront the liquidity difficulties and overhead expenses of enormous institutional speculators. Any little financial specialist with a sound venture technique has similarly as great a possibility of beating the market, if worse than the alleged speculation masters. Try not to expect that you can't effectively partake in the budgetary markets, basically in light of the fact that you have normal everyday employment.

The Bottom Line

If you have the cash to contribute and can maintain a strategic distance from these fledgling errors, you could make your ventures pay off; and getting a decent profit for your investments could take you closer to your financial objectives.

With the financial trade's inclination for creating enormous gains (and losses), there is no deficiency of broken exhortation and silly decision making. As a private trader, the best thing you can do to cushion your portfolio for the long haul is to

279

execute a sane venture technique that you are OK with and ready to adhere to.

Chapter Eight

Earning $15000 Per Month In Stock Trading

The financial trade's normal return is a cool 10% every year — superior to anything you can discover in a ledger or bonds. So what is the reason behind why such a large number of individuals neglect to acquire that 10%, regardless of putting resources into the financial trade? Many don't remain committed long enough.

The way to making cash in stocks is staying in the financial trade; your length of "time in the market" is the best indicator of your complete presentation. Tragically, investors frequently move all through the securities trade even from a pessimistic standpoint potential occasions, passing up that yearly return.

(First of all: You need an investment fund to contribute — and along these lines profit — in the financial trade.

To make cash putting resources into stocks, stay committed

Additional time rises to a greater open door for your investments to go up. The best organizations will in general, increment their benefits after some time, and investors reward this more noteworthy income with a higher stock cost. That more significant expense converts into an arrival for speculators who possess the stock.

Additional time in the market likewise enables you to gather profits, if the organization pays them. In case you're trading in and out of the market on day by day, week after week or month to month premise, you can kiss those profits farewell since you likely won't claim the stock at the basic focuses on the schedule to catch the payouts.

If a market offered about 9.9% returns from 2017 till now, you would make a lot of profit.

Nonetheless, on the off chance that you missed only the 10 greatest days in that period, your yearly return dropped to 5%.

In the event that you missed the 20 greatest days, your yearly return dropped to 2%.

In the event that you missed the 30 greatest days, you really lost cash (- 0.4% yearly).

When the day ends, you would have earned twice as much by staying committed (and you don't need to screen the market, either!) for only 10 extra basic days. Nobody can foresee which days those will be, be that as it may, so investors must remain committed the entire time to catch them.

The more you're in, the closer you'll get to that verifiable normal yearly return of 10%.

Reasons That Prevent You From Making Money Investment

The stock market is the main market where the merchandise goes at a bargain and everybody turns out to be too reluctant to even think about buying. That may sound senseless. However, it's actually what happens when the market plunges even a couple of percent, as it regularly does. Investors become frightened and sell in a frenzy. However, when costs rise, speculators plunge in fast. It's an ideal formula for "purchasing high and selling low."

To evade both of these limits, investors need to comprehend the average untruths they let themselves know. Here are three of the greatest:

1. 'I'll hold up until the financial trade is sheltered to commit.'

This reason is utilized by investors after stocks have declined when they're too reluctant to even think about buying into the market. Possibly stocks have been declining a couple of days straight or maybe they've been on a long haul decay. Be that as it may, when investors state they're sitting tight for it to be protected, they mean they're trusting that costs will climb. So hanging tight for (the impression of) wellbeing is only an approach to wind up following through on greater expenses, and in reality, it is regularly just a view of security that investors are paying for.

What drives this conduct: Fear is the directing feeling, yet therapists call this progressively explicit conduct "nearsighted misfortune repugnance." That is, investors would prefer to maintain a strategic distance from a transient loss at any expense than accomplish a more extended term gain. So when you feel torment at losing cash, you're probably going to stop that loss successfully. So you sell stocks or don't purchase in any event, when costs are modest.

2. 'I'll buy it again when it is lower in a week from now.'

This reason is employed by would-be buyers as they assume that the stock will become lower. However, investors never really know what direction stocks will proceed onward any given day, particularly for the time being. A stock or market could simply go up as well as go down in a week's time. Smart investors purchase stocks when they're modest and hold them after some time.

What drives this conduct: It could be dread or insatiability. The dreadful investor may stress the stock is going to fall this week and pauses, while the insatiable speculator anticipates that a fall yet needs should attempt to improve cost than today's.

3. 'I'm exhausted of this stock, so I'm selling.'

This reason is utilized by investors who need fervor from their ventures, similar to activity in a gambling club. Be that as it may, savvy contributing is really exhausting. The best investors sit on their stocks for a considerable length of time and years, letting them compound additions. Contributing is certainly not a brisk hit game, normally. Every one of the additions come while you pause, not while you're trading in and out of the market.

What drives this conduct: an investor's longing for fervor. That longing might be powered by the misinformed idea that effective financial specialists are exchanging each day to win enormous increases. While a few dealers do effectively do this, even they are savagely and soundly centered around the result. For them, it's not about fervor but instead profiting, so they keep away from emotional decision making.

File Assets Or Individual Stocks?

On the off chance that that 10% yearly return sounds great to you, at that point, the spot to put is in a record subsidize. File reserves contain handfuls or even several stocks that mirror a record, for example, the S&P 500, so you need little information about individual organizations to succeed. The primary driver of accomplishment, once more, is the control to remain contributed.

Truly, you conceivably can win a lot better yields in singular stocks than in bulk stock, yet you'll have to place some perspiration into exploring organizations to procure it.

Putting resources into the financial trade can be an incredible method to have your cash profit, especially in the present monetary atmosphere where investment accounts and long haul certified receipts do not give mega returns. Stock trading is definitely not an activity that is devoid of risk, and a few misfortunes are unavoidable. Nonetheless, with quality research and interests in the correct organizations, stock trading can possibly be entirely beneficial.

1. Research ebb and flow patterns. There are numerous trustworthy sources that report on advertise patterns. You may have to purchase a stock-trading magazine, for example, Kiplinger, Investor's Business Daily, Traders World, The Economist, or Bloomberg BusinessWeek.

You could likewise follow online journals composed by effective market experts, for example, Abnormal Returns, Deal Book, Footnoted, Calculated Risk, or Zero Hedge.

2. Pick a trading site. A percentage of the top of the line sites incorporates Scottrade, OptionsHouse, TD Ameritrade, Motif Investing and TradeKing. Be certain that you know about any exchange expenses or rates that will be charged before you settle on a site to utilize.

Be certain the administration you utilize is respectable. You should peruse audits of the business on the web.

Select a help that has benefits, for example, a cell phone application, investor instruction and research apparatuses, low trade charges, simple to understand information, and all day, everyday client assistance.

3. Create an account with at least one trading site. You're probably not going to require multiple, however, you might need to begin with at least two so you can later narrow down your choice to the site that draws you in the most.

Make certain to look at the base necessities for each site. Your monetary limit may just enable you to make accounts on a couple of destinations.

Beginning with an especially modest amount, like $1,000, may restrain you to certain trading platforms, as others have higher least adjusts.

4. Work on trading before you put genuine cash in. A few sites offer a virtual exchanging stage, where you can analyze for some time to evaluate your impulses without placing real cash in. Obviously, you can't profit along these lines, yet you additionally can't lose money.

Trading this way will get you used to the techniques and kinds of choices you will be looked with when trading; however, by and large, it is a poor portrayal of real trading. In genuine trading, there will be a defer when purchasing and selling stocks, which may bring about unexpected costs in comparison to what you were focusing on. Furthermore, trading with virtual cash won't set you up for the pressure of exchanging with your genuine cash.

5. Pick solid stocks. You have a lot of decisions; at the end of the day, it is very important that you buy stock from firms that are leaders in their specialty, offer packages that people in the stock broking business reliably need, have a stellar and transparent brand image, and have a great plan of action and a proven track record of progress.

Investigate an organization's open budgetary reports to assess how productive they are. A progressively productive organization, as a rule, implies an increasingly beneficial stock. You can discover total money related data about any traded on an open market organization by visiting their site and finding their latest yearly report. In the event that it isn't on the site, you can consider the organization and solicitation a printed version.

Take a look even under the least favorable conditions quarter on record and choose if the danger of rehashing that quarter merits the potential for benefit.

Ensure that you take a careful look into the organization's management, working expenses, and responsibilities. Investigate their monetary record and income declaration and decide whether they are beneficial or have a decent opportunity to be later on.

Analyze the stock history of a particular organization to the presentation of its friend organizations. On the off chance that all innovation stocks were down at a certain point, assessing them comparatively with one another as opposed to the whole market can reveal to you which organization has been over its industry reliably.

Tune in to an organization's profit phone calls. Initially, investigate the organization's quarterly income discharge that is posted online as a public statement about an hour prior to the call.

6. Purchase your first stocks. At the point when you are prepared, dive in, and purchase a few dependable stocks. The careful number will rely upon your spending limit, yet go for in any event two. Organizations that are notable and have built up exchanging narratives and great notorieties are commonly the most steady stocks and a decent spot to begin. Start exchanging little and utilize a measure of money you are set up to lose.

It is sensible for an investor to start trading with as little as $1,000. You simply must be careful so as to maintain a strategic distance from enormous trade expenses, as these can without much of a stretch gobble up your benefits when you have a little record balance.

7. Put generally in mid-top and huge top organizations. Mid-top firms are those that have a market valuation somewhere

in the range of two and $10 billion. Huge top organizations have market valuations bigger than $10 billion, while those with market tops littler than $2 billion are little tops.

Market capitalization is determined by increasing an organization's stock cost by the number of offers exceptional.

8. Screen the business sectors every day. Recollect the cardinal guideline in stock trading is to purchase low and sell high. In the event that your stock worth has expanded, essentially, you might need to assess whether you should sell the stock and reinvest the benefits in other (lower evaluated) stocks.

9. Think about putting resources into shared assets. Shared assets are effectively dealt with by an expert director and incorporate a mix of stocks. These will be expanded with interests in such areas as innovation, retail, money related, vitality, or remote organizations.

Understanding the Basics of Trading

1. Purchase low. This implies when stocks are at a moderately low value dependent on the previous history, you get them. Obviously, nobody knows for sure when the costs will go up or down—that is the test in stock contributing.

To decide whether a stock is undervalued, take a careful look at the firm's income per share just as obtaining movement by organization representatives. Search for organizations, specifically businesses and markets where there are bunches of instability, as that is the place you can rake in boatloads of cash.

2. Sell high. You need to sell your stocks when they are at their height dependent on the previous history. On the off chance that you sell the stocks for more cash than you got them for, you profit. The greater the growth from when you got them to when you sold them, the more cash you make.

3. Try not to sell in a frenzy. When you notice a stock you have drops lower than the value you got it for, your sense might be to dispose of it. While there is a chance that it can continue falling and never rise back up, you ought to think about how probable it is that it might bounce back. Selling for loss is not generally the best thought since you lock in your loss.

4. Concentrate on the basic and specialized market investigation strategies. These are the two very important models of understanding the financial exchange and looking at value changes. The model you use will determine how you settle on choices about what stocks to purchase and when to purchase and sell them.

A principal examination settles on choices about an organization dependent on what they do, their character and notoriety, and who drives the organization. This examination looks to give a real incentive to the organization and, by expansion, the stock.

A specialized investigation takes a gander at the whole market and what inspires investors to purchase and sell stocks. This includes inspecting patterns and breaking down speculator responses to occasions.

Numerous financial specialists utilize a blend of these two strategies to settle on educated venture choices.

5. Think about putting resources into organizations that deliver profits. A few investors, known as career investors, want to put as a rule in profit paying stocks. This is a way that your stock can make money regardless of whether they don't value the cost. Profits are organization benefits paid straightforwardly to investors quarterly. Regardless of whether you choose to put resources into these stocks will depend altogether on your own objectives as a speculator.

Building up Your Stock Portfolio

1. Differentiate your property. When you have set up some stock property, and you have discovered how buying and selling works to some extent, you ought to grow your stock portfolio. This means that you should invest your money in a wide range of stocks.

New firms may be a decent choice after you have a foundation of more established firm stock built up. In the event that a startup is purchased by a greater organization, you might rake in boatloads of cash rapidly. Notwithstanding, know that 90% of new businesses last less than 5 years, which makes them risky ventures.

Think about investigating various businesses also. On the off chance that your unique property is for the most part, in innovation organizations, take a stab at investigating assembling or retail. This will differentiate your portfolio against negative industry patterns.

2. Reinvest your cash. At the point when you sell your stock (ideally for much more than you got it for), you should fold your cash and benefits into purchasing new stocks. On the off chance that you can profit each day or consistently, you're en route to securities trade achievement.

Consider placing a segment of your benefits into reserve funds or retirement account.

3. Put resources into an IPO (initial public offering). An IPO is the first list an organization issues stock. This can be an incredible time to purchase stock in an organization you accept will be fruitful, as the IPO offering cost frequently (yet not generally) ends up being the least value ever for an organization's stock.

4. Go out on a limb when making a decision on stocks. The ideal way to rake in boatloads of cash in the securities exchange is to go for broke and get somewhat fortunate. This does not mean that you should stake everything on unsafe

ventures and trust in the best, however. Contributing ought not to be played a similar route as betting. You should look into each investment altogether and be certain that you can recoup monetarily if your exchange goes inadequately.

On the one hand, avoiding any and all risks with just settled stocks won't typically enable you to "beat the market" and increase exceptionally significant yields. In any case, those stocks will, in general, be steady, which implies you have a lower possibility of losing cash. What's more, with relentless profit installments and representing a risk, these organizations can wind up being a greatly improved investment than less secure organizations.

You can likewise decrease your risk by supporting against losses on your investments. Perceive how to fence in ventures for more data.

5. Be mindful of the draw back of day trading. Financier firms will as a rule charge expenses for each exchange that can truly

add. If you make way more than a specific number of trades every week, the Security Exchange Commission insists that you have to set up a company account with a high least equalization. Day trading is known for losing individuals' bunches of cash just as being unpleasant, so it is generally better to contribute over a significant stretch of time.

6. Converse with a Certified Public Accountant (CPA). When you start profiting in the securities trade, you might need to converse with a bookkeeper about how your benefits will be burdened. All things considered, while it's in every case best to converse with an expense proficient, by and large, you will have the option to sufficiently examine this data for yourself and abstain from paying an expert.

7. Realize when to get out. Trading the securities trade resembles legitimate betting and not a fair interest in the long haul time frame. This is the area where it is not the same as investing, which is longer-term and more secure. A few people can build up an unfortunate fixation on exchanging, which can

lead you to lose a great deal (even the entirety) of your cash. In the event that you have an inclination that you're losing control of your capacity to profit, attempt to discover help before you lose everything. In the event that you see an expert who is keen, judicious, objective and dispassionate, approach that individual for help if you feel overwhelmed.

Chapter Nine

Risk Management in Stock Trading

We should truly go out on a limb look at what risk is. Risk is the plausibility of loss or damage, something that appears to be risky to us. Risk is questionable; it is capricious. At the point when you characterize trading risk, you are computing the likelihood of a stock going up versus that of it going down. This is valuable since it enables you to gauge how a lot of trading risks you are eager to take against the probability of an increase considering the vulnerability. It is fundamental to be happy to accept trading risk orders to accomplish the ideal consequence of profits.

In stock trading, there is a solid connection between risk and reward: more prominent the risk, the more prominent the income for the most part. In monetary wording, risk management is the way toward distinguishing and evaluating the risk and afterward creating systems to oversee and limit the equivalent while expanding the profits.

Each investment requires a specific measure of risk, and for an investor to expect this risk, he must be remunerated properly. This pay is through something many refer to as the risk premium or basically the premium. Risk is thusly key to stock trading or investment in light of the fact that without risk, there can be no gains. Effective traders utilize stock trading risk management techniques to limit the risk and expand the gain.

In stock markets, there are commonly two kinds of risks; first, the Market risk and second the Inflation risk. Market risk results from a plausibility in increment or decline of financial markets. The other risk which is Inflation or purchasing power risks, results from the rise and fall of costs of merchandise and ventures after some time.

The inflation risk is a significant thought in long haul investments, whereas the market risk is increasingly applicable for the time being. It is the market risk that can be overseen and controlled somewhat; inflation risk can't be controlled.

What Is An Appropriate Level Of Risk?

It is troublesome now and again to draw a line between reasonable risk and negligent risk. This will require significant practice, ideally through paper trading. Additionally, you should work at increasing a superior comprehension of the organization you are managing by performing principal examination and specialized investigation, lastly, control your very own mental commitment to the procedure.

On the off chance that you are too risk unwilling, or "trading terrified," you won't have the stomach to hold your triumphant positions sufficiently long to understand the potential benefits that you anticipate. On the other hand, if you are an activity addict and risk excessively, you may get into a round of taking gigantic draw-downs and that can mentally wear on your mind over the trading day. With focus, you can figure out how to endure the vulnerability and brave the awkward inclination that a drawdown presents. After some time, you will start to trade the "zone," a mentality of activity, concentrating on the present time and place, without harping on your past errors or feelings. This will enable you to go out on a limb, equalization and size your trading risk, and endure the questionable idea of the risk.

There are sure systems that can be utilized to alleviate the risk in a stock exchange. The systems are as per the following:

-Defining Goals

An incredible way to handle the vulnerability in the business sectors is to define future situated objectives for yourself and afterward build up an exchanging methodology or exchanging framework that will enable you to accomplish that outcome. It is basic that you remain lined up with your objectives and exchanging procedures; by doing this, you help to take out a portion of the vulnerability and make the risk progressively sensible and perceptible.

-Know Who You Are As A Trader

In the event that you can connect with your center being, you would then be able to shape your trading with no previously established inclinations by any stretch of the imagination. That is the way to progress, to be fluid and change in accordance with various market situations without the conscience and the hard cap.

Numerous dealers state that the brain research of risk is the brain research of certainty. Certainty implies realizing how to trade all circumstances, and this accompanies practice and tolerance. On the off chance that you get that feeling in your gut that you are "betting," you are most likely not certain. Certainty originates from dependable predictable increases. Be calm and pursue your trading plan and certainty will normally come. In your center, you realize that up to 14 days of additions don't make you an expert. Be straightforward with yourself.

-Figure out how to Trade Stocks, Futures, and ETFs Risk-Free

Going out on a limb and vanquishing market vulnerability expects you to be on the bleeding edge, adapting new abilities, and adhere to your exchanging plan even despite the trouble. Drop your self-image, enable yourself to be instructed by others with experience. Try not to be reluctant to ask questions and don't want to be in charge constantly. The best merchants that I have seen are modest, strong, and continually hoping to better their exchanging aptitudes with the goal that they can remain grounded and objective in taking care of their risk.

Also, going out on a limb and disposing of the market vulnerability requires a merchant to take a shot at not getting diverted, augmentative, or even excessively stubborn. Have the option to get littler in trade size when your trades are conflicting with you. Try not to enable your sense of self to assume a major job in your trading exercises by holding losing positions route longer than you ought to be, gambling fiasco. Be fluid and enable yourself to build your range of abilities and adopt new ideas.

-Follow the pattern of the market

This is one of the demonstrated strategies to limit risks in a stock trade. The issue is that it is hard to spot slants in the market and patterns change extremely quick. A market pattern may last a solitary day, a month or a year, and again, transient patterns work inside long haul patterns.

-Portfolio Diversification

Another helpful risk management methodology in the stock market is to broaden your risk by putting resources into a portfolio. In a portfolio, you enhance your venture to a few organizations, parts and resource classes. There is a likelihood that while the market estimation of a specific venture diminishes, that of the other may increase. Mutual Funds are one more way to enhance the effect.

-Stop Loss

Stop-loss or trailing apparatus is one more tool to watch that you don't lose cash should the stock go far a fall. In this procedure, the trader has the choice of making an exit if a specific stock falls beneath a specific determined breaking point. Self-restraint is one more alternative utilized by certain investors to sell when the stock falls underneath a specific level or when there is a lofty fall.

-Proper Risk Management

Ask Warren Buffett, the best financial specialist ever, what is your recommendation to investors, and he says, "don't lose money." But stock market hints risk and luckily, there are sufficient methodologies for a shrewd financial specialist to protect his cash and guarantee gain. A cautious and auspicious exercise of these alternatives causes you to see the risk in question.

Risk management assists with bringing down losses. It can likewise help shield a trader's account from losing the entirety of their money. The risk happens when the dealer endures a loss. On the off chance that it needs to be handled, the broker can open oneself up to profiting in the market.

It is a basic yet regularly disregarded essential to fruitful dynamic trading. All things considered, a trader who has produced generous benefits can lose it all in only a couple of terrible trades without an appropriate risk management system. So how would you build up the best systems to control the dangers of the market?

This part will talk about some straightforward techniques that can be utilized to ensure your exchanging benefits.

-Arranging Your Trades

As Chinese military general Sun Tzu's broadly stated: "Each fight is won before it is fought." This expression suggests that arranging and technique—not the fights—win wars. Additionally, fruitful brokers regularly quote the expression: "Trade the exchange and trade the plan." Just like in war, preparing can frequently mean the difference between progress and disappointment.

To begin with, ensure your trader is right for frequent trading. A few traders take into account clients who trade inconsistently. They charge high commissions and don't offer the privilege of logical tools for dynamic traders.

Stop-loss (S/L) and take-benefit (T/P) focuses speak to two key manners by which traders can prepare when trading. Effective traders recognize what value they are eager to follow through on and at what cost they are happy to sell. They would then be able to gauge the subsequent returns against the likelihood of the stock hitting their objectives. If the balanced return is sufficiently high, they execute the exchange.

Then again, fruitless traders frequently enter a trade without having any thought of the points at which they will sell at a benefit or a misfortune. Like players on a fortunate—or unfortunate streak—feelings start to dominate and direct their traders. Losses regularly incite individuals to hang on and would like to make their cash back, while benefits can lure traders into hanging on for considerably more gains incautiously.

I find that you can ask yourself a couple of inquiries to keep yourself grounded and better comprehend your trading plan. Think about a couple of ongoing trades that you made, audit the stock chart, and ask yourself the accompanying:

- What cost did you enter the trade?

- Did you include extra offers as the stock went in support of you?

- Where did you sell out?

- Would you be able to associate your trading style with the way in which you dealt with the trade?

- Did you purchase stocks close to the base and afterward include more as the stock went up? Or on the other hand, did you purchase and sold rapidly once you handled a little profit?

- What lessons would you be able to find out about your trading style from the manner in which you dealt with this trade?

- How might others have traded this stock chart? What do you have to do so as to develop your trading style and the measure of risk you are happy to expect?

- What is keeping you away from doing this?

- What is a staying point for you that is counteracting you to arrive at that next level, something that you experience difficulty with in light of the fact that it creates a lot of uneasiness and vulnerability?

- Do you experience difficulty purchasing/shorting more offers in any event, when you are extremely certain that you are correct? This line of addressing should assist you with understanding who you are as a broker and what steps you have to go out on a limb to improve your trading risk profile.

-Consider the One-Percent Rule

A lot of day traders pursue what's known as the one-percent rule. Essentially, this dependable guideline proposes that you should never put over 1% of your capital or your trading account into a solitary trade. So in the event that you have $10,000 in your exchanging account, your situation in some random instrument shouldn't be more than $100.

This system is regular for traders who have records of under $100,000—some even go as high as 2% in the event that they can manage the cost of it. Numerous brokers whose accounts have higher limits may decide to go with a lower rate. That is on the grounds that as the size of your account increases, so too does the position. The ideal approach to hold your losses under wraps is to keep the standard underneath 2%—any more and you'd chance a considerable measure of your trading account.

-Setting Stop-Loss and Take-Profit Points

A stop-loss point is a cost at which a broker will sell a stock and write off the trade. This regularly happens when a trade doesn't work out the manner in which a broker trusted. The focuses are intended to forestall the "it will return" mindset and cutoff losses before they raise. For instance, if a stock breaks underneath a key help level, traders regularly sell at the earliest opportunity.

Then again, a take-profit point is the cost at which a dealer will sell a stock and take a profit on the trade. This is the point at which the extra upside is constrained, given the risks. For example, if a stock is moving toward a key opposition level after an enormous move upward, traders might need to sell before the time of solidification happens.

The ideal approach to predefine the risk you are eager to take is to construct a stop loss management plan. Above all else, each time you are entering a trade, you have to have a stop loss so as to secure your bankroll. At the point when you are taking a shot at your trading procedure, you ought to distinguish the level of the trade size you are happy to hazard. At the point when you discover this rate, you ought to do a basic count so as to characterize the level at which your stop misfortune ought to be set.

Suppose your bankroll is $10,000. As such, after the most extreme day trading leverage of 1:4, you will have a purchasing power of $40,000. Presently suppose that the greatest risk you are eager to take rises to 1% of your bankroll. This implies you are prepared to chance 10,000 x 0.01 = $100 most extreme in every one of your trades. In any case, the purchasing power you are overseeing is $40,000, isn't that so?

Presently you have to characterize the amount of your purchasing power. You are eager to put resources into every one of your trades. Suppose you need to invest 1/8 of your purchasing power ($40,000) in every one of your trades. This implies you will put 40,000 x 1/8 = $5,000 in every one of your arrangements. We will risk $100 (1% of the account) in each trade with contributing $5,000. So as to discover the correct area of your stop loss, you have to characterize what rate $100 take from $5,000. We can find this out with a basic calculation:

100/5,000 = 2% (0.02)

As such, your stop loss ought to consistently be at a 2% good ways from the passage cost. Along these lines, you will consistently risk $100, which is 1% of your bankroll.

Instructions to More Effectively Set Stop-Loss Points

Setting stop-loss and take-profit points are frequently done utilizing technical analysis, yet principal analysis can likewise assume a key job in timing. For instance, if a trader is holding stock in front of earnings as fervor builds, the person might need to sell before the news hits the market if desires have gotten excessively high, paying little heed to whether the take-profit price has been hit.

Moving averages speak to the most well-known approach to set these points, as they are anything but difficult to ascertain and generally followed by the market. Key moving averages incorporate the 5-, 9-, 20-, 50-, 100-and 200-day averages. These are best set by applying them to a stock's chart and seeing if the stock price has responded to them in the past as either a help or obstruction level.

Another extraordinary method to put stop-loss or take-profit points is on help or opposition pattern lines. These can be drawn by interfacing past highs or lows that happened on critical, better than expected volume. Like with moving averages, the key is deciding points at which the value responds to the pattern lines and, obviously, on high volume.

319

When setting these focuses, here are some key contemplations:

- Utilize longer-term moving averages for increasingly unpredictable stocks to diminish the opportunity that an insignificant cost swing will trigger a stop-loss request to be executed.

- Alter the moving averages to coordinate objective value ranges. For instance, longer targets should utilize bigger moving averages to decrease the quantity of sign created.

- Stop losses ought not to be nearer than 1.5-times the present high-to-low range (unpredictability), as it is too liable to even think about getting executed without reason.

- Alter the stop loss as per the market's unpredictability. In the event that the stock cost isn't moving excessively, at that point, the stop-misfortune focuses can be fixed.

- Utilize referred to crucial occasions, for example, profit discharges, as key timeframes to be in or out of a trade as instability and vulnerability can rise.

-Reward-to-Risk Ratio (Win-Loss)

In each trade you attempt, you ought to have plainly expressed objectives. This implies you ought to consistently realize the amount you are prepared to lose and what you are focusing on as far as a profit target. However, how would you do that? Simple! A similar route likewise with stop loss management. Be that as it may, this time you deal with your objective.

On the off chance that you focus on benefit equivalent to 1% of your bankroll, you should get a 2% expansion. Along these lines, you will risk 1% of your bankroll (2% of the exchange) and you will focus on 1% benefit (2% expansion). For this situation, you have 1:1 Return-to-Risk proportion, since you hazard 1 to get 1.

1:1 is the base you should focus on if you execute high reoccurrence trading and you open more than one exchange for every day. At the end of the day, don't chance more than you focus on in the event that you are a day trader.

Be that as it may, there is an exemption. In the event that you actualize a high likelihood technique, where the achievement rate is more than 65-70%, at that point, you can put a free stop loss. The purpose behind this is the stop might be intended to shield you from quick value moves against your exchange. The free stop loss could likewise be utilized when you leave your exchanges medium-term (which I don't advise).

Now and again, when you need to trade a major loop, you can extricate your stop loss so as to adapt to amazingly high instability during the opening chime.

Just to explain something on the stop loss, you don't need to enable your order to be activated. In the event that I am searching for a particular increase of supposing 2% and the stock starts to come up short, I will utilize time and deals to pass judgment on the off chance that I should leave an exchange.

Along these lines, after some time, your success proportion will keep on expanding which, will build your per normal exchange benefit. It will likewise put you in a champ's attitude as you get in a steady musicality of hauling cash out of the market.

-Computing Expected Return

Setting stop-loss and take-profit points are additionally important to compute the normal return. The significance of this computation can't be exaggerated, as it powers traders to consider their trades and support them thoroughly. Also, it gives them a precise method to look at different trades and select just the most beneficial ones.

This can be determined utilizing the accompanying formula:

[(Probability of Gain) x (Take Profit % Gain)] + [(Probability of Loss) x (Stop-Loss % Loss)]

The result of this calculation is a normal return for the dynamic broker, who will, at that point, measure it against different risks to figure out which stocks to trade. The likelihood of gain or loss can be determined by utilizing authentic breakouts and breakdowns from the help or obstruction levels—or for experienced brokers, by making an informed investment.

-Trailing Stop Loss Order (TSLO)

Profits will run in support of you to a point, and afterward, out of the blue, things can conflict with you rapidly.

In the event that you are in a trade and the value moves in support of you, there is nothing amiss with altering your stop. Along these lines, you can secure ensured benefits.

The trailing stop is a customary on-chart market order, which gets you out of the trade when explicit prerequisites are met. As you presumably surmise, the name "trailing stop" is connected with the character of the request. The trailing stop essentially trails behind the value activity, when the stock is inclining toward you. Be that as it may, if the stock is moving against you, the trailing stop doesn't move.

Assume you purchase Oracle at $35.00 per offer, and you place a trailing stop at $0.35 (35 pennies) underneath your entrance cost. This implies your trailing stop will get you out of the market at $34.65 if the value diminishes right away.

Notwithstanding, if ORCL enters a bullish pattern and the cost increases to $36.00 per share, at that point, the trailing stop will be consequently balanced at $35.65 per share. Since we entered at $35.00, we will have a secured benefit of $0.65 (65 pennies).

If, in the wake of coming to $36.00 per share, the value starts to drop, the trailing stop holds at $35.65. On the other hand, if the value starts to transcend $36, the trailing stop misfortune will move higher as needs are.

A key thing to recall when putting trailing stops is to account for the instability of the hidden security. This means if a stock has 3% moves per light, a .5% trailing stop will be activated.

-Differentiate and Hedge

Ensuring you capitalize on your trading implies never placing your eggs in a single basket. In the event that you put all your cash in one stock or one instrument, you're setting yourself up for a major loss. So make sure to differentiate your investments—crosswise over both industry part just as market capitalization and geographic area. In addition to the fact that this helps you deal with your risk, however, it additionally opens you up to more chances.

You may likewise get yourself when you have to support your position. Consider a stock position when the outcomes are expected. You may think about taking the contrary situation through options, which can help ensure your position. When trading action dies down, you would then be able to loosen up the fence.

-Downside Put Options

If you are endorsed for options trading, purchasing a downside put option, once in a while known as a protective put, can likewise be utilized as support to stem losses from a trade that goes bad. A put option gives you the right; however, not the investment, to sell the fundamental stock at a predetermined value evaluated at or before the alternative lapses. Subsequently in the event that you possess XYZ stock from $100 and purchase the half-year $80 put for $1.00 per alternative in premium, at that point, you will be successfully halted out from any value dip under $79 ($80 strike less the $1 premium paid).

The Bottom Line

Traders ought to consistently know when they intend to enter or leave a trade before they execute. By utilizing stop losses viably, a trader can limit misfortunes as well as the occasions an exchange is left unnecessarily. Taking everything into account, make your fight arrangement early, so you'll definitely realize you've won the war.

Chapter Ten

Time Management In Stock Trading

There are numerous advantages to being a broker. One of the fundamental reasons we love being a broker is about adaptability. This implies we don't need to get up right on time to get down to business, we don't have a supervisor to instruct us, we can take get-aways at whatever point we need and we can likewise control our very own time.

Numerous traders anyway have a test in dealing with their time, since they don't have the foggiest idea how to oversee it in a compelling way. In this chapter, we will feature a couple of approaches to deal with your time successfully as a broker.

1. A decent rest

A few people like to boast about sleeping for a few hours. 'I will rest soundly when I bite the dust,' they say.

Donald Trump, the United States president, has consistently boasted about how he sleeps for three hours consistently. He contends that it is hard for an individual that sleeps for 8 hours to rival one who rests for 3 hours.

About this, I have an alternate opinion.

I have faith in having a decent night's rest. Rest causes you to remain invigorated during the day. It additionally encourages you to maintain a strategic distance from the burnout that has affected such a large number of individuals. The ideal approach to deal with rest is to rest early and afterward get up right on time also.

2. Have objectives

One of the fundamental reasons why a great many people don't accomplish their time management goals is that they don't have objectives. Having objectives implies having a lot of things that you need to accomplish inside a specific timeframe. Without objectives, you will have a test of time management.

For example, each morning, you need to have a list of things that you need to accomplish during the day. At the point when you have this arrangement of things, you will be in a decent position to accomplish most during a brief timeframe.

3. Organize

You ought to figure out how to organize your undertakings. This implies you ought to consistently attempt to do the most significant things first. For example, if your primary occupation is trading, you ought to do the best to attempt to do or plan your trading early in the morning. This is the place you ought to invest a ton of energy.

Set aside some effort to peruse, watch, and do your trading tasks first. By doing this, you will be in a decent position to make progress. You ought to abstain from trading when you are drained or when you have a great deal going on.

4. Go on breaks

The issue with numerous individuals is that they need to seem occupied. In any event, when they do not have anything to do, you will see them attempt to accomplish something. The test with this is efficiency is exceptionally diminished.

As a broker, you ought to consistently concentrate on profitability. You ought to be content on each one hour spent well. Hence, in your trading day, you ought to have breaks.

5. Stay away from interruptions

Finally, you ought to give a valiant effort to evade interruptions. This is a zone where numerous individuals have a significant issue. For instance, you may wind up caught up in social media networking. You may end up investing a great deal of energy talking with companions. You may likewise be disturbed by TV shows and even music.

To keep away from these interruptions, you ought to put forth a valiant effort to have a decent workspace that is liberated from disturbances. You ought to likewise be sufficiently principled to diminish occasions of being stressed or distracted.

5 Must-Know Time Management Tips for Traders

Low maintenance dealers have it harsh. While we as a whole prefer to consider online markets trading nonstop as a colossal favorable position, it doesn't come without its obstructions. Because a market is open doesn't imply that the time you are available is a fitting time to trade. Nor does it constantly imply that one has sufficient opportunity to really break down the market in the way that it ought to be, and settle on proper choices dependent on the data consumed. The lucky opening for any low maintenance dealer is moderately little, and not many individuals adjust a trading reasoning around this while genuinely figuring out how to make it work.

Managing time is an enormous roadblock for some fire up dealers, as they are just not used to a fixed daily schedule, also experimentation/expectation to learn and adapt gets in the way of clean consistency.

Attached to risk, time is an issue that should take into account one's character type. Basically, if your character type searches for fast activity and for the most part comprises little patience at that point trading low maintenance will be such a lot harder thing to achieve.

Discovering transient opportunities consistently can be simple when you're spending the main part of the day on investigation. That being said, extremely high-likelihood trading dependent on your individual speculation system is, in many cases, rare all through the session. In this manner endeavoring to pack in a full trading session where you end level in 60 minutes or 3 hours with interruptions is heading off to all that a lot harder to sharpen in and center around what you truly need to.

Terrible traders will, in general, be brimming with gaps. Be that as it may, very frequently, those gaps are just inadequacies in information, both present and long haul. With an absence of time accessible, important data can without much of a stretch get skipped, putting the trader at an extreme hindrance.

Here are some quick tips that can conceivably guide you the correct way with regards to dealing with your time as a dealer:

1. Adjust your trading theory with your character type and the time you have accessible

I can't reveal to you the number of traders I witness endeavoring to trade a specific program that conflicts with each embodiment of who they truly are. Elements may meddle with their speculation on this issue, and time is surely one of them.

It is safe to say that you are the sort to show restraint? Is it safe to say that you are restless and can't keep still? If you will, in general, feel fidgety and are a part-time trader, at that point, you extremely just may have one alternative: adjust a transient technique that you can manage serenely in the time you have and compel yourself not to "try too hard." As such, take transient trades, however, don't over-strive regarding the number of sets you are exchanging. The appropriate examination requires some investment, and in the event that you are everywhere as far as what you can sensibly assimilate in during a solitary session, you are likely trying too hard.

In the event that you are a greater amount of the patient, orderly type, at that point, you are likely more qualified towards longer-term objectives. You may utilize the utilization of cutoff orders for execution or basically float in the method for longer-term specialized or principal plays. Stops and go out on limb benefits are large and risk is ordinarily a lot of lower. Individuals without a great deal of time on their plates may favor more extended term techniques as they're just not there to observe each tick, nor do they want to. Full-time dealers that longer-term utilization procedures are generally contributed over a scope of monetary standards, adding more enhancement to the pot (also keeping them occupied all through some random day).

Regardless of whether your character type takes into account a short, medium, or longer-term trading reasoning all depends. In any case, this ought to be stage one with stage two concentrating on fitting that way of thinking inside the limits of time that you have accessible.

2. Never sacrifice sound investigation

If there is one territory that you never need to hold back on is sound examination. Merchants that exclude pertinent pieces of data are truly doing simply aimlessly taking a look at an outline and making an uneducated supposition with respect to what will occur straightaway. Take the brief period that you have and assimilate yourself in investigation. In the event that you don't have the opportunity to think about the setting of all sets accessible, at that point, don't anticipate exchanging them. Sound investigation is basic. In the event that I glance back at any of my deplorable minutes as a trader, they, as a rule, happen essentially in light of the fact that I missed something little preceding execution. When I understand a slip-up was settled on, I would have no real option except to cut the string, a difficult exercise. Utilize your time carefully and possibly execute when your degree of certainty is exceptionally high.

3. Burrow deep and do it quick – maintain a strategic distance from the interruptions

Telephone ringing free, TV blasting out of sight, taking a look at general news sites, or YouTube are basically horrendous for your trading. Likewise, with some other work, they represent an immense interruption and are the snappiest method to get prevented from acquiring essential data that will do just help you as far as execution. Take the brief period that you have and basically dispose of interruptions that represent a danger to perfect, succinct and profound examination that is essentially required for your advancement. Close the door, shut out the clamor and pay attention.

4. Adjust to a methodical method to ingest data

You should commonly utilize a straight approach with regards to investigation with a significant accentuation on the association. Traders that are disorderly in their investigation or just navigate starting with one theme then onto the next will in general, end up dispersed or confounded.

Start with explicit, respectable news destinations: those that generally give me an "enormous picture" sees on current happenings. These are all at the front of my bookmarks and effectively available. "Fun" bookmarks are sorted independently and avoid the ones that issue most.

For a point of interest, you should, at that point, drill down into your intraday news channel action. Go ahead and check relationships and different markets so as to build up a balanced and widely inclusive information bank of the present circumstance. When you make a general assurance that you are happy with your insight into the world of that specific trade, you can start boring into outlines. Do the same straightforward investigation you have been doing for a considerable length of time, looking over numerous time spans and separating everything into littler segments.

While it does not have to be carefully "top-down", it still has to be organized. Start with a large scale picture and make endeavors to separate things into littler parts. Conventional top-down investigation has its inadequacies: on the off chance that you are making conclusions dependent on a full-scale view alone and that view isn't right, everything that follows is a wash and you might be setting yourself up for calamity. Remember a worldwide approach and understand that market timing is similarly as critical as some other part.

5. Try not to drive a window of time

Risk management rule #1: don't do anything by any stretch of the imagination. Straightforward? Indeed. Easily done? No.

In the event that you happen to lean toward a short window of time as far as normal trade length, you need to comprehend the consequences that accompany it: you will have days where you are basically not happy with any trade, paying little mind to the time you put resources into investigation. Experts are marketers and bend over backward to drive action down the throats of perusers each possibility they get (also most are specialists = you exchange, it is beneficial for them). The reality, be that as it may, is if you can't profit from what you know, you shouldn't do anything. You ought to appreciate trading and everything that accompanies it, so don't attempt to constrain something that simply isn't right.

Throughout time, I have seen a huge scope of trading methodologies that incorporate various windows of time.

However, a trader shouldn't pick this way of thinking dependent on this factor alone. Spare time is something that is valuable to every one of us, however, utilizing it admirably and positive P&L is about the main thing that will enable us to have a greater amount of it. In a business where "timing is everything," dealing with your work process is similarly as essential as any arrangement of trade execution.

Chapter Eleven

Becoming a Great Stock Trader: Getting Started and Best Practices

Numerous individuals fantasize about profiting with stock trading, and others just marvel every once in a while in the event that it very well may be finished. A huge number of financial specialists make cash playing the business sectors consistently, and however the greatest additions are the most energizing and what stands out as truly newsworthy, there's a lot of subtlety and loads of moderate structure wins for stock traders. Figuring out how to make money trading stocks will require some serious energy; however, it is a reachable objective.

Stock trading is a risky movement. If you give it a shot, you'll have to anticipate misfortunes — a few organizations win, and some lose each day. In any case, with continuous research and a comprehension of which organizations merit putting resources into and why you can make money trading stocks.

Beginning as a Brand-New Stock Trader

Beginning and making money trading stocks are two unique things. In case you're new to the game, pursue these means to set yourself up for progress as you gain understanding:

- Research market patterns: Even the best brokers don't rest with regards to research. You have to find out about market inclines just as trustworthy sources where you can remain current on breaking news. "Kiplinger," "The Economist," and "Bloomberg" are a couple of trustworthy stock-trading magazines to add to your day by day understanding list. It's likewise worth after the web journals and web-based life records of industry specialists, including effective brokers, business analysts, and different experts.

- Create an account with a trading site: Once you're prepared to begin trading, you'll have to make a record with an exchanging site — a site like Scottrade, TradeKing, or TD Ameritrade. Prior to picking a help, read through client audits and BBB evaluations, if accessible, to affirm that the site is respectable. You'll additionally need to perceive what exchange expenses and different charges you'll pay for utilizing the administration. In the event that you need assistance narrowing down your decisions, search for benefits that will enable you to trade, for example, financial specialists examine instruments, portable applications, or client care administrations.

- Work on: Trading stocks isn't simply researched, and it's significantly something other than exchanging stocks. If you need to show signs of improvement and see an arrival on your ventures, you have to rehearse. Before you profit, create an account on a site like ScottradeELITE or OptionsHouse and profit. This will assist you with getting acquainted with how trades are set and what choices you'll make when a stock is doing ineffectively or well. This can assist you in figuring out how trading functions before utilizing genuine cash.

In case you're a new investor, you may be moving toward the market from a general point of view. This is incredible, yet after some time, you'll need to concentrate on a territory that you're a specialist in or love finding out about. The market is brimming with a great many alternatives, and it's difficult to bounce on each great exchange that travels every which way every day. It's basically better to concentrate on a little region of the market as you gain understanding as a dealer.

Fortunately, as another broker, you can inquire about and investigate uninhibitedly without adhering to a specialization immediately. Simply realize that sooner or later, you'll need to pick and ace a particular piece of the market. Likewise, in case you're a fledgling looking for a trading site, recollect that you don't need to pick one immediately. A few people create accounts with two or three sites and afterward thin their decisions later when they have a more clear comprehension of which pleasantries, administrations, and expenses are best for their trading technique.

Some Frequently Asked Questions

I'll address a portion of the more typical inquiries and remarks here:

- How would you pick the correct stocks?

This may sound more difficult than one might expect — all things considered, if everybody picked the correct stocks inevitably, there wouldn't be any misfortunes. In all actuality, the correct stock isn't generally the most outstanding or the most energizing. Prior to choosing to put resources into an organization, ask yourself these inquiries:

* How gainful is the organization? In case you're purchasing stock and need its value to build, you'll have to assess the organization's budgetary reports. These records are accessible online for any organization that is traded openly. In case you're experiencing difficulty discovering this data, you can contact the business to get a physical duplicate of the latest yearly report.

* Is the organization prone to be beneficial pushing ahead? Regardless of whether the yearly report didn't show any productivity, an organization may even now merit putting resources into. Check the business' initiative, its yearly costs, and its obligation. You can likewise survey its monetary records and salary explanations to evaluate whether the organization is probably going to be or remain beneficial later on. You may likewise discover, for instance, that another or low-benefit organization has as of late obtained some veteran officials. This kind of progress is a convincing motivation to put resources into a business.

* What brought on any losses? On the off chance that you locate a poor quarterly exhibition in the money related report, it doesn't really imply that it's not worth putting resources into the organization. Research and reveal what added to this low execution, and solicit whether there's a hazard from a rehash. What's more, if there is a risk of another poor quarter, you'll

have to choose whether the potential result merits contributing in any case.

* How has the organization done contrasted with its friends and industry? In the event that you go over a loss or gain, it's conceivable that variables identified with the business — not really the organization — added to these outcomes. Contrast the organization's stock history with its rivals to perceive how it has fared over the previous years. Likewise, see industry patterns. When stocks were up or down for the whole business, did the organization proceed true to expectations? Or, did the endeavor exceed expectations or pass up development that contending organizations delighted in?

As you gain understanding, you'll add your very own inquiries to this list so you can vet a stock and ensure it works for your trading procedure. You may likewise have criteria to advise when it may be satisfactory to veer off from your technique.

This is the kind of subtlety that you can just create through broad research, practice, and genuine exchanging. For complete apprentices, however, it's prescribed to stay with surely understood organizations that have loads of information about their exchanging chronicles, initiative, and productivity. It's additionally a decent practice, to begin with only a limited quantity of cash.

Note that a few people likewise have rules about things like just trading with an unmistakable brand or an endeavor with long periods of accomplishment. Contingent upon how moderate or extreme you need to be as a broker, you may receive a portion of these techniques or relinquish them for different conditions, such as having a strong plan of action paying little mind to time in activity or offering a specific kind of item or administration.

- How would you purchase your first stock?

After you've investigated a few organizations and working on purchasing stocks for all intents and purposes for no particular reason (and experience), it's a great opportunity to attempt the genuine trade.

Sign on to your trading site account, and search for some well-investigated, dependable stocks.

It may be enticing, to begin with, something dangerous or contribute a major sum, yet it's ideal to consider making the plunge with a little exchange.

It's normal for amateurs to invest as meager as $1,000 while regardless they're learning.

Make sure to check for exchange expenses, however. Since you're currently working with an official record and exchanging genuine stocks, these sorts of charges will apply.

- Would you be able to Trade Stocks for a Living?

351

A great many individuals trade stocks as their all-day employment, and a great many others appreciate trading part time. How you approach stocks is totally up to you. You can make sense of how to make cash exchanging stocks at home, or you can seek after day trading as a profession.

A few people likewise appreciate trading all the more inactively through a mutual fund or working with a specialist to encourage trades. In a mutual fund, you arrange with a gathering of different financial specialists and pull your money together for contributing by an expert reserve supervisor. These investments are regularly expanded over an assortment of ventures and areas. Another decision is to join a stock trading group or online network where you can discover understanding and backing — which is surely significant for new traders.

- What Amount Can You Make From Stocks in a Month?

How much money you would be able to make from stocks relies upon your trading technique, your specialized area, how the business sectors are performing, and endless different elements. Proficient, full-time traders can make over $5,000 in a month. The definite return rate likewise changes, relying upon the sum contributed. In case you're simply beginning or just trading on the low, you can even now make hundreds or thousands per month. In addition, as you gain expertise and reinvest your profit, you can procure substantially more on a month to month premise.

Tips for New Traders

New brokers have various techniques and logical strategies to research and attempt as they approach the market. Below are some tips to help.

1.) Take Out Time to Peruse Different Types of Markets, Strategies, and Analysis Methods

Traders with more experience can return to the procedures they use, as well, and check whether they can change their way to deal with start turning a benefit. These are only a couple of options you can seek after as a broker:

- Trading penny stocks: Penny stocks are low-esteem stocks traded for under $5 per share. The profits are commonly low, but at the same time, there's less hazard since you won't need to invest a great amount in beginning trading. It's additionally conceivable to make a tremendous benefit in trading these reasonable stocks. You'll need to find out about over the counter markets and put additional work into examining an organization's money related history since organizations that trade penny stock don't need to meet the severe monetary prerequisites of the New York Stock Exchange or NASDAQ.

- Day trading: As a day trader, you'll open and close a few trades inside the same session. Since these traders are taking a look at variances inside a little time span, they're scanning for various signs of a decent exchange than long haul investors. Day trading is commonly not advised for learner investors.

- Putting resources into long-and transient techniques: You would someday be able to trade, clutch stocks for a considerable length of time, or locate a stock methodology someplace in the middle. There's heaps of adaptability by the way you exchange, and individuals have made a benefit utilizing different systems, approaches, and procedures in the stock trade.

Notwithstanding investigating various kinds of trading or procedures that might be more qualified to your character or money related objectives, you can take a look at various market examination techniques to give you an edge or put you on track to benefit.

The essential examination techniques are fundamental and technical. Both are utilized to foresee value changes and consequently educate which stocks to purchase and when.

The thing that matters is that a basic examination takes a gander at the organization — its initiative, benefit history, foreseen increases, future objectives, notoriety, and so on — to check the stock's worth.

A technical analysis, nonetheless, sees market patterns and what drives financial specialists to settle on stock choices. You may discover accomplishment by moving your concentration starting with one investigation technique then onto the next or by attempting a blend of the two to educate your trade decisions.

2.) Trade in Dividend Stocks or Initial Public Offerings

Another choice for turning a benefit as a broker is to put resources into high return profit stocks. With this kind of venture, the organization delivers investors profits — a percent of organization benefits — each quarter. Financial specialists get a profit paying little mind to whether their stock has acknowledged in value.

Beginning open contributions are another decision. These are the primary stocks an organization ever offers, and however, most new businesses come up short, it tends to be an awesome chance to get a stock at its least ever cost. Since the organization won't have earlier benefit information, however, you'll need to accomplish more research about elements like administration and the organization's field-tested strategy and course before deciding if the first sale of stock is a decent risk.

3.) Perfecting Your Trading Skills

You don't need to be a specialist to make money trading, yet as you place more ventures and continue rehearsing and inquiring about, you'll normally show signs of improvement at trading stocks. On the off chance that you find that you're reliably not profiting on your trading — paying little respect to whether you're another dealer or have some understanding — you can pursue these pointers to help make something happen.

4.) Follow Some Stock Trading Best Practices

On the off chance that you find that your trades aren't getting positive returns, return to the inquiries you pose to assist you with picking an organization to put resources into. You may need to include or change the criteria you use to pick organizations.

You can likewise attempt some other accepted procedures for profiting in online stock trading, for example, putting resources into mid-and enormous top organizations. The previous have a market capitalization between $2 billion and $10 billion, and the last has a market capitalization of over $10 billion. Putting resources into these organizations is regularly productive on the grounds that market capitalization means that the organization's stock value contrasted with its extraordinary offers.

Another choice is to add an additional progression to your due tirelessness when examining organizations: tuning in to an organization's profit telephone calls. In the event that you've just evaluated the organization's quarterly profit discharge, this extra advance will give you a more clear comprehension of the business' authority and plan for pushing ahead.

5.) Monitor the Markets Every Day

Individuals beginning their first day of trading and those who've been in the business for quite a long time share one significant duty regarding all intents and purpose: observing the business sectors consistently. This will assist you with remaining over creating patterns, but on the other hand, it's vital to the time tested exchanging mantra of purchasing low and selling high.

Regardless of whether you plan on being a traditionalist, forceful, present moment, or long haul merchant, this general guideline should control your contributing choices.

6.) Buy Low and Sell High

Purchasing low and selling high is anything but difficult to recall, and it's a demonstrated technique for mesh a benefit as a merchant. In any case, you would prefer not to settle on motivation choices at whatever point a stock value climbs or dips. Truth be told, it's imperative never to freeze when a stock dips under the value you paid since the sum may bounce back.

To choose whether a sum is high or low enough to warrant an exchange, do this:

- Take a look at the organization's income per offer and representatives' buy action.

- You likewise need to take a look at the business' administration, benefit history, and life span.

You need to purchase low. However, you likewise need to put resources into an organization that will recoup — ideally directly after you've gained their stock.

A similar guideline applies to selling high.

In the event that you need to sell the stock so you can reinvest the benefits, you need to ride the flood of the stock worth expanding for whatever length of time that conceivable. The organization's prosperity may likewise imply that the business can reinvest in itself, which may additionally drive share value.

Persistence is thus important, however, you additionally need to know when a value is probably going to level or decrease. Following industry patterns and experts' actions can assist you with pinpointing the best time to sell.

361

In case you're keen on day trading or short selling, purchasing low and selling high will be imperative to your prosperity. You'll additionally be generally intrigued by unpredictable markets since frequent increments and declines in stock worth open the entryway for frequent gainful trades. There are loads of intrinsic risks, however, in unstable markets.

7.) Diversify

In spite of the fact that you'll, in the long run, become a specialist in a specialty advertise, a great arrangement for seeing predictable additions is to expand your portfolio. This is just prescribed once you have a strong comprehension of how the market functions and how to purchase and sell stock.

Diversification is significant since it secures you against industry changes. For instance, if every one of your stocks were in tech and an administration guideline or new development contrarily influenced stock costs in that part, the entirety of your speculations would be affected. A various portfolio is insignificantly influenced by such patterns.

This methodology is likewise a decent method to adjust high-risk and preservationist ventures. Putting resources into new companies is commonly risky, for example, since most are covered inside five years. On the off chance that you've put resources into a built-up organization in a specific industry, however, you can purchase stock in a startup in a similar section.

Their shared gainfulness could be all-around useful for the business, or maybe the greater organization will procure the littler one — netting you a sizable benefit.

8.) Reinvest

It very well may be enticing to leave trading once you've made a benefit. Nonetheless, on the off chance that you need to prevail in the long haul, it's shrewd to reinvest your income into other stock or into something less productive, however okay with solid, long haul benefits, similar to reserve funds or retirement account.

In Closing: Learn by Doing

To a novice, picking stocks may appear as though finding an organization that is performing great or searching for a startup venture flaunting an amazing item or administration and putting resources into them. For sure, a large number of the best stockbrokers bounced on great chances and left with tremendous additions. In any case, these individuals didn't fall in reverse into these examples of overcoming adversity.

Master traders carry their insight into the market each day. They realize what patterns to look for, and they recognize what makes a decent trade or awful trade — and when it merits disrupting their own guidelines. Certainly, a few people do luck out trading stocks.

In the event that you need to move unhesitatingly realizing that you can make cash exchanging stocks, however, you'll always have to be taking a shot at your methodology, watching out for showcase patterns, and standing prepared to strike at the correct chance.

Regardless of whether you're absolutely new to trading or have been bringing about certain losses and need to make something happen, probably the ideal approaches to succeed and make money trading stocks is to watch what trades specialists make and figure out how they're computing their options.

The key is to comprehend why the trade is being made — regardless of whether a pro isn't trading a region you're acquainted with, on the off chance that you can contemplate their philosophy, you can apply their methods and way to deal with your own subject matter. Truth be told, this is the ideal approach to figure out how to make money trading stocks.

Conclusion

I believe congratulations are in order because you have made it to the end of this book, and you have been equipped with the knowledge you need for effective swing and day trading.

From what you have read, you would realize that the definitive objective of this book is to give you a superior chance to productively utilize the opportunities you encounter the same way a specialist trader would. Regardless of whether you are a regular broker that has lost a great deal of money before, this book will make trading quicker, simpler and multiple times increasingly productive for you.

And the sky is the limit from there!

ABOUT OPTIONS

There are a lot of trading titles out there, including those focused on option strategies. This book focuses primarily on risk management approaches, the best option strategies, the consistent theme all through. By configuring it this way, you can approach different topics, keeping this main objective in mind. So, go ahead, go to the areas that interest you.

This book can be read from one end to the other or used as a reference guide. Each strategy provided identifies the risks and benefits associated with the position. It also identifies alternative strategies to consider in risk management, if any. There are millions of ways to succeed in trading markets, but some challenges are universal for all. Tools and techniques to address these challenges are also provided.

This book offers options strategies for managing risk and navigating various market conditions. I really believe in taking care of the risk first, the profits will follow. With this in mind, the approaches you find here focus on reducing the potential losses of traditional equity positions and creating a repertoire of option strategies that can make gains as the markets go up, down, or fall. To integrate the complete steps required during the negotiation, it also provides discussions on market and industry analysis, as well as elements to look for when trying out a new strategy.

Whether you're new to trading or that you are an experienced investor, the listed options on stocks and indices are excellent vehicles to manage risk and increase your assets. The wide diversity of strategies available using these titles makes them suitable for just about everyone - as long as you understand how they work and apply them correctly. I started trading options many years ago and found that by using different strategies, I could implement business profiles with reasonable risk-reward over the years.

Trade and investment are usually differentiated by deadlines. I believe that investing is something you accomplish to achieve long-term financial goals. Whatever plan you personally create to achieve these goals, the options provide a way to protect long-term assets during periods when markets face them.

Although I primarily use the term trading to invest or trade, I consider it to be a market approach to achieving superior returns to help build these investments over the long term. Higher yields mean taking additional risks, but I certainly want to say measured risks. At the very least, the approaches proposed in this book should reinforce the focus you need to keep on the risk, reward, and effective management of positions, no matter which financial asset you choose to use.

Trading times may be shorter, but do not get me wrong. . . I am not talking about hyperactive day-trading, where you are glued to your screen. Stock options and indices offer strategies that require day-to-day management, as well as those that can be reviewed weekly or more. It's up to you to implement the appropriate approaches to your risk tolerances and preferences, as well as your schedule.

UNDERSTANDING OPTIONS IN 2021

Options are financial tools that derive their value from another underlying asset or a financial measure - here, I focus on equities and market indices. Because options are in two forms, calls and calls, adding them to your current trading and trading tools allows you to benefit from up and down movements on the underlying movements you select. You can do this to limit the total assets at risk or to protect an existing position.

To truly understand the stock options and indices, you must also have a solid understanding of the asset on which they are based. It may mean looking differently at movements of stocks or indices - for example; volatility is an essential component of the value of the option. By comparing options with the underlying securities or other securities, your learning curve is directed towards their application.

The main purpose of trading any security is to understand its risks, including all of the following:

- Know the conditions to consider when analyzing a trade
- Use the right commercial mechanics when creating a job
- Recognize trading rules and requirements
- Understand what makes the position win and lose value

The following sections discuss these key options components to provide a good platform for creating rewarding positions.

KNOWING OPTION ESSENTIALS

A stock option listed is a two-party contractual agreement with standard terms. When you create a new position, buying an option gives you rights, and selling an option leaves you with obligations. These rights and obligations are guaranteed by Option Clearing Corporation (OCC), so you never have to worry about the trader is on the other side of the contract.

A major risk you face with options is the risk of time because contracts have a limited life. A call option becomes worthwhile when the underlying stock increases, but if the move is too late, the purchase may expire worthlessly. On the plus side, options have expiration dates ranging from 9 months to 21/2 years.

Your rights as an appellant include all of the following:

- Buy a specific amount of underlying shares
- Purchase until a certain date (expiry)
- Purchase at a specified price (called strike price)

This is why the purchase price increases when the stock price rises - the price you are entitled to is fixed when the stock itself increases in value.

A put option becomes valuable when your stock falls, but the timing is the same. The change must take place before the expiration of the option contract. Your sales contract rights include the sale of a specific quantity of stock before a certain date at a specified price. If you have the right to sell a stock for $ 60, but the bad news about the company lowers the price to $ 60, those rights become more valuable.

Acquiring skills as an options trader means selecting options with expiry dates that allow time for the intended moves to occur. This may seem very difficult at the moment, but some basic rules are helpful. These rules include good transaction management, which means leaving a position if it moves against you and reaches its predetermined exit point.

Each stock with options present has a variety of expiry dates and exercise prices. When searching for options, you will find the following:

- A longer time-out option is more expensive.
- An option with a lower exercise price is more expensive.

Information on all available options can be found on the Internet from various sources, including your broker. The selection of the best, given the current conditions and their point of view on the actions, takes a little time, but it's not rocket science. Your biggest problems are those associated with any type of negotiation: managing your own emotions and exercising discipline.

GETTING COMFORT WITH OPTION MECHANICS

Options differ from actions in terms of what they represent and how they are created. This results in additional rules for

373

negotiation and decision-making beyond basic buying or selling considerations. You may decide to simply leave the position in the market or exercise your rights under the contract.

Are these additional complications worth it? For many people, yes. The differences in the mechanics of stocks and options are very simple and manageable. A big advantage of these securities is the way they provide leverage. By controlling share rights rather than the stocks themselves, you significantly reduce your risk.

From the beginning of this book, I have identified the factors that affect the value of an option, as well as the most appropriate conditions for buying and selling different contracts. By understanding how options provide leverage and reduce your trading risk, you begin to understand why I use the term risk initially measured.

RECOGNIZING RISKS AND REWARDS OF OPTIONS

The main risk associated with options is the risk of time. You have the tendency to lose your entire investment if the change you expect is too little or too late. It's not an all-or-nothing proposition for you. You may decide to exit an option position if an adverse movement occurs in the underlying stock before expiration. It all comes down to disciplined negotiations.

The valuation of equity risk versus call and put risk creates a strong foundation for understanding the risk and benefits created by more complex option positions. Visualizing these risks on a chart develops your ability to evaluate an option swap. The risk graphs, which represent the value of the position in relation to the price of the underlying stock, are a trading tool that will be valuable to you throughout your trading career.

INTEGRATE OPTIONS INTO YOUR ROUTINE

Understanding the options and what motivates their prices offers another view of the stock market. In addition to the sentiment information provided by options trading, the conditions that you must understand as an options trader can help your stock market analysis. These market features also help you analyze and select sectors to achieve your goals.

As with any new market approach or strategy, adding options to your trading means the following:

Understand the benefits and risks associated with them Test them safely or at low risk

Options can be "tested" by monitoring price changes, using paper trading strategies, and focusing on a limited number of strategies adapted to current conditions. In addition to these steps, it allows you to take into account the negotiation costs associated with this security.

ADDING OPTIONS TO YOUR ANALYSIS

The analysis of trading options can easily integrate with your current market analysis, complementing it with sentiment tools. Market-wide tools and sentiment analysis often focus on extreme conditions to identify periods when there is the greatest potential for market reversals. Basically, when the last trader gets short, it's a bullish signal for the future. Optional measures that help recognize extreme conditions include contract volume and implied volatility readings for key market indices. So, by adding sentiment analysis to an amplitude analysis, you get a nice confirmation of pending changes.

The options analysis focuses on two aspects of the market:

- Trend conditions
- Volatility conditions

Although stock traders are also aware of trend conditions, they may be less in line with volatility conditions. Or perhaps there is a strong emotional feeling of greater volatility, but not quantitative.

A technical analysis designed to provide insight into trends and volatility helps you focus on stock options or trading. Adding information to the industry analysis allows you to use underlying groups that behave differently to diversify your holdings better and spread your risk. The combination of industry analysis and options also offers good low-risk alternatives for capitalizing downside movements through the use of put options.

TRYING OUT INVESTING AND TRADING STRATEGIES

Option values are not based solely on the price of the underlying stock you are trading. Other factors affect the market price of an option. Reading these other factors is a good start, but to better understand price dynamics before you have money at stake, you can take other steps.

There are various techniques at your disposal designed to provide the following:

- A better intuitive understanding of changes in the underlying stocks (and the market in general) that affect the price of an option.
- Practical knowledge of simulation mechanics

Therefore, becoming proficient in option strategies requires practicing through paper trading - similar to stock trading. But before that, you really need to understand how real market changes affect the values of options over time. Once you have done this, you can get a lot more from the paper exchange. You can concentrate on other trading costs, including slip and margin requirements, as well as ways to better execute trades.

Paper trading is not the only method you can borrow from stock trading to look into a new strategy. Back - Testing an option approach may take a little longer than a stock approach, but it could certainly save you a lot of money. By having a plan that slows you down to face different nuances of trading options in advance, you will define disciplined trading skills.

PUTTING OPTIONS TO WORK

option contracts can be used for financial tools or hedge for speculating. When buying an option contract, you are able to

377

exercise your rights or simply trade away the rights. Needs and conditions dictate different art. You want to be prepared to assess the situation and do what is best. Exercising an option to minimize stock market risk is just one way for you to put the options at your service.

Reasonably minimizing risk is the name of the investment game, so it is very useful to know how to protect existing positions and strategies by adding options. The hedge can be implemented position by position or covering the entire portfolio. If instead of a short-term bearish outlook that requires protection, your opinion becomes so negative that you are looking for downside trading opportunities, the options offer a much safer approach than selling an action or a short-term sector.

Another way for options to make big efforts for your investments is to use leverage. By spending less on the initial investment, you are responding to a reduced risk approach, but that does not mean you should get reduced returns. Basic strategies can help you accomplish both. And if speculation is part of your modus operandi, you can risk even less when you are ready to limit your profits.

UNDERSTANDING THE OPTION STYLES

There is a major focus on stock options in this book, but it's hard to ignore another important segment of the stock market. This is the index market. The striking difference between a stock and an index is that the stock is a tradable stock. An index can not. This means that the exercise of the index option takes on a new dimension. Since this is not the only difference between the two types of options, it is important to understand how your rights and transactions are affected by the option style you choose to use.

USING OPTIONS TO LIMIT YOUR RISKS

Comparing the risk profiles of stocks and options is a good start to appreciate the value that options bring to your investments, but the use of strategies to capitalize on these stocks is much better. Assessing the many protection options available is one of the first steps in implementing all strategies. Spend some time understanding why some will better serve their goals than others will turn theoretical discussions into real applications:

The risk for an existing position: The risk for existing positions can be reduced to varying degrees, ranging from reasonable protection to full hedges, adjusted to market conditions.

The risk for a new position: The risk for new positions can be reduced similarly to a very little amount using a combination of options or less significantly with unique long-term options.

Account approvals for strategies that make use of long options combined with stocks or individually are usually available for most traders. As you acquire experience and have more strategies, you can actually customize a position risk profile using combinations of options. This includes:

- Vertical debit spreads
- Vertical credit spreads
- Calendar Spreads
- Diagonal differences

Access to different strategies involves implementing approaches that are best suited to existing market conditions.

APPLICATION OF OPTIONS TO SECTORAL APPROACHES

ETFs can be one of the most effective investment products introduced in decades. They offer great diversification, like mutual funds (MF), but far surpass both areas:

Ability to leave an ETF as needed with a quoted market price during the day (not when calculating the value at the end of the day)

EXISTENCE OF OPTIONS USING ETFS AS SECURITY

Needless to say, I really like this second. Portfolios can be built using ETFs and ETF options for protection or making use of ETF options for the entire portfolio.

USING OPTIONS IN DIFFICULT MARKETS

Equities and ETFs offer a great way to participate in bull or bear markets, but there is still a third potential price trend - which is lateral. By adding strategies that let you capitalize on this third trend alternative, you are taking a step further to allow the market to dictate your approach.

In addition to responding to a third potential market trend, option strategies allow you to reduce directional risk by taking advantage of upward or downward movements rather than

380

one direction. You can create a combined position and adjust it over time as prices change. This approach responds to market movements rather than trying to predict.

REDUCING YOUR DIRECTIONAL BIAS

Stock positions, long or short, have a directional bias as they depend on movement in one direction for profit. Options allow you to minimize directional bias by creating combined positions that can be profitable if the underlying moves up or down.

Therefore, not only can you better control maximum losses with options, but you can also reduce directional risk by using strategies that can be achieved with two of three possible directional motions. These approaches are based on neutral delta trading styles, which introduce a new way of thinking about the market.

BENEFITTING WHEN MARKETS ARE EVERYWHERE

A stock can remain in a lateral trend channel for an extended period, offering option traders a way to take advantage when most traders can not. Although the lateral model may be long-term, the option strategies that take advantage of it are shorter in nature. These extended models also tend to cause strong movements away from the recessed channel and generally test the model before continuing. This prepares you for a change of strategy from the beginning of a new trend.

CONSIDERING YOUR OBSTACLES

Whether you trade stocks, ETFs, currencies, or options, there are similar obstacles to success that need to be overcome. The main thing is your makeup. Negotiation evokes certain emotions that can wreak havoc on your bottom line unless you actively manage it.

You might consider exciting new trading strategies, but be careful when you jump the weapon. Good preparation is required. Three steps to follow before using a new marketing strategy:

- Understand the risks and rewards of security
- Practice Strategies
- Analyze a trade

Although this book covers many topics of "learning" and " analysis, " this chapter presents tools and techniques for practicing strategies. First, by monitoring the different options pricing components and paper trading, you simulate the actual conditions. This gives you a more intuitive feel for price changes and helps you avoid costly mistakes. Then, by developing your backtest prowess , you implement only the greatest approaches, allowing you to stay long enough in the game to gain valuable experience. Through experience and practice, you finally achieve mastery of the strategy.

MONITORING OPTION GREEK CHANGES

Understanding basic option strategies is a much faster learning curve than recognizing the right price for options used in strategies. But among the most effective techniques to really understand the value of these bonds is to monitor the price and the Greek changes in conditions. real.

TRACKING PREMIUM MEASURES

Developing your skills with any option strategy really means understanding how option grants are affected by changes in the following:

- The price of the underlying
- Expiration time

A great method to get a better intuitive feel for their impact is to track daily changes in all the different components. All you have to do is access market prices, an options calculator, and a spreadsheet. By taking note of a few different options, you should learn a lot about how changing conditions affect prices in general. By including the Greeks in the process, you also understand what factors play the most important roles at different times.

Ideally, you will end up reviewing the markets and monitoring prices over a period when prices move a little. This makes it possible to highlight the delta, gamma, and theta impacts on the price. Before putting your money at risk, set up a spreadsheet to track the following:

- Price of underlying
- Price for calls ITM, ATM, OTM and e foreshore maturity ed variables
- Days before expiration
- Intrinsic value option, delta, gamma and theta

By following these values, you can identify the metrics that have the greatest impact on option strategies.

The delta can be displayed on the basis of values from -1 to +1 or from -100 to +100.

CHANGING VOLATILITY AND OPTION PRICES

The impact of volatility on option prices is sometimes somewhat difficult to understand because implied volatility (IV) includes price factors that vary over the life of the option. IV includes the following elements:

- Past volatility (historical)
- Expected future volatility (implicit) and
- Request for a contract

Past volatility

Crowd behavior can inflate option prices when demand for some contracts increases as news of a company arrives.

Implied volatility (IV)

Implied volatility (IV) is the implied volatility of the option price. Does this cover everything for you? Given that the IV is a very important option price factor, it is probably a good idea to expand this definition a bit.

In terms of trading and IV:

- It is best to buy options when the IV is relatively low.
- It is better to sell options when the IV is relatively high.

The problem with these basic rules is that you can not always follow them. By maintaining a long-term ownership position, you want to protect; you just have to throw caution in the wind, and put IV high? Certainly not, especially considering that increasing the IV often results in a growing fear in the market. When you are faced with call options in a highly volatile environment, you may need to evaluate a wider range of months to maturity and strike prices.

When the implied volatility (IV) is relatively high, then it decreases considerably, it is called IV crush.

Remember that IV can vary:

- Until maturity, which contributes to more uncertainty about the value of the option.
- For the exercise price: Usually, the cashier IV (ATM) is the lowest, but it does not always work that way. Asymmetric charts provide IV at the strike price and can speed up the process of selecting options when you have to buy contracts, while IV is relatively high. An option price can be divided into two components: the intrinsic and extrinsic value. The value is entirely determined by the value of the option, but IV does not play any role in this value. The deeper the option (ITM), the lower the IV will have an impact on the total price of the option.

By using short option strategies, time reduction works in your favor. Trading options with 30 to 45 days to expire accelerates this deterioration for you.

PAPER TRADING AN APPROACH

The pursuit and implementation of new strategies naturally develop your trading skills. With paper trading, you can move safely in the new strategic learning curve.

When trading on paper, be sure to incorporate the trading costs associated with the position to get the best value for the profitability of the strategy.

Paper trading: advantages and disadvantages

Paper trading is a great way to minimize losses by learning the mechanics of the strategy or by slightly modifying your trading routine. Looking at a long money-out option (OTM) decreasing the value as the implied volatility decreases is much less painful when it's on paper. However, it does not really prepare you for the battle of greed and fear inside. However, this forces you to face it before you have money online.

Establishment of electronic paper exchanges

The paper exchange can be done in a spreadsheet, electronic platform or. . . You have it, paper. Do what's best for you If you plan to create your own diary, also include the Greek option.

Many financial sites allow you to enter different positions in a portfolio tracker that is updated late in the day or late in the day. Unfortunately, not everyone accepts option symbols. A basic tracker will give position information that includes price changes with the result. A more advanced platform may include displays of risk charts and other transaction management tools.

USE OF TRADING SYSTEMS

A trading system is a tactic with precise rules of entry and exit. Even if you are currently using a systematic approach to a strategy - that is, you only buy a call when the implied volatility is relatively low - a trading system is more narrowly defined. When using a system, you must do the following:

Set a position for all purchase signals generated by the rules
Exit each position when the output signal is generated

Know what you get

There is no decision making when implementing the system - you never think about accepting an input or output signal. If you accumulate losses or something seems wrong, you shut down the system completely. The two greatest things about a formal system are:

- It minimizes your trade emotions
- It allows backtests to get an idea of expected performance.

If you start to exercise discretion in deciding what to do, these two benefits will disappear. Emotions appear, and their results may differ considerably from test results. As with any trading strategies, an essential key to system trading is working with systems that are tailored to your trading style and the size of your account.

Although the rules of a system are strict, flexibility is common by varying the speed of the indicators or by adding filters. A filter is an additional rule for exchanging inputs or outputs. Indicators and comparable system components are defined as system parameters.

The characteristics of a good trading system include:

- Profitability in various markets, securities, and market conditions
- Overcoming a purchase and maintenance approach
- Stability with manageable drawdowns
- Diversify your trading tools
- Adapted to your style and the availability of your time

Be extremely careful when designing a system and put it on the autopilot. Always watch the negotiations.

PERFORMING A BACKTEST

A backtest uses historical data to determine whether a system generates stable earnings. You can perform backtests using data downloads or mechanical transaction tracking, but the most efficient way to do this is to use a software application for backtests. You just have to make sure you test what you think you are testing.

When backtesting a system, include longer periods to capture bullish, bearish, and lateral markets. In this way, you get results in the worst conditions and experience (in a test environment) realistic downshifts. Drawdown is the term used to define accumulated losses on accounts resulting from consecutive loss transactions. Evaluating lifting is just another way of managing a man and his risk.

A robust trading system works for a lot of markets (stocks, commodities, etc.) under a variety of conditions (bull and bear markets).

By examining the results of the backtests, you are looking for profitability and stability. Stability refers to the consistency of the results - you want to know if only a few operations generate all the profits or are spread over a variety of operations. A stable system:

- It has winning deals with average profits that exceed the average losses of lost trades.
- At an average system benefit close to the median system benefit (low standard deviation)
- Suspends manageable samples
- Do not trust some profitability trades

Note that a system does not need to have more winning operations than losing trades. Many trend systems rely on the ability to run profits for fewer transactions while quickly reducing losses on lost trades.

After creating a system with reasonable backtest performance, you perform advanced tests by running the rules in a shorter time. Typically, you start the test on the last backtest date and run at some point before implementation. Expect diminishing returns in advanced tests. System trading is not an undisclosed key that generates profits. It is a way of minimizing harmful professional emotions. Consider this approach that deserves your attention if you're ready to roll up your sleeves and explore.

Following the right steps

Follow these steps when re-testing a system:
- Identify the basis of the strategy (i.e., enter trend conditions).
- Identify incoming and outgoing trading rules.
- Identify the negotiated market and the backtest of the period.
- Identify the assumptions of account (system and commercial allocations).
- Test system; evaluate the results.
- Identify the reasonable filters to minimize the loss of trades (number and / or size of these trades)
- Add a filter based on the results from step 6; test system; then evaluate the results.
- Add a risk management component.
- Test system; evaluate the results.

Check the average value of the trading loss as well as the maximum and consecutive losses to determine if a system is suitable.

System time as the rate of change (ROC) was tested by using a simple displacement cross means (ADM) for signaling the entry of the trade [ROC 34 SMA: 13] and output [ROC 21 SMA: 8]. As a faster signal was used for the release of the trade, a second parameter had to be added to the trade entry, requiring that the 21-day ROC be greater than its 13-day SMA. Otherwise, the appropriate commercial output may never be reported. It is a trend system that seeks to capitalize on a long-term upward momentum. To limit profit losses and erosion, a faster moment signal is used to exit the position.

The backtest was conducted over a six-year period that included periods of highs and lows (1999-2005) in a group of six semiconductor stocks, including SMH, an ETF for the sector. US $ 20,000 was used for the system, with 50% of the money available used for each bargaining. $ 10 per sales commission has been added to the costs. No stops were part of the initial test of the system.

A system need not be robust to be effective. Since volatility and trend characteristics vary for different securities, some are better suited to certain types of systems.

Review of system results

Risk management is the main theme of this book; evaluating a non-stop system may seem counterintuitive. However, when you think about it, stop levels are pretty arbitrary - the market really does not care if you enter a $ 45 position. It may or may not be supported at 5% or 10% below. Allow the system to recognize a viable stop-loss point by retesting it and decide if it presents an appropriate risk to you.

The results of the system have been very favorable in many measurements for the initial execution, so no filter has been added. The maximum adverse excursion percentage was revised to determine if a reasonable stop level could be added. A 15% downtime was added, and the system test was run again. The results were just a little less favorable, so the parade was incorporated.

Graphics packages can use different calculations for the same indicator. If you change systems, compare the values of the indicators that provide signals to exchange the same system being tested. Always think about retesting the system on the new platform.

Two advanced tests were also performed, with and without stopping. Both - periods of the year were used for each, and the system remained viable with much lower profitability. Expect this to happen with actual system performance and advanced tests. This is due to changing inefficiencies and conditions that are developed from the markets. It's one of the reasons why you need to review the performance of the system periodically and integrate reasonable stops whenever positive.

A lower percentage stop can be considered as an approximation of average and median returns, but since average incomes are greater than average losses (allowing profits to work), you must first compare the mean and median to earn and lose. business separately.

You can make use of a standard deviation evaluation to evaluate profit stability for any market approach.

ADDING RISK MANAGEMENT TO A BACKTEST

All business approaches must consider risk management. Put the emphasis on the largest adverse movements for a strategy trying to identify cases that still allow the working strategy. If adding this downtime maintains cost-effectiveness and system stability, and fits your risk tolerance, consider implementing the strategy or system.

Cutting losses

A systematic but non-mechanical approach can still be tested. Regardless of how you perform this backtest, you should keep an eye on the major adverse moves that have occurred in the generated transactions. This allows you to identify reasonable filters and systematic stops designed to minimize losses.

A stop-loss order can result in a higher loss percentage when a transaction is executed. The worst case occurs when a signal is generated at the close of trading one day, and the security shows a price difference on opening the next day.

Taking profits

Identify risk-loss stopping points that are probably already second-hand. On the other side of this, have you ever been to a lucrative business that is starting to move in the wrong direction? At this point, you realize that you do not have a specific exit plan to make a profit. Sometimes you focus so much on the risk that you forget to identify the target prices favorable. Or you may have identified a lucrative exit point, but conditions begin to deteriorate before that price level is reached.

In addition to identifying a stop loss level, identifying a stop percentage or a dollar value to minimize the number of profitable transactions that turn into losses. The trailing stop should be built into your system, or the strategy is the strategy and tested. If you had like the system to generate the trailing value, consider trading with large moves that are favorable that earned much less in terms of profits (or transformed into losses). After completing your exam, you can do the following:

- Add a filter that speeds up your trips
- Generate a percentage right using the most favorable tour data

Letting the benefits run

An effective business approach does not have to have more gains than transaction losses. It only needs profits to overcome declines. This is indeed the case for many trend-oriented platforms. You end up with additional losing trades, but the average value of the loss is well below the average value of the trades. And so , go the mantra, "Make sure you reduce your losses while letting the profits run."

Sorting the highest loss or profit transactions makes it easier to see the statistics for both.

Although you need to identify a method to make a profit, you should also avoid lowering profit levels so that they no longer make up for losses. Successful trading requires a little pre-work. You will see your trading evolve, focusing on the following points:

- Reduce losses.
- Prevent profits from turning into losses.
- Leaving the profits running.

SHIFTING FROM KNOWLEDGE TO MASTERY

Controlling strategy does not mean that all the transactions you perform for a given strategy are profitable - it means that the right conditions were in place when executing a particular transaction, placing the odds in your favor for a particular strategy. profitable operation. Proper management of the position is also another element that highlights discipline when leaving a trade if conditions change. It sounds very easy, but mastering the strategy can take years to evolve. Your objective is to stay in the trading game long enough to reach this area.

By focusing first on the basics and mechanics, you create a solid foundation that allows you to understand advanced techniques more quickly. You implement new strategies through paper trading to avoid the most costly mistakes. When you're ready to announce the new strategy, you can further minimize the cost of errors by reducing the size of your position and remembering to make a profit. This approach allows you to stay in business longer, allowing you to find and develop strategies that best fit your style.

SETTING THE RIGHT PACE

There are a number of good choice strategies in this book, some of which are likely to pique your interest more than others. Start by negotiating some of the simplest approaches on paper, then go on to negotiate with them. After that, discover the strategy you prefer, again by the paper trade. There is no guarantee that the market conditions are favorable to this strategy is the strategy; Therefore, you may prolong your days of paper trading until the market changes or you are ready to explore a new strategy. But, It is really important to keep this in mind. You want to put the focus on the strategies that have meaning to you and agree the best for your style. This is how you will finally develop the domain.

Starting with some strategies

I hope that learning new strategies will please you. It's amazing to discover all the different ways to make money in the markets. But not all strategies and tactics work in all market conditions. More importantly, they will not all fit your style. If you are new to options trading, follow one or two basic strategies to develop a good understanding of change and premium mechanics.

There are a variety of strategies at your disposal that allow you to make money in the markets. In addition to your preferred method of analysis, you will find that you are developing a preferred list of strategies that favors you.

Experienced option traders must recognize current market conditions and then explore one, perhaps two, exceptional strategies considering these conditions. Start trading with paper and progress from there. If there is a specific strategy that really intrigues you or speaks to you, but the conditions are not good, just change it to paper. In the long run, it's best to focus on the market approaches that are right for you.

Adding strategies as market conditions change

I see markets as a permanent pursuit because conditions are always changing. Although there is a continuous cycle of ups and downs, the market is never exactly the same. It seems that you have already recognized it by buying the book first.

When the strategies that generally work well for you are starting to weaken, take the time during the weekend to perform a full market assessment. You can detect the first signs of a change in conditions.

Option trading lets you implement strategies that can be profitable regardless of market conditions. A sample includes:

- Low volatility (long base call, married sex)
- High and high volatility
- Low, low volatility (base selling, debit spreads
- Low and high volatility (collars, credit spreads
- Low volatility, limited by range (butterfly, condor)
The combination of stocks with options or options with options offers really great options. This can be bad or good news, as each approach takes time to master. Be careful when checking a strategy at random. rejecting it because it "does not work."

It is likely that you will not trade all available strategies. Most traders experiment differently along the way and then master a smaller number. The experience gained allows you to maximize profits on your favorite strategies (knowing when to keep them) while minimizing your losses (knowing when to double them).

Deciding which option strategies to use is like a market analysis - there are many ways to approach it, none of which is the "right" way. The best tactic for you is the one that makes the most sense intuitively, so when conditions change and things get harder (and better), you'll have the confidence to stick to your plan.

REALIZE MASTERY THROUGH LONGEVITY

The experience of different markets and the exploration of appropriate strategies require longevity in the markets. Rising markets may run for years, and volatile conditions may also remain stable. Expect additional losses when markets transition or when implementing a new strategy. Risk management using limited loss and unlimited gain strategies, to the extent possible, lays the foundation for longevity.

Paper switching provides a technique for minimizing learning curve losses. A second method is to size the position correctly. Starting with smaller starting positions, the potential losses are manageable. Adding rules that include making a profit is the icing on the cake.

Successful trading will never happen overnight. Be prepared to observe different market conditions, spend time making low-cost mistakes, feeling different levels of emotion, and developing your business skills.

Determination of appropriate business sizes

There are different techniques for identifying appropriate commercial sizes. Many go beyond the scope of this book simply because of space constraints. Two easily embeddable are:

- Identification of a maximum amount allocated per transaction
- Identification of a maximum percentage amount allocated per transaction

I prefer it because it changes automatically depending on the size of your account.

The options represent a leveraged position, so you do not have to allocate the same value to the option positions as for the stocks. In fact, it's probably not the best idea to do it. Using your stock allocation plan as a basis, you can estimate an initial allocation value by recognizing an option position that controls a similar amount of stock. This is a starting point that should be tested and revised.

Establish trade allocation values before analyzing a specific trade. You must know in advance the maximum amount available for an individual exchange to minimize the risk of your account.

When you try a new policy (after changing roles), further reduce the size of the transactions so that the errors are more tolerant. If it means negotiating the size of an option's contracts, so be it. Remember, you're not here to impress Wall

Street with the size of your business - you're here to make money in the markets.

As your skills grow, increase the size of the positions for the tested allowances. This will increase profits as option trading costs are generally higher than the percentage of trading costs. If you have been well prepared and continue to manage your risks, increasing the size of the positions should not be a problem. In fact, this should improve results because you will get economies of scale with transaction costs.

Focusing on profit

Throughout this book, the focus is on risk management. In this chapter, however, there is an added emphasis - making a profit. It is not enough just to have a large number of lucrative businesses. Your profits must include the following:

- Exceed trading costs
- Exceeds prudent investment approaches
- Exceed your losses

This is not just for nothing; you must have a plan that includes a review of the strategy and business results to implement the best rules of profitability. These rules should minimize the number of profitable transactions that turn into losses and make profits. Developing these skills means that you evolve as a trader.

There are many different prices that can provoke an emotional response during a negotiation. Make sure to identify exit points for a loss and exit points for profits.

Trade is partly art, partly science. The development of rules and specific steps to be part of a process that puts you on the path to skillful trading. Implementing them with a focus on risk management gives you the time to develop your business. A great first step on the scientific side is to create a list of strategies. This lets you methodically approach a new type of trading to gain as much knowledge and experience as possible.

To begin, I wanted to provide a list of ten major option strategies. The common point with these strategies is that they have limited risk and are alternatives to consider. The unlimited or limited but high risk - risk strategies that could potentially replace are provided with the summary strategy.

Each of the top ten strategies includes:

- Name and components of the strategy
- Risks and rewards
- Optimal market conditions (trends, volatility)
- Advantages and disadvantages
- Basic risk profiles
- Additional information by strategy

By all means, think of adding notes to make them yours.

MARRIED PUT

A married put combines a long stock with a long put for protection. The position is created by buying shares and placing them at the same time, but the key is to create protection against sales. The purchase of a put option for existing shares or the launch of an option for a subsequent expiration month is consistent with this strategic objective. Long Out-of-Cash (OTM) options must be sold 30 to 45 days prior to expiration.

COLLAR

A collar combines a long stock with long-term protection and a short call reducing the cost of protection. An ideal scenario is when you can buy long-term stock and the call option in conditions of low volatility, allowing long-term protection. Calls are sold as volatility increases, and the expiration time is 30 to 45 days, so time decay accelerates short call gains.

LONG PUT TRADER

A long put is a low-risk limited position that wins when the underlying falls. This replaces a short position of unlimited risk stock that requires the establishment of more capital. The downward movement must occur when the option expires, and non-cash sales (OTM) must be discontinued 30 to 45 days prior to expiration.

LEAPS CALL INVESTOR

Long-term Equity Anticipation Security (LEAPS) reduces the costs and risks associated with a long stock position. The position is better established when the implied volatility is relatively low. The owner of LEAPS will not participate in dividend distributions that reduce the value of the shares.

DIAGONAL SPREAD

A diagonal gap combines an option from next month's short with a month's long option of the same type. When the exercise prices are the same, we talk about calendar spread. A short-term, neutral view can sell the short option to offset the costs of the long option. A diagonal call is described here, but a sales diagonal works as well when you are short-term in the long run.

CREDIT PROPAGATION BEAR CALL

A bearish spread combines a short and short strike price purchase with a longer and higher purchase ending in the same month. Create a credit and replace

a short call with unlimited risk. It is best applied when implied volatility is high and 30 or 45 days or less before expiration.

STRADDLE

A straddle combines a long purchase with a long sale, using the same exercise expiration and price. It is built when volatility is low and should rise and win when prices rise or fall sharply. Since there are two long options, exit from the expiry position of 30 to 45 days to avoid a deterioration of time.

CALL RATIO BACKSPREAD

A call ratio backspread combines longer exercise prices for calls and higher with a lower number of lower strike calls that expire in the same month. It is best to implement it for a credit, and it is a potentially unlimited reward position with a limited risk that is more profitable when a bullish movement occurs.

LONG PUT BUTTERFLY

A long-selling butterfly combines a bull put spread, and a bear selling spread expiring in the same month for a debit. The two short positions have the same exercise price and make up the body. The two long positions have different exercise prices (above and below the body) and make up the wings. Deteriorating weather conditions contribute to trade.

TEN DOS AND DON'TS IN OPTION TRADING

Trade is partly art, partly science. Development as a trader begins with the use of a formula approach for different markets and strategies. The skillful application of an experienced professional requires practice, patience, and experience. It is a trip that you receive ideally.

I hope this book contains many rules, steps, and concrete methods. I sincerely hope this has also provided you with some important nuances of trading. Things that can not be applied mechanically. This seems to be the perfect point to focus on those who are here.

Do Focus on Managing Risk

The game is known as risk management. In fact, when people ask you what you do and what you do, say that you are a risk manager. Become one with him. Now, if it's not nuanced, I do not know what it is.

By exploring only option strategies, you are actively addressing other financial risks in your life. This includes the risk of inflation, income risk, and even the market risk associated with buying and maintaining the investment.

When your trading is based on risk management, you:

- Understand the risks and benefits associated with the markets in which you trade. Learn and test strategies before putting money at risk.
- Create a plan that identifies the entry and exit approaches of the enterprise size and the maximum allowable loss. Be aware of how the plan will be implemented to meet your risk parameters.
- Understand how to manage trade and establish positions.
- Have a plan to make a profit
- Ask yourself, "What if I'm wrong?

Other more general risk considerations include sector diversification and negotiated strategies. You can correctly allocate trading sizes, but if you enter five trend trades using the same strategy on stocks in the same sector, you are going against this trading size rule. That's the nuance. By extending these portfolio-based guidelines, you are acting more like an effective risk manager.

Don't Avoid Losses

In one way or the other, you will have losses in your trades. This is not a feature for beginners; It's just a cost to do business. In fact, suffering small losses is a skill developed by experienced traders. Try to reach this level sooner or later.

Avoiding losses is one way to increase them. You can make use of your rules and see positive results with a series of small wins and losses, just to clear the board (then some) with a big loss. This is a discouraging setback.

By shifting your vision of what constitutes successful trading from one profit to another following its rules, you are on the road to true success. Initially, you can tell yourself to do it, but you often become a true believer with experience. When this happens, you become more involved in a rules-based approach, and that's when change happens.

Do Trade with Discipline

Disciplined trade means following your rules in every trade. Not in part or most of the time, but always. Will you have a perfect record in front of the discipline? Probably not. . . Somewhere along the line, your human feelings will improve you. If you do not have the discipline at the beginning, and you have the chance to stay in the commercial game, your best discipline is continually improving. Otherwise, it only takes a short period of time before your luck runs out.

Unfortunately, those who have been successful initially can delay the appreciation and commitment to disciplined negotiation. Initial success can give you a false sense of being right, and that's not the point.

The characteristics of a disciplined trade in each trade are as follows:

- Allocate a reasonable amount to an operation
- Identify a maximum business risk
- Identification of input and output signals
- Run an order when your plan requires it

These are the elements of the checklist, but the disciplined trade goes beyond that. Do your homework, review your business, evaluate your plan. . . I do not think I could create a complete list. It's about learning what you need to do to negotiate successfully, mapping out how you're going to do it, and putting it into practice.

Don't wait to withdraw your emotions

Some traders assume that successfully trading means completely defeating your greed and your emotions of fear. I am here to tell you that that day means that you will have no emotion. . . It is certainly not a good thing. Eliminating emotions when negotiating is not a reasonable goal; However, their management is.

Things that can trigger emotions include:

- Negotiate using a discretionary approach
- Make business decisions when markets are open
- Use a stock or an underlying sector that owes you a transaction due to past losses

The ways to deal with these specific elements include:

- Focus on more systematic approaches
- Identification of non-worked hours for examination and management of operations
- Move away from a specific stock or industry, even if you generally trade successfully

There are even times when not negotiating for a certain period is the best way to adjust your attitude and your approaches.

Tracking your emotions is the first step in their management. Remember to add a note to your business records to follow them. Also, watch your emotions outside business hours... if you wake up grumpy or worse, can not sleep at night, your emotions control you.

Do Have a Plan

Many Wall Street statements have been around for quite some time, as they simply stay loyal to graduates year after year. Other sayings also include one that fits perfectly here: "When you do not plan, you plan to fail."

The creation of a baseline must certainly be considered a process and not a one-off event. Think of the "draft" and start by writing a plan. Completing it with a word-processing document or an easily editable spreadsheet can be great, but if you feel like you're on too much computer, a good old paper and pen are fine. The obsolete approach allows you to take notes along the way without hesitation because the computer is off. The essential thing is to create something.

When carrying out your first trading plan, set a deadline for completion and return three months later. This gives you a chance to throw the wheels, identify what seems to work and not work. It also highlights the elements that may be missing. Schedule a second review about six months later, then set a regular schedule that makes sense.

In addition to key risk management elements, start incorporating items such as general rules (for example, buying weak implicit options and selling high default options where possible) and the steps you will take to do so (for example, review historical and implied volatility graphs and verification of implied volatility levels with an options calculator).

Identifying other aspects of your trading work also helps (for example, analyzing market situations for long-term investments discretely from short-term trading) and again how you will get there (e.g., monthly Saturday analysis investments, Sunday Weekly Analysis for Negotiations).

As markets and your personal circumstances change over time, expect your trading plan to change as well. Better yet, plan it.

Do Be Patient

Because the focus is on risk management and creating a plan, you can feel a lot of pressure to create the "right" plan. Try to understand that there is almost always more at stake when there is no plan, as opposed to a plan that requires some work.

Part of the trading plan process includes adjusting your rules. This is certainly something you do outside of office hours, and that is the result of evaluating the strategy's performance and working to improve your overall trading plan. This can mean an increase in trading allocations or stop loss percentages or trading fewer strategies at the same time.

Your plan can be very aggressive or very conservative, but at least it serves as a basis for adjustments. Sketching two will be better? Probably, but market conditions can affect the effectiveness of your adjustments. Okay; At a particular time, you will have traded in a variety of conditions and learned techniques to take advantage of them. This is called experience and takes time.

Patience is not just for trading plans. Sometimes the best thing a professional can do is nothing. . . Waiting for trading or expecting profits are valuable skills that can have a big impact on trading profitability.

Don't undergo analysis for paralysis

If you like to play with the numbers, the economy and the financial markets provide an infinite number. You could probably spend years looking for relationships between different metrics, trying to get market timing signals. Then you can backtest and test in advance all the existing indicators to see which ones give you the ideal trading signals.

The paper business all the time will not necessarily bring you closer to a successful business. At a particular point in time, you will need to know the markets where you, the human trader, will react differently when trading live.

As mentioned, part of trading is managing your emotions and not deleting them. There is another aspect of that because there are also great emotions and characteristics that you bring to the table. Trust becomes so important when the market image begins to fade - that's what makes you follow your reasonably proven rules.

Therefore, the market with all your data can provide interesting diversions, but it keeps you from the task at hand. After all their learning, exam, testing, the practice, and analysis are made to a policy, in taking the experience provides live solidifying their understanding of everything. If this is your first trading option, use limited risk strategies and appropriate trading sizes to gain this experience. And if all goes well, you will also earn money along the way.

Take responsibility for your results

Never change the responsibility for your business results to anyone or to yourself. Why put your success in the hands of someone else? This makes it very elusive.

Throughout your trading career, certain situations or issues that affect the profitability of the business will surely arise. If there is a problem with executions, think about how you order and discuss it with your broker. If problems persist, correct them by transferring some of your assets to another broker and measure those results.

When you only have limited time for your standard exam due to work restrictions, personal appointments. . . Anyway, move on to strategies that you have time to do the right way. If there is still not enough time, getting away from trading is your only responsible option. Do not worry; the markets will always be there when you can reach them. And when you do, you will have kept some assets for trading.

Always recognizing that you are responsible for your own results, you seek solutions faster and take control. No need to wait for another person to take action or an event to happen. Doing this at the beginning of the game makes it possible to assert a much wider command on your learning curve and accelerates successful negotiations.

Do not stop learning

The changing nature of markets makes it almost impossible to avoid this. Since the economic conditions, the ups and downs of the market, and international markets are never exactly repeated, there is always the possibility of learning.

There are a variety of analytical tactics for trading, and each has a greater variety of techniques and tools to explore. Add to the mix new products introduced periodically, and you will have your work ready for you.

It may seem that there is a contradictory message here; I suggested focusing on some strategies rather than adopting a variety of different approaches. The objective was the control of the strategy and remains important. However, when you are on this path, a manageable number of new strategies must be explored. Market conditions dictate it simply.

It is useful to have a game plan for continuing education. . . especially if you want to have a good relationship with your friends, family, colleagues, etc. (also known as balance in your life). Here are some quick opinions to help you create yours:

By mastering the strategies, you will find topics that you want to understand better. Address these questions in a targeted way through self-study (books, CDs, periodicals).

Move to other forms and analysis strategies through more formal education if needed (live classes or DVDs, book manuals) or self-study.

Start the year with general objectives (for example, learn two strategies and more about technical analysis), as well as more details (for example, find strategies that benefit from markets with lateral tendency, better understand -markets).

Many traders naturally continue to learn as they turn to books, articles, news programs, conversations. . . deal with the markets. This is a perfect introduction to my last comment on what, in my opinion, is essential to your success in the negotiations.

I love the game

As with many other traders, I like to read about markets, trade, and other traders. As I check the discussions about the characteristics of successful traders, I often see "love the game." Believe me

The key factors for successful traders really include the challenge of understanding the markets, applying the right approach, and being disciplined. It's not about linking them or making money for them. This is partly because you have to love something that requires such intense work - not necessarily long hours but certainly focused. And in terms of money, this single-engine will eventually lead to big losses for most traders. The long and practiced path for all others must be appreciated.

There is a chance that you think you understand what I mean, but I feel that you know exactly what I mean. Be passionate about your trading, and accept your challenge. There is a healthy excitement about this activity that you have chosen throughout your life.

Is it possible to trade options for a living? That's what everyone wants to know.

It seems that everyone hates his work and wants to relax and exchange options for a few minutes a day and get a very good income.

And why not? That is what I want. But is it feasible? Is there anyone who trades options for a living?

Answer: YES.

There are many people who exchange life options. But most traders do not just hang on to options or stocks only. The ones I know trade all things - options, stocks, bonds, commodities, and even forex from time to time.

CAN YOU MAKE LIVING SELLING OPTIONS?

Yes again. If you do not extract anything else from my emails, I hope you will find that earning 10% on a commercial sale like an iron condor or a butterfly is not that difficult. We do it monthly. The trick is to avoid losses and manage your positions because not all trades win.

Many people make a living or supplement their retirement income with trading options. And the numbers continue to improve - just look at the trend of the volume of options. More and more options are exchanged each year. Volume figures are breaking records every year.

And if others can, you too. You do not need a rocket scientist or a genius. I know very stupid people who make good trading options. And thanks to technology upgrades, anyone at home has access to all the trading tools and data they need - almost all of them are available for free from your broker. Option trading fees are also lower than ever. So, consider trading options to make a living.

SO HOW MUCH CAN YOU EARN?

Most hedge fund directors would sell their first child with returns of 20% per year. Warren Buffet averages 22% a year and has been the richest man in the world for many years.

Before, I was aiming for 10% per month; now, I want 5% more per month. But even if we want less, say that 3% is still 36% per year. Try this at the bank.

HOW MUCH MONEY DO I NEED TO BEGIN TRADING OPTIONS FOR A LIVING?

It all depends on your lifestyle. If you reside in Texas, a 3,000 square foot home can cost $ 250,000 in a nice neighborhood. The same house would cost $ 750,000 in California. Do you need to ride a Porsche or Honda Accord that's right for you? Do you have 5 children to send to college?

The amount required depends on your expenses.

But to provide an answer to the question, let's say you want to make $ 100,000 a year. Cool.

If you want to earn $ 100,000 before taxes and commissions and get an annual return of 36%, you will need $ 277,777 in mutual funds. Now, I do not always use 100% of the money on my account. I leave about 20 to 30% in reserve. So, say you leave 20% in reserve too.

If you only redeem 80% of your account, you will need $ 347,500 in your account to earn $ 100,000 with a 36% return on risk money. Let's round that up to $ 350,000.

That's it? No, at least I do not think so. I think you should also have a decent amount of money for savings and other investments. For example, I have money from real estate and dividends, as well as some companies in which I have investments. So, if something bad happens to my trade or markets, I still have enough revenue to survive.

BUT WHAT IF YOU CAN TAKE RISK?

Ok, so you want to play and go bankrupt. I would always try to keep a 20% reserve on my account to overcome the losses and use it for adjustments and any good trading opportunities that may arise.

But if you take risks, get a portfolio margin. The margin of the portfolio is for traders who know what they are doing and allow you to trade in larger sizes with little money. So, with $ 100,000, you can trade up to $ 600,000 in options. WOW

This allows you to make money faster because you have more leverage, but you can also lose much faster - so be very careful. Greediness can make you do stupid things.

HOW LONG WILL IT TAKE ME TO LEARN TO TRADE OPTIONS?

It's a delicate question. It took me several years. I did not have any mentors or people to watch. There were also not as many websites, books, and videos available. I would say that if someone were serious and spent a few hours a day learning and negotiating, he could learn to change his life in a year. It will not be true for everyone, but I think it's a safe number to look for.

WHAT IF I DO NOT HAVE TIME TO LEARN HOW TO TRADE?

I don't like giving my money to other people to manage and then not knowing fully what they are doing with it. So, even if you are using a service like mine, which has self - trading, I think you should still know how negotiations work, how to use your broker's platform, and keep an eye on what's going on in your account. Some members told me that they only wanted to check their accounts once a year - that's stupid. It's your money. You worked hard there. And you have to work very hard to make sure that a) you do not lose it and b) keep growing.

SO, HOW POSSIBLE IS TRADING OPTIONS FOR A LIVING?

Yes, but it takes time, effort, and desire. Trading for a living is not always a hobby, or anything other than running your own business. It's not like in movies where they scream at their brokers over the phone to buy 1000 shares of this or that and earn a million dollars.

Take your time to learn how to trade. Remember, the markets will be here tomorrow. And with put options, each month is a new game; so if you miss this month, wait a few days.

You have two basic options when you trade stocks - you can create a long position to benefit when the price of a stock increases or create a short position to benefit when it falls. Along the way, you can get or pay dividends here and there, but that's pretty much the side of the bargain. The options allow you to benefit from stock movements up and down while offering some additional ways to capitalize on price changes.

By establishing a basic option position, it is possible to gain higher stock (buy) and lower (sell). In either case, your original investment is usually much lesser than a similar stock position. Also, to option positions, these securities can be combined to reduce costs further. This chapter provides ways to negotiate for less money and less risk.

LEVERAGING ASSETS TO REDUCE RISK

Generally, when you think about leveraging assets, you think about increasing your risk - at least on the equity side. The options allow you to leverage your assets while reducing your risky investment. It's a good combination. With options, the paid premium allows you to price a stock without placing 100% of its value. While there is no assurance that stocks will move in the desired direction, this is the case if you trade options or stocks. So why not do it cheaper?

DETERMINING YOUR TOTAL DOLLARS AT RISK

The options reduce the risk because less money is invested - that's the end result. Once a position has been created, anything can happen - stocks can go up quickly, fall like bricks, or sit down with minimal movement while the rest of the market is active. You do not know. Nobody knows what will happen next.

Any action can fall to zero; therefore, any long action or long position you hold may also be reset. Therefore, your initial investment is your maximum potential loss. In fact, I take it back - if you buy a stock using the margin, you could lose twice your initial investment.

The risk of a long equity position is considered limited but high. Indeed, an action can not fall below zero. Unfortunately, there is a probability of loss between zero and the price of some stocks.

However, there are many possibilities between a total loss and no loss. The main argument here is that when you invest with less money, in the beginning, you usually have less to lose. It is rare to have such a distinct advantage without any inconvenience. The distinct disadvantage of the options is that you can not wait for the change you expect from your investment because there is a time constraint.

Calling risk out when bullish

When you're optimistic about an action, you can:

- Create a long inventory position

423

- Create a long call position

If the stock goes up, you can take advantage of one of these positions - the extent of the benefit depends on the actual change. Your risk is reduced when you buy a call because it has reduced your total investment.

Two main things to note on the risk graph are:

- The significant difference in losses
- Profits increase faster with stock position

Because there are a number of trade - out in this business, I am going to take the slow accumulation of earnings with a lower total risk. It is certainly possible that the stock remains inactive for months, which makes me leave the position to begin a serious upward movement. Again, it's a business - off I'm ready to take.

A risk chart provides a very effective way to understand the risks, rewards, and trade-offs associated with a specific strategy.

By monitoring the values of the options, you will find that if the action moves slightly over time, the option can acquire and lose value as follows:

- Decreases or increases or as stock price rises or falls
- Increases or decreases as the implied volatility of the option increases or decreases.
- Decrease overtime

Price alone does not determine the price of an option. Implied contract volatility (IV) also plays a significant role in its value, with higher IVs resulting in higher contract values. The deterioration of time plays a minor role daily, but the cumulative effect may undermine the value of the option.

Establish long-term positions when implied volatility (IV) is relatively low to increase profitability and minimize losses due to IV reductions. Keep in mind that a relatively weak IR environment does not guarantee that the IR will increase during the lifetime of the option.

Making use of LEAPS for long-term option positions

This is a Long-term Equity Anticipation Security. It's not a new type of trading instrument; it's just a time-consuming option - more than six months to two years. All option stocks do not have LEAPS available, but for those who make the month due, it's almost always January. You will notice different root symbols for these options.

LEAPS goes something like this:

- LEAPS contracts are made in May, June, or July; it depends on the option cycle.
- The new contracts come due in January about 21 /2 years from the date of creation so that in August 2008, there are options available to 2 January 2010 and January 2011. 2011 is newly created jumps.
- When new LEAPS are released, the closest January LEAPS (due in 2009) becomes a regular option, as

Options Clearing Corporation (OCC) revises the symbol to include the root of the regular option.

The root symbol of a LEAPS contract is different from the root symbol of a specific stock to differentiate it from other January options that expire in different years. This approach to name LEAPS could become obsolete when the new option symbol program came into effect in 2008.

The abbreviation for a LEAPS contract comes from the security of anticipating long-term stocks. These contracts are simply options with a lot of time until maturity.

The more time you have for an option to expire, the more money you pay. Therefore, you should assume to pay more for LEAPS contracts. Your risk maximizes with this increased cost, but the extra time gives you a greater chance of maintaining a contract that is at stake (ITM) upon expiration. LEAPS are:

- Available for some stocks and indices that have regular options.
- An investment alternative was offering up to 21/2 years to benefit from your contractual rights.

In addition to giving more time to investment strategies, LEAPS offer extensive asset protection guarantees. The combination of LEAPS with a long stock significantly reduces the cost per day of protection. You must balance the reduced cost with the desired level of protection because, ideally, the inventory will increase over time as you hold it. If this occurs, the sales value decreases during this period, while the strike price remains the same.

More volatile stocks generally have a higher number of exercise prices available each month, as shares are more likely to reach a strike price further away.

Put limits on a bear in motion

When you are out of stock, you can:

- Create a short stock position
- Create a long sell position

If stocks fall, you can take advantage of any of these positions. Rewards are reduced because a stock can only go to zero. Similarly, the rewards are potentially great if the stock becomes worthless.

Two main things to note on the risk graph are:

- The significant difference in losses
- The less than a significant difference in earnings

TRUSTING MARKET TIMING

After trading for an indefinite period, you realize that it is very difficult to identify the future direction of security, let alone where it is going and when. But selecting an appropriate term for an option is clearly an important part of trading these securities. This means that you need:

- Recognize the role that ratings play in stock and option trading
- Be ready to be "wrong" and limit your losses.

- Pay the right price for realistic moves.

Basic option trading requires that you correctly predict the direction in which the underlying will move, the magnitude of the movement, and the maximum time it takes for the movement to take place. All of these things are also needed for stock trading - the difference is that you can keep a long position on stocks for months while trading. Managing a position in this way does not necessarily mean that you are trading successfully.

There are times when an action leaves a limited range, side channel, to return to the channel. If you have created a directional position based on the break, you must leave the position (action or option) if the action returns to the channel because the conditions that justified the trade no longer exist.

Predicting the right direction

To capitalize on a stock position or a single option, you must correctly identify the direction of the underlying stock movement.

Predicting the right direction is a challenge that you face, regardless of the security you choose, so it seems adequate to favor one that uses less of your capital for at least a portion of your transactions. Only you know the answer to that.

Here are some general rules to increase your chances of success:

428

- Trading with the trend using technical tools,
- Or (for competent opposites) negotiate against the trend when the moment is weakening, and its indicators point to a pending curve,
- Negotiating undervalued stocks that garner positive attention by using fundamental tools,
- In all trades, limit your losses with unbiased exit strategies.

Predict the extent of the move

The risk of time is the main disadvantage of trading options, but there is another risk that requires discussion. You may be right about the direction and timing of a stock move, and yet you have too small a range to make your option position profitable. This happens to all option operators.

How can you minimize these deficits? For the most part, it is useful to have some tools - technical or fundamental - that provide estimated price projections.

Your overall business profitability can be improved by focusing on more likely transactions (higher deltas indicating that the movement is more likely to occur) rather than less likely home run transactions. Let the gains accumulate over time, and you will probably have the chance to get a home run or two along the way.

Consider taking some of the profits from your table on a portion of your total position when the game you have planned is partially completed.

Options pricing models also help identify the most likely transactions by providing:

- Expected implied price evolution of the option (implied volatility)
- An estimate of the probability that the option will be ITM at maturity.

By using these option components in your trading analysis, you can determine whether the price of the option is relatively high or inexpensive by taking into account stock history, past option prices, and market conditions. This is shown later in an example.

Predicting the right moment

Time limits for an option give young traders their first rule-based system when risk is properly managed. It means both:

- Negotiation is a reasonable part of the account
- The position is closed before accelerating the decline

A long option position has a clear and integrated output rule. Ideally, this is not the only direction you use to get out of a position.

There is no one size for all maturity selection criteria, as they may vary depending on the strategy and your trading style. The most direct time horizon for options trading is associated with press releases or reports that may result in strong movements on a specific date. This includes:

- Economic or industrial reports, such as unemployment figures or semiconductor orders

- News Releases

Some technical tools also give estimated time projections, including price models or cycles. First, identify your time horizons and check the option strings.

COMBINING OPTIONS TO REDUCE RISK

A put was combined with long stocks to protect it, limiting the risk of the position. This was also accomplished when a call was added to a short stock position. In both cases, the cost of the position has increased.

The equilibrium level of a stock is simply the price of entry. Since option premiums cost you more than the contractual rights of the exercise price, an equilibrium value must be calculated using the strike price and the option price.

When you create positions that focus on specific market opportunities, you can combine the following:

- Stock options
- Set of different call options
- Different mounting options
- Call and collect

Adding long or buy options was the only combined positions discussed so far, but short options can also be used to minimize the risk:

- Further reduction of net position cost and / or
- By increasing the potential directions, the underlying can trade while making profits.

When a short option is correctly combined with a long option or the underlying stock of the same kind, it is said to be hedged. Indeed, your risks (obligations) under the short contract can be satisfied by using the shares or exercising your rights under the long contract. Without this protection, the short contract is called naked. It looks good for your exhibition.

Simple option trading allows you to receive a credit when opening a position - this credit is equal to the option premium. If all goes well, the option will expire without money (OTM), and you can keep the credit. Different newsletters encourage naked option strategies, and this may look like a great way to generate monthly revenue, but the seller needs to be aware of it.

Getting a naked call is the riskiest position you can create, and I strongly advise against this type of trading. Instead of creating a limited risk, an unlimited reward compatible with good risk management, a simple call is an unlimited risk, a limited reward position.

Unfortunately, what usually happens with these strategies is that months of small credits are eliminated with losses of one or two operations only against you. I am not opposed to the creation of a credit exchange; I just do not like to expose myself completely from the risk point of view.

The risk can be limited by combining credit or debit options using hedged option positions. This section presents limited risk allocation operations and combined limited rewards positions.

SPREADING THE RISK WITH A DEBIT TRADE

A vertical gap is a position that combines two options:

- A long option and a short option of the same type (buy or sell)
- Have the same month of maturity and different exercise prices.

This is called "vertical" because that's how exercise prices line up when you look at a chain of options. You can create a vertical gap for an initial debit or initial credit. In each case, the position presents a limited risk and reward.

Each option position in a vertical gap is called the leg.

The type of vertical spread you select depends on the outlook of your market. You Vary risks and benefits altering the strike prices used to establish the position too. You can create two kinds of vertical spreads for one debit, one using calls and the other using put options. They are referenced by inventory prospects and include:

Bullish Spread: You create a **bullish** spread by buying a call and simultaneously selling another call that expires in the same month. The short call has a greater exercise price. Short-term purchases eventually reduce the price of long-term purchases, so this spread trading is less risky than purchasing a purchase on its own.

Bear put spread: you make a bear put spread by buying a put and simultaneously selling another put expiring the same month. The put has a lower exercise price. The price of this

433

lower strike being cheaper, you pay a net debit for trading. Short selling while reducing the long-selling price, so this spread trade is less risky than buying long sell options alone.

Exposing yourself is a very risky position, even if you are willing to buy the shares at the exercise price of the short sale. The sale of short selling generally occurs when the inventory is down or bad news is published. The acquisition of stock on the market or that the assignment in a time like this - it goes against reasonable risk management principles.

Risk Assessment and Reward for a Call Flow Spread

Your maximum risk for the upward spread is the initial debt you paid to create it, similar to a basic long position. Because the position combines a short call to reduce the cost of the long call, it also reduces the risk of the position. Because you get nothing for nothing on Wall Street, reducing your risk in this way has a price in terms of reduced rewards.

If ABC trades at $ 37.65 and you're up, you can create a higher spread by doing the following transaction:

- Buy on January 1st, call 35 @ $ 4.20 and
- Sell January 1, 40 Call $ 1.50

The buyer's long-term debt is $ 270 ([$ 4.20 - 1.50] × 100). This is also the maximum risk that occurs when ABC closes at $ 35 or less upon expiration. At this price, both calls will be useless.

Unlike a basic long call, your all-out reward is limited by an increasing call spread because the short bond prevents you from getting unlimited rewards. Your maximum reward is the gain you get from year-end transfer transactions less than the initial debit paid for the $ 230 [($ 40 - 35) × 100 - 270.00] position. The maximum reward occurs when ABC is trading at $ 40 or more at maturity.

Your actual gain or loss can be between maximum risk and maximum reward if the ABC closes between 35 and 40. The calculation of the difference in profitability is similar to a long purchase. Using the Long Call Exercise Price, you add the difference between the two option prices (the initial charge without the multiplier) to determine your equilibrium level. In this example, the breakeven point is $ 37.70 (35 + 2.70).

Given that a vertical throughput differential is a net long position, its value will experience the same accelerated deterioration of time in the 30 days to maturity as a long default option position. Integrate a spread exit method before this period if the position may lose value in this way.

The risk map identifies the following important areas:

- Maximum risk $ 270 displayed by a lower horizontal line
- Maximum reward of $ 230 displayed by the top horizontal line
- A stock price of $ 37.70 displayed by a dark vertical line.
- A profit loss range, represented by a diagonal line ranging from the lowest strike price to the highest strike price.

Risk, reward, and balance calculations for vertical spreads are made assuming that you have been assigned your short bond and exercise your long rights.

Risk assessment and reward for a placed debit spread

Your maximum risk for the term spread is the initial debt you paid to create it, similar to a long base selling position. Because the position combines a short sale to reduce the cost of selling in the long run , it also minimizes the risk for the position.

If XYZ trades at $ 50.85 and you have lost stock, you can create a downward selling spread by doing the following:

- Buy on January 1st 50 put @ $ 2.75 and
- Sell on January 1st, $ 45 to $ 1.30

Net debt is also the maximum risk. The risk, reward, and profitability calculations are similar to those of the upward spread:

- Debt = maximum risk = (2.75 - 1.30) × 100 = $ 145.00
- Break-even = $ 50 - ($2.75 - $1.30) = $50 - $1.45 = $ 48.55

- Maximum Reward = [($ 50 - 45) × 100] - $ 145.00 = $ 355.00

The maximum reward occurs when XYZ is redeemed at $ 45 or less upon expiration.

The risk map identifies the following important areas:

436

- The maximum risk of $ 145 displayed by a bottom horizontal line
- Maximum reward of $ 355 displayed by the top horizontal line
- Price 48.55 $ breakage displayed ed on a dark vertical line
- A range of a loss of profit, displayed by a diagonal line ranging from the highest strike price to the lowest strike price.

Consider entering a vertical debit when there are at least 60 days left to expire to allow the position to become profitable.

Never leave the long leg of the vertical spread without also leaving the shortest side of the spread - otherwise, you significantly change your risk profile. This applies even when it seems that the short leg will expire worthlessly.

Summarizing your debit risks and rewards

In the two vertical debit spreads, your risks and benefits are limited. Each spread is less risky than the corresponding long base position because you reduce the initial debt of the short option price. Risk reduction comes in the form of greatly reduced rewards for you because of the short position of the option also limits your profits.

A transaction risk graph provides specific risks, rewards, and tradeoffs associated with a specific transaction.

When ordering a new vertical flow differential, consider using a lower limit value than the cited price for the combined position to minimize the impact of slippage. You probably will not be able to trade at mid-spread, but you can probably get the order filled if you reduce the amount of debt a little bit.

HOW TO SPREAD THE RISK WITH A CREDIT TRADE

Debit spreads are not the only kind of spread trading that you can create using calls or put options. You can switch the purchased exercise price, and the one sold on the debit spreads to create a credit spread. Once again, the spread requires you to buy one option and sell another of the same type, expiring in the same month. You can build two different vertical credit spreads:

Bear call spread: You create a call distribution by purchasing a call and simultaneously selling another call that expires in the same month. The short call has a lower exercise price. Because the price of a lower strike call is higher, you get credit for trading. The long call ends up surpassing the short call, so this spread trade presents a much lower risk than a naked call option.

Bull put spread: You create a bearish spread by buying a put and simultaneously selling another put that expires the same month. The put has a higher exercise price. Because the price of a higher strike is higher, you get credit for trading. Long sales eventually cover short sales, so this spread trading is significantly lower risk than a short sale.

Risk Assessment and Reward for a Call Credit Spread

438

Your maximum risk for the bearish spread is limited to the difference between the strike prices of the options minus the credit you received when creating the transaction. The position uses long calls to limit the risk of short calls, which in itself is unlimited. Instead of placing an XYZ put spread for a debit, you can create a call spread call XYZ bear for a credit.

You create the bearish spread by buying the highest and cheapest call and selling the most expensive and lowest call:

- Buy on January 1st, 55 calls at $ 0.95 and
- Sell January 1st 50 Call @ $ 3.20

For credit spreads, net credit is also the maximum reward. The reward, risk, and break-even calculations for a bearish spread call are as follows:

- Credit = Maximum Reward = $(3.20 - 0.95) \times 100 = \$ 225.00$
- Break-even = $\$ 50 + (\$ 3.20 - 0.95) = 50 + 2.25 = \$ 52.25$
- Maximum risk = $[(\$ 55 - \$ 50) \times 100] - \$ 225.00 = \$ 275.00$

A short purchase gap reduces risk by limiting short-lived losses. Reducing your risk means that your rewards are reduced. Your maximum reward is the initial spread credit. This occurs if XYZ closes below the exercise price of the short purchase at maturity, causing both worthless options to expire.

The risk map identifies the following important areas:

- The maximum risk of $ 275 displayed by the bottom horizontal line

439

- Maximum reward of $ 225 displayed by the top horizontal line
- A stock price of $ 52.25 displayed by a dark vertical line.
- A profit loss range, represented by a diagonal line ranging from the lowest strike price to the highest strike price.

If the original stock is close to the strike price on the last trading day prior to maturity, you may be given the short option on the weekend, but you may not have the option opportunity to exercise your contractual rights. long Close a vertical credit spread for debit on the last trading day before maturity if the underlying price is close to the short strike price.

Risk assessment and reward for a put credit spread

Your maximum risk for the Batch Spread is limited to the difference between the exercise prices of the options minus the credit you received when creating the transaction. The position uses the long sale method to significantly reduce the risk of short selling, which is high. Instead of placing a high ABC purchase gap for a debit, you can create a high ABC sales gap for credit.

You create a bullish spread by buying the lowest exercise put and selling the highest put:

- Buy on January 1st, 35 sales at $ 1.70 and
- Sell Jan. 1, 40 put @ $ 4.10

For credit spreads, net credit is also the maximum reward. The reward, risk, and break-even calculations for a stock gap are as follows:

- Credit = Maximum Reward = ($ 4.10 - 1.70) × 100 = $ 240.00
- Maximum risk = [($ 40 - 35) × 100] - 240.00 = $ 260.00
- Balance = $ 40 - ($ 4.10 - 1.70) = 40 - 2.40 = $ 37.60

A bull spread position reduces the risk by limiting the short put losses. Reducing your risk means that your rewards are reduced. Your maximum reward is the initial spread credit. This occurs if ABC closes above the strike price of the short sale at maturity, resulting in the expiry of the two options with no value.

Always watch the trading conditions after the close of trading on the last trading day before expiration. You never want to allow a limited-risk position to turn into a high risk or unlimited position because you can not manage the trade until the end.

Summarizing your credit risks and rewards

The risk chart for a vertical credit spread is similar to the vertical debit spread with limited risk and reward. It dramatically improves the short-term risk graph or short sale, which limits the risks are unlimited or limited, but high. This is done by creating a position that covers the short option instead of leaving it naked.

Although you can perform a spread operation at a price that is more favorable than the present market price, always remember that if your risk settings indicate that you need to leave a position, simply move out of the position. This can almost always be achieved by placing a negotiable term order.

When overall averages rise sharply, most equities and sectors do the same, and when they fall sharply, most stocks and sectors follow. The sectors do not move exactly in conjunction with the indices. Economic conditions often favor a group over a period of time, and as conditions change, so do sectors that show strength or weakness. Focusing on strong or weak areas allows you to apply the best strategies to the conditions. First, of course, you must know how to find them. Technical analysis provides tools to analyze sectors, including those to identify strengths and weaknesses. In this chapter, I present the fundamentals of technical analysis you need to achieve your sector trading strategies.

GETTING TECHNICAL WITH CHARTS

Chart analysis is an aspect of technical analysis that uses price and volume data to provide an overview of trends for market valuation purposes. There are a variety of graph types and data views, providing an extremely broad list of analysis tools. By focusing here on some industry-oriented and option-trading tools and techniques, novice traders in chart analysis should accelerate quickly, while those familiar with this will receive a review.

Basics of charts

The charts use price data to provide an overview of the trading activity over a period of time. A shortlist of common chart types includes the following:

Line chart: uses the price as a function of time. A single price data point for each period is connected using a line. It usually uses a close value, which is generally considered the most important value for the period (day, week, etc.). Line graphs provide excellent general information on price movements and trends, filtering the noise of smaller movements during the period. period.

The disadvantages of line graphs are that they do not provide information on the strength of trading during the day or whether deviations have occurred from one period to another. A spread is created when trading a period is completely higher or lower than trading in the previous period. This happens when important news affecting the company comes out when the markets are closed. Does not it seem like a good piece of information to have when you negotiate?

Open-High-low-closed bar graph (OHLC): Uses the price as a function of time. The trading range for the period (from bottom to top) is displayed as a vertical line, with opening costs showed as a horizontal tab on the left side of the range bar, and closing prices in the form of a vertical line. horizontal tab on the right-hand side of the beach bar. break. A total of four price levels is used to build each bar.

OHLC charts provide information on the strength of the trading period and price differences. Using a daily chart as a reference point, a relatively long vertical bar informs you that the price range was wide enough for the day.

Another method to look at it is to say that stocks were volatile that day - good information for option traders. It also suggests a stock strength when stocks close near the high of the day and weakness when stocks close near the low of the day.

Candlestick chart: uses the price as a function of time. Similar to an OHLC chart with the open to the closed price range of the period highlighted by a thick bar. Unique patterns in this chart can improve daily analysis.

The candlestick charts have distinct interpretations of motifs that describe the battle between bulls and bears. It is better to apply them to a daily chart. Candlesticks also display price ranges and gaps.

See the graphs using both:

- Long-term linear graphs observing price trends
- OHLC chart or candlestick to better understand price action over the period, including the strength and volatility of a security

A wide variety of technical graphics packages are available as standalone software programs or web applications. The prices range from free to thousands of dollars, depending on the features of the package. When using technical analysis for the first time, consider starting with a free web package, identifying your specific needs, and developing from there.

REGULATING YOUR TIME HORIZON FOR THE GREATEST VIEW

Before you focus on a specific range of the chart, think about your investment or trading horizon. What you want to see when valuing your 401 (k) investment is different from your focus on active trading.

Technical analysis puts a different emphasis on deadlines. Long-term trends are considered stronger than those in the short term. To get the greatest view of trends, it's extremely useful to change the time range used for your charts. The typical chart pattern is a daily chart, but others also exist.

When performing a market analysis to find strong sectors, an ideal progression includes evaluating the following:

- Key Long-Term Trends Using Monthly Charts and Sector Charts
- Intermediate, major, and minor trends using weekly charts covering broad indices and industry sectors
- Small, short-term trends using daily pie charts

By first recognizing major and intermediate trends, you are less likely to be involved in the emotion associated with short-term movements.

A horizontal support line can be traced after lower prices to double the price level. The line is confirmed when the third ring of this price level is successfully maintained, and the purchase request returns to the title that submits the price.

VISUALIZING SUPPLY AND DEMAND

Charts can be seen as a display of supply and demand:

- Demand for purchase drives up prices
- Supply creates sales pressure that drives down prices
- The volume shows the magnitude of the supply or demand

446

Markets do not move up and down - the battle between bulls (demand) and bears (supply) causes different types of price movements.

A horizontal resistance line can be drawn when the price increases to reach the price level twice. The line is confirmed when the third ring of this price level is successfully maintained, and the sale of supplies returns to safety, which lowers the price.

Support and resistance areas

Support and price resistance are breaking the current trend:

- Support represents a transition from supply-induced price declines to price increases when renewed demand comes into play at this price level.
- Resistance represents a transition from rising prices, driven by strong demand, to lower prices when selling pressure reaches that price.

When negotiating, note that these transitions align over time, sometimes creating lateral trading channels as the price moves between the two. The more the price serves as support or resistance, the more it is considered strong.

The use of support and resistance to identify entry and exit points is a basic trading system. Also, consider using them in the price projections to identify stop losses and outflows as well as to calculate risk-reward rates.

Previously supported price zones tend to serve as areas of resistance in the future and vice versa.

Trend Analysis

I use the concept of trend a lot before reaching this formal definition. This is because I am sure you have an idea of what is an upward and downward trend for any asset. Painfully, if you held this asset in the latest trend. More formally, the trend identifies the direction of prices:

Upward Trend: the price go up and down so that a line on the rise can be traced in indentations that show higher lows. Higher highs are also characteristic of upward trends.

Downward trend: Prices fall and fall in such a way that a line of decline can be traced above the top of the retracement peaks, which have lower peaks. Low troughs are also characteristic of downward trends.

Create a trend line by connecting two lower (uptrend) or two lower (downtrend). When the price successfully tests the line for the third time, the trend is assured. Making use of these lines as entry and exit points is an effective application of the tool, similar to support and resistance levels.

Consider drawing two trend lines using a long-term chart , such as a monthly chart, to highlight a zone of resistance against a single subjective trend line. One can use close data while the other uses market lows. Follow the action of the market near everyone.

Moving Averages

Moving averages are lines constructed on a graph using an average closing price over a given number of days. These lines are considered late indicators because historical data follow price action. The two major kinds of moving averages are:

- Simple moving averages (SMA) using a basic average
- Exponential Moving Averages (EMAs) that integrate all available pricing data, adding weight to the latest data

Simple moving averages also weigh all closings over the selected period, while exponential moving averages are calculated so that the most recent data has more weight on the line.

SMAs and EMAs can be created using a variety of parameters and ranges of graphics. As a result, you can display a five-day SMA on a daily chart or a ten-week EMA on a weekly chart. Moving average lines are considered as unbiased trend indicators because the lines are derived from objective calculations.

The three most common parameters for any moving average are:

- 20-day moving average indicating short-term trends
- 50-day moving average indicating medium-term trends
- 200-day moving average showing long-term trends

You may have heard the financial media report that the price is close to the 200-day moving average. Indeed, a break in this line is considered significant and can confirm a reversal of the trend.

Exponential Moving Averages (EMA) incorporates all available price data for the underlying security, with newer data having a better weight on the EMA value for the period. Because of this, they are more sensitive to price changes.

IDENTIFYING RELATIVELY STRONG SECTORS

Bullish or bearish movements in the market generally lead to gains for most sectors and bonds. However, during more moderate trends, some sectors and stocks outperform the market, while others underperform. A sector or security may also move in the opposite direction during these periods. Your objective as a trader is to find relatively strong and weak groups so that you can apply lucrative strategies to the industry.

Relative ratios

You create a relative proportion line by dividing one title into another. This allows you to objectively show the performance of one security against another because the line increases when the main security exceeds the second and decreases in case of underperformance. Adding an overlay graph to a relative relationship allows you to display both titles in a graph. Ball ladders generally provide a better view of the movements of others.

Trend lines plotted on a log chart appear differently when you move to an arithmetic scale.

Shorter moving averages (i.e., a low setting) are considered faster and closer to price. You can distinguish these lines in a graph because they are a little jagged.

By including relative indices in a graph, you have a clearer view of the performance of two titles. When it seems that both indices have been moved in a similar way until very recently. But a look at the line of relative proportion tells another story. For much of the three year period, SPY outperformed the XLF, significantly from June to October 2007.

Relative report lines are also called relative force comparisons.

In a month of deterioration of the relative reason line, the XLF fell below the 200-day EMA and shortly after the 50-day EMA. Although unlabeled , the shorter EMA is identified by observing the one closest to the price. When the downward trend conditions are optimal, prices and MAs are aligned with the lowest price data that appears on the graph, followed by the shorter EMA then the higher EMA - just like this graph shows.

Some traders use moving average crosses as signals of the trading system. This approach has its place in the negotiations, but note, where the price was at the moment the cross occurred - almost at its lowest point. Keep in mind that moving averages delay price data. I like to use crosses to identify a change in inventory conditions and as a strategy filter. Once this crossing is done, I am in favor of downside strategies.

Before moving away from this particular graph, note that trend lines can be applied to relative proportions. The same rules apply:

- Draw upward trends using troughs
- Draw downward trends using trend highlights

In addition, the previous support areas can become robust and vice versa.

When you use overlay features in a chart, the indicators added to the chart are based on the primary security.

When using relative proportions, it is good to identify a group of indices or related sectors to monitor. Cash flow from one market or one industry to another as economic conditions change. Portfolio allocations should favor more efficient and underperforming markets. This results in the reversal of a market leader in another market for varying amounts of time.

The broad range of ETFs that track different assets (for example, the dollar or oil) allows you to use an asset allocation plan in the markets using only one type of security. Add options to many ETFs, and you have reduced the risk of accessing commodity and currency markets.

The curves trend can be used in the power lines comparison report to identify better the changing areas and conditions of support and resistance. Similarly, broken support will often serve as resistance in the future.

By focusing on the sectors, selecting an optional Family Family ETF allows you to assess industry trends and relative performance quickly. For example, Select Sector S & P Depository Receipts (SPDR) includes ten ETFs based on the S & P 500 Index:

- SPY follows the entire S & P 500 index

- Nine ETFs track each of the nine main sectors that make up the index

Collectively, the nine ETFs in the industry make up the SPY ETF. By examining ten graphs, you can conduct a broad market and industry assessment that can serve as a basis for overall investment or negotiations in the industry. The search for a liquid ETF fund family and optional your first goal, you do so a follow-up confirming the liquidity of ETF options.

A relative proportion line only compares the performance of two titles - it does not indicate a trend for either title. A rising line may indicate that the headline has an upward trend at a faster pace than the second headline or that it is trending downward at a slower pace.

RATE OF CHANGE INDICATOR

Relative proportions provide a good visual approach to evaluating sectors. A change rate approach allows you to quantify and rank the performance of these sectors. The rate of change (OCR) of a title is the speed at which it moves - when calculating safety returns, you use a type of OCR. There is also an OCR indicator that can be drawn on charts for the analysis, trading, or scoring of securities.

To calculate a ten-day OCR, use the following formula:

- (Price of the day ÷ Prices 10 days ago) × 100

As an alternative approach to industrial trade, you can expand the list to include industry groups, investment styles (small or large value, value, or growth) or countries, among others. The main objective is to develop a group of ETFs with related inflows and outflows.

By using OCR trends, you really want to capture the cash flow from one market or industry to another. Remember to check different times, such as weekly or monthly OCR, and see how notes change each week. Relative strength trading approaches aim to build upside positions on relatively strong performance and bearish positions on relatively poor performance. This worked best when the periods used entail ranking that persists for more than a week or two, so you stay in a strong position.

During trading, the ROC is used with a simple moving average (SMA) as a commercial alert. The ROC crosses above your SMA are bullish, and the ROC crosses under your SMA are a bearish alert.

The term normalizes refers to the process of expressing data so that it is independent of the absolute value of the underlying. This allows a comparison with other titles.

USING SECTOR VOLATILITY TOOLS

Technical analysis displays volatility in a number of ways, including historical baselines and volatility (HV) charts. The objective technical indicators available in many graphic sets and covered in this section are:

- Statistical volatility
- Average True Interval
- Bollinger Bands
- Bollinger %b

These tools offer different views of volatility and allow you to check the markets for securities that can prepare for a change. Although volatility may remain high or low for long periods, these measures may provide the following:

- A purchase alert in case of decline
- A sales alert with higher heels
- A tool to help identify the appropriate strategies
- Seasonal motion detection

The value used for the technical indicators is called the parameter. Commonly used parameters are called default values.

Volatility display with indicators

Statistical volatility and the real average range are two different views of price movements. See how they differ:

Statistical Volatility (SV): VS, another term for historical volatility that makes use of closing values to show an annualized standard deviation line that signifies the degree of the price movement of the security. As various periods of time can be used in a chart, SV reflects the period of the chart, not necessarily a daily calculation, as you see on option HV or SV charts.

Average True Range (ATR): ATR used a true range value (TR) to define the price movement and was developed by Welles Wilder. The TR incorporates extreme movements, such as spreads, to better reflect volatility. TR uses the previous and the last closing and closing values to calculate three different ranges. The widest beach for all three is the TR for the period.

A rate of return calculation is a measure of the rate of change. It allows comparisons of securities at different prices, creating value regardless of price.

ATR is an exponential moving average that smooths TR. A big change in ATR incorporates price differences and provides traders with important information on price volatility that may be missed by other smoothed indicators. As ATR uses historical prices and a smoothing process, it is a lagging indicator and does not predict volatility. However, a strong upward movement of the ATR of a bond is often accompanied by an IV increase in its options.

When using brokers to identify low bandwidth inventory, check the chart to see what is happening with the stock. The price may have fallen due to an ongoing securities transaction such as a stock purchase and is less likely to change from this point on.

The nine sectors ETFs hit the lowest on the same day, with each ATR peaking in the next day. The SV profile of ETFs varied more, but most also peaked a few days before the bottom. When reviewing charts, note the following about XLI:

- The price has evolved over a very wide range, closing the day in style with a slight net gain.
- SV was moving away from a peak two days earlier
- ATR always went up
- The 14-day SMA ROC was flat, suggesting a possible end to decline.

Although XLI ranks fifth on the 14-day ROC, closing at its highest for the day was extremely optimistic, given the variety of trades that day. The situation deserved surveillance to confirm a reversal.

The price continued to climb, while the ATR appeared to decline, and SV conditions remained high. The ROC exceeded its 10-day ADM, which was a bullish signal. The only strategy discussed so far that adapts to these conditions (high volatility, high) is a long and short buying position.

By buying the close ETF at $ 38.55 and selling the September 39 exercise price at $ 0.80, you created a moderately reduced risk position. Instead of $ 3855 on the line, you reduced your exposure to $ 3775 or 2%. In fact, there are better strategies to take advantage of this situation - ones that allow you to limit your risk a lot more - but this is appropriate for now.

You can create a short-term covered call strategy in order to be excluded from the position. This is the case here, so you want the XLI to trade above 39 by the September due date. That's exactly what happened. At maturity, Friday XLI closed at 40.63, and you would have been affected. That means you bought the position for $ 3,775 and sold it for $ 3,900.

ANALYZING VOLATILITY WITH BOLLINGER BANDS

The Bollinger Bands provide another interesting insight into relative volatility levels. This technical tool makes use of a simple moving average (SMA) surrounded by upper and lower ranges, both derived from a standard deviation calculation. John Bollinger, the developer of the tool, uses the following parameters as default settings:

- SMA 20 periods
- The upper band (SMA + two standard deviations)
- The lower band (SMA - two standard deviations)

Bands expand and contract as price volatility contracts and spread.

Two additional Bollinger Band tools are:

Bandwidth (BW) for measuring the distance between the two bands using the calculation: BW = (BB higher - BB lower) Average moving average

Bollinger has shown that when BW is at its lowest level in six months, a tightening candidate is identified. It is a security that consolidates before a potentially strong leak, bigger or smaller. It is common for a false move to occur so that comprehensive strategies can provide a way to remedy this situation.

% b to know where the price is relative to PV, calculated using a variation of George Lane's stochastic indicator, with values ranging from:

- 0 to 100 when the price is equal or between ranges
- Less than 0 below the lower band
- Greater than 100 above the upper band (high)

Review the news when you come across a chart with a sharp rise or fall in prices, as well as a narrow bandwidth in the Bollinger Bands.

A value of 75 reflects the price in the bands and a quarter below the lower band in terms of total bandwidth. % b normalizes the price to the size of the bandwidth and allows you to compare apples with apples from different stocks for sorting purposes.

Different industries are experiencing bullish and bearish trends at different times. Although large ups and downs in major markets often move all securities in the same direction, the strength and duration of movements of these different securities may vary considerably. In general, the following applies:

Sectors and securities with very high values for% b are optimistic when confirmed by other technical tools.

Securities and sectors with values too low for% b are low when confirmed by other technical tools.

Bollinger noted that instead of prices being raised when they are close to a Bollinger Bands, the condition actually reflects the strength and a leak that can continue. Look for setbacks towards the moving average line to establish new positions in the direction of the trend after such a break.

PROJECTING PRICES FOR TRADING

There is no guarantee on the markets. Options with low levels of implied volatility may remain low, downside stocks may continue to decline, and options with a 75% chance of making money at maturity, depending on the model, may expire worthlessly. That's why risk management is your first job as a trader. Using resistance areas and support areas and trend lines is a simple way to manage your risks.

Price projections can include those that identify outputs for a loss or profit. Both are important. Sometimes we focus so much on risk management that we also forget not to forget to make a profit. By identifying areas higher and lower than the current price before establishing a position, you simplify the management of operations. Consider using objective strategies like price channels, retractions, and extensions to identify output levels. The following sections present the two sides of the coin: methods for projecting price movements (magnitude and time) as well as risk management tools. Exactly what options traders need.

SUPPORT AND RESISTANCE

Support and resistance provide subjective tools that identify:

- Actual output levels for loss
- Potential exit levels for profit

Although the support and resistance lines are subjective, they represent a reasonable approach to manage your risk because they identify a maximum loss. As your skills develop, the application of these tools and exit points will be improved.

The reason I use the "potential exit" on the profit side is that changing conditions can guarantee an anticipated exit from partial profits or allow you to increase revenue based on the change. Suppose you embrace a bullish position - if your indicators become bearish, you may receive an alert requesting a position exit earlier than expected. Similarly, you may have already received a portion of your profits when the title reaches its original projection price. If the chart stays bullish, you can review your price target for additional profits.

The extent of the exit only applies to the profit; the exit points for a loss must be fixed in the stone. You can move earlier, but you absolutely can not revise the output level in a way that increases losses. It is essential to identify a maximum loss price for the position and execute it if it is reached.

As the trend lines are traced by the analyst, a certain degree of bias can be introduced. Consider giving yourself some freedom when using these inbound and outbound pricing areas to help reduce the impact of bias.

Making use of a moving average crossover system, you decide to take a long position in the XLF (Financial ETF) the day after the 20-day EMA cross-over by the 50-day EMA. An output signal includes a 20-day EMA cross below the 50- day EMA. Because this output does not identify a specific output for a loss, you add a helpline below the present price to manage your risk.

In the previous uptrend, $ 36.58 support, but this zone was halted when the XLF went down a few months ago. Since then, the market has reversed, and the same level of $ 36.58 had served as resistance when the XLF began to rise. The ETF has recently surpassed this level, making it a reasonable area of support for future stop loss. Since the ETF trades around $ 37.10, it represents a 1.4% loss in risk parameters.

To display a 200-day moving average on a weekly chart, you must use a setting of 40 because there are five business days in a week.

Longer moving averages are considered slower and less sensitive to price changes. You can distinguish these lines in a graph because they are softer. The calculation of a moving average is called the smoothing process.

TRENDS

Trend lines are ascending and descending moving lines drawn through higher troughs (upward trend) or lower troughs (downward trend). These lines can also be used for price projection purposes. The actual price level used with these lines is estimated because the lines tend rather than horizontal.

Many technical analysis packages include a targeting tool that allows you to identify the price and date for different areas of the chart. Using the same XLF EMA cross entry technique, a trendline output can be identified with the crosshair tool.

Many trend tracking systems have more small losses and fewer large profitable transactions. These systems depend on the use of the system output rather than physical stop-loss output levels. To properly manage risk while letting the system function properly, it incorporates the percentage of loss outflows in its back-test to determine if the system is viable when a stop loss is included.

The options come with an expiration period, so the time it takes for a stock to reach a projected cost is as important as the projection itself.

There are many technical tools that generate input and output signals but not price projections. When identifying a maximum loss exit point, be sure to consider basic risk management techniques.

CHANNELS

Price channels include those designed using two different trend lines and those built using a regression line - here I show the last one to focus on objective tools. A regression channel:

- Uses a specific number of previous prices to create the chain
- Includes an intermediate regression line representing the expected value of future prices (without guarantee)
- Corrects the data period, then extends the channel lines forward in time.

A regression line is fixed, which means that it is constructed using data with a start and end date rather than adding and deleting data in the same way as a moving average. The price should reverse the average with these channels.

A regression line is also called a line of best fit. This is the line that represents the shortest distance between each data point and the line.

When building a regression channel, you make use of an existing trend that must remain intact. The price contained in the channel confirms the trend, and the outgoing price of the channel suggests that a change of trend could develop.

There are several ways to create a string. Here I focus on a basic approach to linear regression. After recognizing the trend period, the regression line is drawn, and the limit lines are created as follows:

- The upper limit uses the distance between the regression line and the highest point on the line.
- The lower limit uses the distance between the regression line and the lowest point on the line.

The very wide canals reflect volatile tendencies, while the narrow canals reflect quieter tendencies. Often the price will stay in the upper or lower channel for periods of time. If the price comes out of the channel and returns to it without going to the median regression line, a change of trend could develop.

Suppose you created the regression channel using a weekly OHLC bar graph for XLB. The data range for the channel is indicated above, and a long entry point in the trade is identified by the arrow.

As the trend progresses, you can identify an increasing exit point using the lower limits of the channel and the regression line. Your exit rules may include the following:

- Exit the position Monday after the price closed the lower channel line on the weekly chart (projected at 25.36).
- Make a profit if the price rises above the upper channel line then return to the channel.
- Make partial profits on the middle regression line if the price is not shifted to the upper channel line.

See the help links in the chart set for information on creating and applying metrics.

Using the crosshair tool allows you to identify realistic price projections that correspond to points in future time.

Try building regression channels on weekly and monthly charts, then switching to daily and weekly charts, respectively, to apply robust trends to the relatively shorter period.

Although very hard to see in the image, the reticule tool also identifies March 12 as the corresponding date for moving to the lower boundary line. In other words, assuming the price continues to behave as in the past.

You may think it's a very big assumption, but it's the one you make every time you get into a trendsetting position. This approach of a temporal projection is subjective but provides a good check of reality when considering the possible movements.

Trends are not considered predictive. They exist on the market, but they do not predict the price because they can continue or fail. The technical tools provide guidelines for risk management and profitability, not guarantees.

Retractions and price extensions

Rewind tools use existing trends to identify potential areas of support and price resistance. The trends and market conditions are largely associated with two primary human emotions: greed and fear. Technical analysis recognizes the impact of this crowd-based behavior and uses tools that attempt to quantify it when possible. One of these applications includes the use of Fibonacci rates for retraction purposes. These proportions are derived from a numerical series of the same name, originally defined by Leonardo Fibonacci.

Series Examples and proportions are found in nature and are used by many traders. How different market players take ã measures when certain n e levels before ç Fibonacci are met, you need to be aware of these levels. A basic understanding will probably help you evaluate the market action.

WD Gann was a successful product trader who also developed a number of widely used indexes and retraction and extension tools. Gann's ratios include, among others, 0.125, 0.25, 0.50, and 1.00.

Series and proportions of Fibonacci

The entire Fibonacci series is generated starting with 0 and 1 and adding the two previous integers in the series to get the next integer

Fibonacci rates are values obtained by dividing an integer in the series by previous or next integers specific to the series.

As prices do not increase up or down, contractions develop, which are counter-trend movements. A retracement includes:

- A retraction of prices during an uptrend
- A rise in prices during a period of decline

Fibonacci levels are often used to define withdrawal zones. Extensions use the same aspect ratio process to identify projections beyond the starting point of the base trend.

Fibonacci numbers can be used to configure indicators to make adjustments to the default value.

Time extensions

A second method uses Fibonacci numbers or proportions to identify future dates of possible turns. Projections are determined using

- A ratio based on the time needed to create the original trend.
- A count using progressing Fibonacci integers.

Another approach commonly applied to time objectives is the use of market cycles. Similar to the economic cycle, the stock market goes through ascending and descending cycles, which are measured from bottom to bottom. A low cycle can then be used to estimate the next low potential for the market. One of the best-known cycles of the stock market is the four-year cycle, with a recent trough in 2006. For the future, this means that another important minimum is expected to develop in 2010.

PROJECTIONS AND PROBABILITIES

By aligning different high probability factors, you create a situation where you place the odds in your favor for a specific strategy or operation. By managing your risk, you minimize losses and make larger gains . The process involves some science (supported by rules) and some of the art (supported by experience).

467

Possibility of weighing versus probability

Although basic tools can be subjective, a valid trend line makes it easier to identify intact trends and provides a sensible exit point when the line is broken. This interruption is a sure sign that the original reason for entry into the trade is no longer valid. However, you can still encounter problems when the time comes.

What happens if the trend line you drew was on a weekly chart, and during the week, the trend line was broken? Technically, you do not have a weekly close below the trend line, but that does not mean you should just continue to see the price deterioration. The technical methods rely on the confirmation of the indicators to help align the ratings.

Identifying an exit point before entering a position helps to reduce your excitement during trading.

During an uptrend, if the volume increases as the price fall towards the trend line, it will be a downward warning. A line break with increasing volume is another proof of bearishness. This action on a daily chart allows you to leave an established position using weekly data.

There is no assurance that the trend will remain intact.

Waiting for all the tools to become optimistic will generally not lead to negotiations. Or those who are marked will be created at the end of a movement. Try to evaluate the conditions and use their experience to put all the chances of your name. Although XLI has increased and trade has progressed, the same conditions on a different day may lead to continued downward movement. That's why risk management is essential.

React to the anticipation of a movement

Anything can happen on the markets next week or the trading day. . . even when the market closes. Trends can continue, reverse, or simply stop. The more time goes by, the more uncertain things become, so it's always good to remember that you just do not know what's going to happen tomorrow. The best you can do is to identify the rules of risk management and to maintain the odds in your favor. When conditions change, take the necessary steps and continue.

Practice disciplined trading through these strategies to gain the experience necessary to hone your skills in different market conditions:

Sector Analysis: When performing an analysis, use tools that provide objective information about current conditions for different time periods, including moving averages and Bollinger bands. This lets you stay in step with what is happening with what might happen next. Consider the general movement of the market and the evolution of the industry in relation to the market.

After assessing the current trend and volatility conditions, incorporate other tools that provide insight into the strength of these conditions and possible changes. Then develop your strategy accordingly.

Only accept new positions if you can effectively manage all your open businesses.

Commercial   evaluation: When evaluating potential business use tools that provide reasonable projections to evaluate reward : risk rates. Consider only the position with the risk levels that is within your guidelines.

Operations Management: When managing a position, be sure to monitor the conditions - do not stray from an operation that requires your attention. Use order types that automatically perform a stop-loss exit when possible .

By adding option strategies to your investment and trading portfolios, you minimize trading stress. Trading is quite difficult, but when market conditions threaten your long-term holdings, distraction can be quite destructive. Stress reduction is very vital to better decision making in both aspects of your portfolio.

Options protect portfolios and trading positions. Because there are several strategies available, you must have an implementation plan. In this chapter, I discuss some protection strategies and some things to consider when you put them into practice.

The last part of the chapter discusses a unique risk that adjusted options represent for investors and traders. Adjusted options are contracts with a non-standard delivery package due to securities transactions that occurred during the term of the option. I discuss the options defined here as they may add risks even to the conservative and protective strategies included in this chapter.

PUTTING PROTECTION ON LONG STOCK

I usually focus on short-term options trading strategies in this book, but the options are also definitely geared to long-term holdings. Applying protection strategies to your existing reserves can turn anxious, sleepless nights into quiet nights during market crises. Since no one knows when these slowdowns will occur, integrating protection strategies as a regular consideration in your investment planning can mean the difference between reaching your financial goals in time or standing by for the next bull run to get there. arrive.

COMBINING PUTS WITH LONG STOCK

The purchase applied to existing equity investments provides insurance against large losses in the event of a major downturn. As with other forms of insurance, it's frustrating to write a check for something you may not need, but it's great to have it when the time comes. Two strategies that combine a long inventory with a long investment are:

- Married put (stock and sale bought together)
- Protection put (stock and product purchased separately)

The two positions are basically the same but are different in the pure- chases calendar. Each consists of a long purchase for every 100 shares held. It is not necessary to distinguish the terms. What is important for you is to understand why and how you protect your assets. I use the term protection post for the rest of this chapter.

A put gives you the right, but not the obligation, to sell the underlying shares at the exercise price of the contract until the business day preceding the expiration date of the option. Until now, you can also sell this right on the market.

Protection considerations

The phrase is sometimes used to describe the stock market and its tendency to all actions "all boats of rising tide raises" to raise together during a bullish run. Unfortunately, the opposite is also true. Whatever the merits of individual action, when a low market reaches, it does not take prisoners - to fall quality actions.

It is almost impossible to anticipate market fluctuations, so the best thing to do next is to protect the reserved shares in the long run. Suppose you bought ABC shares a few months ago for $ 34.00 and want to keep them for the long term. You can, at any time, set a selling price for this stock by buying a sale. It does not matter whether you intend to exercise some of your losses or simply offset them with option gains.

When considering two different equity investments with similar growth potential and prospects, check the available options. This can facilitate your investment decision if one allows you to buy protection while the other does not.

Instead of an all-or-nothing approach that includes selling ABC and attempting to buy back in the event of a market downturn, the position can be protected in the short or long term using the put. Before considering specific options, you must decide to continually protect a position or do it intermittently, depending on your market prospects.

Suppose you are looking for temporary protection for ABC (30 to 60 days). When reviewing option strings, you will need to evaluate the options 60 to 90 days before they expire. This gives you the flexibility to move away from the position before the decay of time speeds up 30 days before expiration. The next thing to consider is the level of protection you want to have. Table 10-1 provides partial sales chain data for ABC to assist in this decision.

Open interest implies the total number of open contracts for a specific option contract. Since option contracts are created on-demand, they reflect information about the trading activity of the day before.

One size does not fit all

Because you are concerned about the market action in September and October, it is reasonable to focus on the October and January options to cover the downside. You must then identify any losses that you wish to accept. You bought the title for $ 34, and you are currently trading at $ 37.50. Do you want ABC protection at the current price or the level you bought it? These are questions that you face every time you consider protecting a position.

The longer the time it takes to mature, the more uncertain the share price will be at maturity. An in-the-money (ITM) has more time to become an out-of-the-money (OTM) and vice versa. The price of options uses the movements after the inventory to assess the different probabilities for the future movement of the pre ç them. Use delta as an element to check the probability that the option will be ITM upon expiration, given its past movement.

Although protection is a relatively simple strategy, there are many ways in which protection can be provided. To help you in your analysis, identify your horizon of protection and the maximum loss you are looking for before viewing the option strings. This will help you make decisions.

Price of exercise of put options - Prime purchase – POS options (purchase value at the point of sale - purchase price) × 100 = Net income

Unless otherwise indicated, the multiplier of a stock option is 100. When trading with a combined position that includes 100 stocks, be sure to incorporate this value into the formulas.

From that moment, the actual option selected for the strategy is definitely a personal decision. You may prefer long-term protection and include April options in your valuation. You can only search for catastrophic coverage , in which case you can also add exercise prices below 35.00.

To close the example, warning 37.50 must be selected if you do not want to see a lucrative position turn into a loss during the exercise. If you are pessimistic in October, the ABC Jan 37.50 put option offers protection for the entire period.

There are many things to ponder when looking for protection for an existing inventory position, including:

- Term of protection (month due)
- Level of protection (strike price and the option price)

You can also consider the probability that an option will be ITM at maturity by referencing the delta. By using the options most likely to be ITM at expiration, you may find that you can get out of the protective position and use the product to help fund new protection.

You can still sell a hedging option before it expires if you believe the markets have calmed, and the intermediate outlook for your stock is back.

Since nobody knows what the next day will bring to the markets, an investor may decide to maintain a certain level of protection in-stock positions, regardless of the short or intermediate perspective. To minimize expenses, lower strikes can be considered as part of a plan that offers a cover catastrophic - a type of protective approach against collisions.

Accelerated decay of time

When negotiating options for this or other policies, you must consider the impact of time lag on the position of the option. Theta is the Greek option that identifies the daily loss of option value associated with the current price of the option.

Using an ABC Out 37.50 put option with 60 days to expire, you can get a theta by accessing an options calculator such as the one located on the ICO website (www.optionscentral.com).

The theta value of the option traded at $ 1.05 is -0.0078. This means that if everything stays the same tomorrow, the option will lose 0.0078 in value. This may not be much, but it may increase.

In addition to the cumulative impact of weather deterioration, this rate accelerates as the expiry approaches, particularly during the last 30 days of an option's life.

The impact of weather deterioration accelerates the last 30 days of an option's life. This means that the extrinsic value will decrease more quickly with the value of the option - assuming all other circumstances remain the same.

To reduce the impact time decay within 30 days of expiration, long-term option trading strategies must incorporate an exit plan that resolves the problem. Generally, I leave an option 30 days before maturity to avoid accelerated losses of its extrinsic value.

If you think that $ 0.02 / day is manageable, consider what it means in terms of percentages. In ten days, 0.0216 represents 4.8% of the value of the contract.

The way you protect your positions is similar to any other investment decision - it depends on your personal preferences or risk tolerance. Find an approach that suits your style.

Weighing protection cost versus time

When you have a specific and reasonably short time horizon to protect a position, the month selection is quite simple. Once you look for long-term protection, the analysis requires a little more effort. Because you expect security to increase in the long run, ATM options must be OTM by maturity and can be very inefficient. You must weigh the cost of protection against the duration of the validity of the protection.

The investment process requires that you balance risk and reward. No risk, no reward, but that does not mean you have to risk everything. Consider protection positions as a way to limit your losses while letting your profits run.

Long-term protection

Suppose you have observed that XYZ shares have recorded steady annual gains of 8%, even over the years, with a 2% drop in the course of the year. How do you protect this position? A $ 2.15 GAB offering five months of protection was used in the ABC example. Since ABC was $ 37.50, the sales premium represents 5.7% of its value.

Balancing the cost of protection and returns is difficult and requires a game plan. Again, this is not a unique proposition for all proposals. If you regularly buy put options, you may sacrifice the returns stock and more. On the other hand, completely ignoring protection can cost a large part of your initial investment.

The simple solution to this issue is that you need to find the right balance for you. You can decide to use the intermittently put options when it emerges weak periods, but if you can synchronize the markets as well, probably not need protection. Think about it.

When buying products to protect your investments, be sure to balance the cost of protection against the net returns of the protection position.

By carefully evaluating the different options, rather than simply looking for the cheapest alternative, there is a greater chance that the option will be worth 30 days before expiration. As part of your plan, consider:

- The net exercise value and the level of protection provided
- The net impact on returns versus the cost of protection

- The statistical chance of the option being ITM at expiration (delta)

Being clear about your strategic goals from the start should definitely help you.

Calculation of costs per day

Finally, when selecting the protection elements:

- Be careful when buying seemingly cheap products that do not offer adequate protection and will likely expire worthlessly.
- Consider the cost of protection during the maintenance period of your actions.

Using ABC's strike price of 37.50, you can calculate the daily protection cost for both options. This is done by dividing the option premium by the number of days before expiration:

- ABC October 37.50 put @ $ 1.05 = $ 1.05 × 100 = $ 105
- $ 105 ÷ 60 days = $ 1.75 per day
- ABC $ 37.50 put @ $ 2.15 = $ 2.15 × 100 = $ 215
- $ 215 ÷ 150 days = $ 1.43 per day

The selling price of ABC Jan 37.50 translates into a cost of approximately $ 0.014/share for the option if held to maturity.

Try your best to manage your positions by responding to market conditions without reacting excessively. Nobody can completely control their emotions when the markets go up or down. Do what you can to manage them by completing your analysis when markets are closed whenever possible.

LIMITING THE RISK OF SHORT STOCK WITH CALLS

Long options offer a way to protect your investments for a specific period of time. Although you probably do not have short equity positions in your investment portfolio, you can periodically trade strategies that use short overnight equity positions. A long call can protect you against losses due to ascending nocturnal breaks.

Protecting a short position

Just as a long sell option protects a long stock position, along with buy, protects a short stock position. An appeal gives you the right, but not the obligation, to buy shares at a specific exercise price on the maturity date. You can exercise your purchase rights to close a short position if the shares increase rapidly.

Because a short stock position is generally maintained for less time, it is much easier to select protective purchase options. Generally, you can evaluate options as soon as possible until the expiration or next month. Shares with options will have two months available.

The option months closest to expiration are usually called *next- month options* and those that expire shortly thereafter are called *next-month options.*

In addition to paying less for the call, the selection of the strike price should be easier because the stock is less likely to move away from the entry price in the moderately short period the position is held. Try to use options that meet your criteria for maximum loss.

Continued reduction of the risk of short stock

If you are really want to reduce the risk of out of stock, why not consider setting up a long sales strategy to capitalize on your bearish vision for a specific stock? Suppose you do not have ABC shares, and you have low stocks. How does a long sell position compare to a short stock position? Assuming ABC is trading at $ 37.50.

Here's what you need to consider:

Cost of inventory: The initial cost for the short stock position is 50% of the current stock price because selling a margin required 150%. 100% is credited to the account for the sale of shares, and the remaining 50% is the money you need for the position.

The maximum risk of inventory: Because the inventory can theoretically increase without limit, the risk for a short seller is also considered unlimited. You can try to limit this risk by asking that the shares be bought back if they exceed a certain price, but overnight deviations inaction may cause this maximum level of risk to be exceeded.

Risk of maximum option: the maximum exposure for a long option position is the premium paid. In this case, it's $ 105.

Option Maximum Reward: If you have the right to sell one share for $ 37.50, and you are currently trading at $ 0, the intrinsic value of the option will be $ 37.50. Theoretically, you can buy shares on the market for $ 0, then exercise your right to sell them for $ 37.50. The $ 1.05 you have paid for this right must be subtracted from the gain of $ 37.50 per share of the stock transaction to determine the maximum reward for the position of the option.

Option Break-even   Level: The break-even point   of the option's position is the strike price option minus the option price, or $ 37.50 to 1.05 = the US $ 36.45.

The value of the places increases when a stock falls and represents a bearish position. Although they waste assets that are adversely affected by the deterioration of time, they have limited risk and limited but high reward potential.

Looking first at your risk, the short position limits the maximum risk to $ 105. This equates to an amount of $ 1.05 per share that can easily be overcome with a night inventory gap. From the point of view of the reward, you reduce the maximum gain by the cost of the sale ($ 105), but you have the potential to far exceed the small reward in stock by comparing the margin gains.

HEDGING YOUR BETS WITH OPTIONS

You can use the following options to hedge stock positions:

- A long position with a long stock position
- A long call with a short position

The option may be exercised to close the position of the shares, or optional gains can be used to offset the losses in the shares. The term *hedge* talks about a position used to

482

offset losses on security resulting from adverse market movements.

Securing a position or portfolio with options is a form of hedging. But not all covers are created equal. . . some are more perfect than others. A *blanket perfect* is a position that includes a title that earns the same value as a second title. The gain outweighs the loss. As a result, a $ 1 decrease in ABC coincides with a $ 1 increase in XYZ.

The Greek options delta obtained using an option calculator provides the expected change in the value of the options given a $ 1 change in the underlying stock.

Protect a portfolio. . . partially

You partially protect a position when you have a security that gains value when the hedged position loses value. In general, when you combine two titles that tend to move in opposite directions, you find that it is not always an individual relationship. A gain of $ 1 on one share may be a loss of $ 0.75 on another security. Assuming that the relationship between the two continues, their combination offers a partially protected position.

Delta can be used to help create partially or completely covered positions.

Coverage of shares with stock options

The ABC 35.00 put has a delta of -0.186. Assuming you own 100 ABC shares and sell on October 35, the expected impact on your account with a $ 1 drop-in ABC is calculated as follows:

- (Underlying change) × (Delta) = Change of option (- 1) × (-0.186) = +0.186

When the stock drops to $ 36.50, the option is expected to increase to about $ 0.54. The stock position lost 100 dollars, and the option position gained about $ 19. Since the entry into force on October 35, when the value of the shares has lost value, she has provided coverage for ABC. However, the gain on the option was less than the loss of shares, so it is only a partial hedge of the position.

The listed indexing options have characteristics different from those of listed stock options. For example, a hint is not a security for you, not something you can buy and sell. As a result, index options are settled in cash rather than when transferring a physical asset.

Cover a portfolio with index options

Since listed options are available for stocks and indices, portfolios can be hedged individually or with index options, assuming that the portfolio is well correlated with a specific index. Securing your portfolio may actually require an index option for a group of shares and individual stock options for others that are not well correlated with a particular index.

Correlation is used to describe the relationship between sets of data. Values range from -1 to +1, and once it's been applied to actions, you provide the following information:

- Equities whose returns move in the same direction of the same magnitude say they are positively correlated positively (+1)
- Equities with returns moving in the opposite direction of the same magnitude that would be perfectly correlated negatively (-1)
- Stocks whose returns do not change consistently in terms of direction and magnitude are considered uncorrelated (0)

For example, suppose you have a well-correlated $ 150,000 OEX portfolio trading at around 680. A quick partial hedge approach uses the value of the portfolio and the strike price of the index to estimate the hedge. OEX index options are obtainable for different months in five-point increments of the exercise price. When trading at 682, a purchase of 680 will have an intrinsic value of $ 2 because the value of the option is the same for index and equity options.

A common multiplier for an index is also 100, so the total option premium for the March 670 sale is $ 1,050 ($ 10.50 × 100). The basket of options is valued using the strike price and the multiplier, or $ 67,000 for sale on March 6 (670 × 100).

The option multiplier is the contract valued to determine the net premium of the option (market price of the × multiplier option) and the value to be delivered from the set of options (strike price of the option). ' option × multiplier).

Suppose you decide to protect your portfolio against market declines of more than 2%. You can estimate the hedge by starting at the current index level (682) and subtracting the

485

decline you want to accept to get a starting point for the strike price selection as follows:

- 682 - (682 × 0.02) = 13.6
- 682 - 13.6 = 668.4

Exercise prices 665 and 670 can be taken into account. Using the 665 Put Option:

- Protection offered by 1 put: 1 × 665 × 100 = $ 66,500
- Protection offered by 2 Puts: 2 × 665 × 100 = $ 133,000
- Protected Portfolio: $ 133,000 ÷ $ 150,000 = 88.7%

If OEX falls below 665, your sales are gaining intrinsic value at a rate equal to the sales delta. As the OEX decreases, the peaks are closer to a 1: 1 movement with the index. The time remaining before expiry will also affect the actual coverage gains.

Cash options (ATMs) have deltas of approximately 0.50. Once an option is passed from ATM to in the money (ITM) or out of money (OTM), the delta changes value. The Greek option that gives an idea of the amount of delta change is gamma.

A set of stock options generally represents 100 shares of the underlying stock. When you use the strike price and the 100 multipliers to evaluate the options package, it is common to think that you pay the strike price for each stock. It is normal to apply it to stock options, but this is not very specific when considering index options or adjusted stock options. In both cases, it is better to consider the value of the options package as simple:

- Price of exercise × Multiplier

A stock option package usually includes 100 shares. When the rights of the sales contract are exercised, the owner of the stock option receives the exercise price multiplied by the multiplier options - usually 100. The value that the holder of the put option receives is also called the *Option Pack Exercise Price*. Other terms that you may see for this value include:

- Assignment value of the options package
- Optional package delivery value

It depends on which side of the option you are on. All of these terms mean the same thing, the money that is traded when the rights to an appeal or a sales contract are actually exercised.

Protect a portfolio. . . completely

To further discuss the coverage, it is useful to use the alternative range from 0 to +100 and from 0 to -100 for the delta. Indeed, action has a delta of 1. Using this information and ABC's example, Oct. 25, with a delta of -0.186, provides the almost perfect coverage for 19 ABC actions.

ATM calls typically have deltas slightly above 0.50, while ATM investments are typically slightly below 0.50. The use of 0.50 as an approach is generally good for the initial evaluation of the strategy.

Stock hedge

Starting with a perfect stock cover using ABC, let's say you've allocated about $ 5,000 for a combined position (more stock). Since ABC trades at $ 37.50, you expect to own about 100 shares. Using the ABC option data, you focus on the January 35 exercise price option with a five-month maturity. The put gives a delta of -29.1. Since the three put options do not cover 100 stocks, you evaluate a potential position using four put options. The delta for four versions from January 35 is:

- Delta position = number of contracts × Delta = 4 × (-29.1) = -116.4

Like 1 action at +1 delta, a long position of 100 shares represents +100 deltas. A perfectly protected position has a combined delta of zero, requiring 116 ABC actions. You calculate the position delta as follows:

- 116 shares × +1 delta/share = +116 deltas
- 4 whores × -29.1 deltas per put = -116.4 deltas
- Delta position = +116 + (-116.4) = -0.4 Deltas

The cost of the job is calculated as follows:

- 116 shares × $ 37.50 = $ 4350
- 4 positions × $ 1.35 × 100 = $ 540
- Cost of the position = $ 4350 + 540 = $ 4890

This nearly perfect coverage will not stay intact for long; every time the ABC goes up or down by $ 1, the delta changes to approximately its gamma value. Part IV proposes ways to take advantage of this changing situation.

Remember that the delta of an option is changed by range for every $ 1 change in the underlying stock. For this reason, the options are called for *delta* security *variables*. The delta of action, on the other hand, remains constant. A long portion of the shares will also represent one delta is called *the fixed delta* security.

Portfolio hedge

You approach a perfect portfolio hedge the same way, but the fact that not all portfolios are perfectly correlated with an index is problematic. The perfect hedge becomes difficult to reach because the option delta changes as the value of the index changes, and there is an incorrect movement between the index and the portfolio.

Using a delta approach to protect the portfolio of $ 150,000 will bring you closer to a perfect hedge against the strike price estimate. Using an index level of 682, March 690 sales are ITM 8 points. The market price for these sales is $ 20.85, which corresponds to a delta of -0.549. One of the goals is to get closer to 1: 1 protection, so the March 2, 690 purchase gives the following results:

- 2 × 690 × 100 = $ 138,000
- 2 × -0.549 = -1.10

In this case, for every 1 point decrease in OEX, the value of the combined sales increases by 1.1. Over a short period, this translates into 1.1 times the protection of a $ 138,000 portfolio. The multiplication of $ 138,000 by 1.1 provides protection for a portfolio valued at $ 151,800. Given the variable nature of the delta of an option, you will probably be satisfied with slightly less precise portfolio protection.

AVOIDING ADJUSTED OPTION RISK

The adjusted options are those that existed when certain securities transactions took place. As a result of these actions, the terms of the contract required adjustments to reflect the action. Commercial activities that may require it include:

- Share divisions
- Significant cash dividend distributions
- Mergers and Acquisitions
- Spin-off

Most dividends do not result in an option contract adjustment.

Justify option adjustments

The two main reasons why options are adjusted after different securities transactions are:

- To ensure that existing contracts retain their value
- As a result, the contract reflects the securities transaction in your delivery package.

Without modifications, the stock option market could be riskier. Maybe exciting is the right word... Imagine one of your calls losing all its value after a stock split and a doubling put option after the distribution of a large cash dividend.

Corporate action 1: Stock splits

490

Adjustments due to stock split is the fastest to understand. When a stock you own divides two by one (2: 1), you get one additional share for each share you take on the record date - the date used to identify existing shareholders. The day you receive the additional interest, there is nothing very different for the company in terms of its financial statements. To properly evaluate the stock, its price is halved in the market on the day of the stock break.

Option adjustments resulting from a 2: 1 stock split are treated in the same way as stock splits:

- The number of contracts held is modified (similar to shares)
- The price at which the owner has rights (strike price) is adjusted

A new option agreement is created to deal with this corporate transaction and receives a new symbol. When you have an option with the underlying stock going through a 2: 1 split, you will see 2 new option contracts in your account for every 1 contract you had before.

In the current nomenclature of option symbols, the adjusted options are almost indistinguishable from the ordinary options. The problem arises when the delivery option or multiplier has to change to reflect securities trading, which is the case with a 3: 2 split. Modifying an option after a 3: 2 split requires many more adjustments to get the correct score.

When you make a sale without keeping the underlying stock in your account, you create a short position. In fact, the sales rights allow you to sell the underlying shares at the exercise price of the contract. Selling a stock that doesn't belong to you reverses the typical order of a stock transaction and leads to a short position.

Corporate Action 2: Mergers, Splits, and Dividends

Major mergers, acquisitions, spin-offs, and cash dividends change the underlying set of options when an option contract is adjusted. Indeed, the 100 original shares can now represent the delivery of the owner to:

- 100 original shares + shares acquired (merger)
- 100 original shares + new shares (split)
- 100 original shares + cash surrender value (large cash dividend)
- No original shares + acquisition shares (acquired)

In the latter case, the underlying stock may not exist if the company was acquired by another company. Adjusted options are now based on a share of the company that acquired it.

If you think you have found a business option that seems too good to be true, you may very well have stumbled on an option play. Traders on the stock exchanges that are very familiar with corporate actions taken by the actions they negotiate and know how to evaluate adjustments. There is no free money on Wall Street, so do not go into these options without understanding them.

The way you value this type of contract adjustment is more complex. It is essential to understand your rights, obligations, and position assessments if your contract is adjusted. Contact your broker if this happens. And never create, ever a new job using an adjusted option contract that you do not fully understand.

Whenever a combined position (option plus stock) you have is adjusted, be extremely careful when exiting the stock or option position separately. The combined position maintains the appropriate stock option indices created initially, but by selling a portion of the adjusted equity position , you can create great risk in the option position. Talk to your broker to discuss any position changes.

ADJUSTING FROM ADJUSTMENTS

It's good for option markets to have a way to approach contract valuations and delivery packages for different corporate actions, but what does this mean to you? Two things:

When reviewing the adjusted options in your account, check the contract specifications to understand your new rights or obligations, if any.

More importantly, be aware of the adjusted options when creating new positions to evaluate traded securities properly and know their rights and obligations.

Whenever an option quote does not look right, check the details of the contract.

Avoid building new option positions by making use of adjusted options. There is no money hidden in these contracts, just an extra effort to understand and evaluate them.

Detection of an adjusted option

The Options Symbology Initiative proposes a revised approach to option symbols that should more clearly identify the adjusted options. Until all option chains switch to the proposed system, you must know how to detect the adjusted options. Here are some things to check:

- An abbreviation "ADJ" that appears after the symbol in a quote.
- An option root symbol different from the default root
- The optional parcel details may be partially listed with the quote header - see the full quote for any changes to the package
- An exercise price appears twice a month with different symbols.
- Atypical exercise price appears for one share (46375)
- The market price of the options seems to be offline, high or low

These are the main ways to distinguish market-adjusted options. As for all safety, when something does not seem right in terms of price or volume, be sure to dig deeper to see why this is the case.

Evaluating your adjusted options according to the distribution

When an option is modified due to a 2: 1 split, new contracts are valued in the same way as ordinary options. Atypical divisions, like a 3: 2 division, need a little more attention. To evaluate an option after a 3: 2 split:

- Use the adjusted strike price and the multiplier to calculate the value of the set (JKL 60: 60 × 150 = 9000 bonds).
- Determine the underlying package value in the market using current quotes (150 JKL × 62 $ = 9,300 shares).
- Subtract the value of the package from the market value to obtain the intrinsic value of the option ($ 9,300 - 9,000 = $ 300).
- Assuming an option quote of $ 3, what remains after subtracting the intrinsic value is the the extrinsic value ($ 3 × 150 = $ 450, $ 450 - 300 = $ 150).

While people often think of markets moving in one of two possible directions, they also spend a lot of time moving in a third direction: laterally. Individual averages, sectors, and headings show different degrees of trend (up or down) and trend (side).

Option strategies are unique in that they allow you to make a profit when lateral movement is in place. By using options, you can earn additional rewards on existing positions or trade-in limited-risk markets. Long butterflies and condors are two of the strategies presented here.

WINNING POSITIONS IN SIDEWAYS MARKETS

You have two dilemmas when markets move laterally:

- Manage stagnant returns from existing positions
- How to win new positions

You may be agitated when lateral movement persists, asking if you should close your current positions and when things will go back (and in which direction). Although I do not know the exact statistics on the time the market goes into the "no-trend" mode, I know that because I negotiate options, it does not really matter. First, consider the management of positions when the market stabilizes in a parallel trading range.

MANAGE EXISTING POSITIONS

Long calls allow you to earn gains with rising trends, while long options allow you to earn gains with declining trends. When markets spend time moving sideways, you can make gains by matching positions. I hope you are now contented with the combined positions, as there are so many different ones available. As a starting point, options can be included in existing stocks or exchange-traded funds (ETFs) to increase returns when markets seem insane.

As a general rule, to start new positions, you want to sell a premium when the implied volatility is relatively high and purchase it when it is relatively low.

COMMENTS ON THE STRATEGY

It turns out that DELL had a daily shutdown further below the lower regression channel line at the end of July 2002 and that some fences over the upper regression channel at the beginning of November 2002, before eventually May 2003. The price remained in the range of channels except for a few days for 18 months.

The covered call strategy could have continued to generate profits throughout this period. If the shares were withdrawn during the May 2003 break, they could have been redeemed later in the month, when DELL returned to test the upper line of the channel, which now serves as support.

Do not place a permanent stop-loss order for the underlying stocks used in a hedged purchase strategy. If the stop is triggered, you will have a short call naked, which is an unlimited risk position.

In reviewing the DELL case study, I hope you have noted the following important points:

The short call does not protect the position of the stock; generally, only reduces the cost base, which moderately reduces the risk

You must minimize your risk by identifying a stop loss output level, even if it means buying a short purchase out of stock

Historical volatility and implied volatility generally decrease when security is within a trading range.

Earnings reports and other news related to the economy and society can significantly affect the implied volatility, even when the price moves essentially laterally.

You should consider your vision long term of the position on the shares long term because there is a limited potential loss but higher with this strategy.

As an alternative approach, it is possible to buy a long-term put while calls are sold each month to protect the disadvantages.

Cash Closing Calls (ITCs) can be launched for one month and increase the exercise price to a modest gain when stocks increase

Commissions can have a significant impact on business results

Other business costs, such as tax consequences, must be taken into account when implementing this strategy or any business strategy.

Trading rules based on stop loss exits and regression channel breaks help implement a successful strategy in risk management.

portfolio trading provides problems that can occur when in working a new strategy, as the impact of the IV compared to the price of time

When a long-term consolidation leak occurs, it is common for the stock to come back to test the model.

If you leave or are called from a position when implementing a covered call strategy during a consolidation, a return to the default value may provide the opportunity to establish a new directional position in the 'inventory.

A LEAPS contract is a long-term option obtainable for certain underlying indices, exchange-traded funds, and equities. These contracts generally have more than nine months to 21/2 years to expire and become regular options once this period has elapsed.

By selling calls on long stocks or the ETF position, you increase the number of ways in which stocks can move while allowing gains. You also reduce your potential gains if an upside-down explosive movement occurs. It's just a strategy exchange that you need to consider when considering different business approaches.

Option Strategies for Lateral Movements

The covered purchase strategy is only one that can generate gains during the parallel trading periods. As mentioned in the comments on the strategy, you can choose to protect the stock position with a long put option, and then sell the calls monthly until a break occurs or the expiration month of the long sale is over. approach.

In addition to the combination of stock positions and options, you can extend the same concept to a single combination of options using LEAPS
contract positions (long term stock anticipation shares)   on the leg of the venue. Action. This approach generally reduces the risk by reducing the total cost of the position.

Risk management occurs before generating revenue. If you experience a prolonged lateral movement of a title you hold, you can create a lower perspective for action, move out of position, or protect with a put.

What to consider with the combinations of options

One of the benefit options generally on individual stocks and exchange-traded funds (ETFs) that underlie the options is that they generally require less investment. The bottom line is that you have less money at risk. The disadvantage is that any asset can expire worthlessly. And this is for you on the commercial side - there are a number of things to consider for each type of asset you decide to use. That's why managing your risk is a common thread. The only collateral considered risk free is a US Treasury Note.

When a stock moves laterally for a period, it is said to be in the consolidation phase. The greater the consolidation, the greater the chances of a strong leadership moving away from this consolidation.

Instead of a portfolio of individual stocks or ETFs, you can keep LEAPS contracts for different stocks or sectors. A covered call strategy may be applied using the LEAPS option as a secondary mobile asset from which you increase your revenue. There are little things to consider if you follow this path:

Using a LEAPS contract as the underlying will subject you to margin requirements since the position technically represents a spread, not a pure short position covered.

Spread strategies require a different level of option approval from your broker - you may be able to access these strategies or not, depending on your type of account (for example, IRAs).

Since LEAPS are also subject to the same price factors as an ordinary option contract, Implied Volatility (IV) conditions favorable to the sale of calls are not necessarily ideal for LEAPS purchases. The strategy can work better on an existing job.

The double-edged sword IV may result in conditions in which it is better to sell your LEAPS contract, which may have decreased less than the underlying asset itself.

In addition to a LEAPS strategy, additional revenue can be generated from a calendar strategy simply by using an existing long call. In this case, the short-term calls are sold against a long call by the underlying. The risk is moderately reduced by reducing your net position investment, and the same considerations apply to those listed for a short call LEAPS approach.

The term deployment option refers to the process in which an existing option position is closed by a clearing transaction, and a similar new position is created for a month later.

Strategy short-list

Some of the strategies discussed in this book that can provide gains in secondary markets, moderately reduce risk, or both, include:

- Purchase of long-term shares (limited but high-risk position)
- Credit spread (a little money)
- Put the credit gap (a little money)
- Calendar of calls
- Put the calendar
- Distribution of the call ratio (unlimited risk position)
- Increase the sale rate (limited-risk position, but high risk)

Here are two limited risk strategies designed specifically to benefit from secondary market action - the butterfly and the condor.

Understanding Butterfly Positions

A butterfly is a strategy designed specifically to win when security or ETF trades sideways. Some features of the strategy are:

- Limited risk and limited reward
- Can be created using calls or put
- Combines two vertical gaps
- It's short term in nature
- Usually created for a debt

Maximize gains when the underlying security remains within a trading range dictated by option strike prices

A variation of the basic butterfly is the iron butterfly that combines calls and bets. This post is usually created for a time-saving credit in your favor .

A market in lateral movement can also be called without trend or direction.

DEFINING THE LONG BUTTERFLY

As with some of the strategies discussed in this book, the butterfly comes in two varieties:

- Butterfly long call
- Long butterfly

Both strategies combine a vertical credit spread, and a vertical debit spread to capitalize on lateral market movements. The policy name comes from the three options used to create the item, as follows:

- Body: 2 short options of similar type

503

- Wing 1: a much lower exercise price option
- Wing 2: a much higher exercise price option

Generally , the price of exercise of the options are short in cash (ATM) or near-cash, profits are maximized if the underlying closes below to maturity in the exercise price of the short options.

Always consider different strategies adapted to current market conditions. You may decide that an alternative strategy better reduces your risk.

Creation of an iron butterfly

The long iron butterfly is a touch of service and places butterflies that allow you to create a position for a credit. To do this, you use a redemption spread and a rising spread, both for credit. The position remains with limited risk and limited reward. He also has lateral movements to maximize the gains. In the "you get nothing for nothing" category, these spreads require an extra margin because the two vertical spreads are credit positions.

The put and call butterfly

The Iron Butterfly combines two vertical credit spreads to capitalize on the lateral movement of stock as follows:

- A bearish buying spread with an exercise price of the close short or cash option (ATM)

- An upward selling spread with an exercise price close to short or ATM and the same exercise price of short purchase

Brokers can base their margin requirements on the iron butterfly on a short overlap-strangling combination instead of two vertical credit spreads. Check with your broker for specific requirements before creating a position.

Vertical spread spreads are the same for both credit spreads; The maximum risk for the position is the difference in the exercise price of a vertical spread less than the initial credit. The long iron butterfly has exercise prices that line up like this:

- The lowest strike price is a long option.
- The next lowest exercise price is a short sale.
- The same exercise price is used for a short call.
- The highest strike price is a long decision.

When creating the iron butterfly, you use the same exercise price for the short option. The initial credit you get to establish the position is your maximum reward.

Risk of the iron butterfly

Making use of an iron butterfly with a wider spread minimizes the risk-reward rate for this position. The following example uses an action that typically moves more silently (historical volatility at 100 days - 12%), with slightly lower levels of implied volatility (IV) over the past 12 months.

Securities transactions may lead to adjustments to existing option contracts. Be sure to check the specifications of the options you use, especially when prices seem low.

Example of a long iron butterfly

We are in mid-June, and after a sharp drop in equities three months ago, the MO has returned to a more distinctive trading range. It turned out that there was a fallout

This changed the valuation of the company. The MO is trading around $ 70 and, having decided that the split should not have an impact on stocks in the future, you evaluate the following iron butterfly:

- Long 1 Jul.60 Put @ $ 0.05
- Short July 1 70 Put @ $ 1.20
- Enjoy July 1, 70 Call at $ 1.30
- July 1, 80 Long calls @ $ 0.05

Therefore, instead of a $ 3 spread on the index shares trading around $ 106, you have improved the spread to $ 10 on a $ 70 share.

An iron butterfly combines four different options - be sure to consider your trading fees before entering a position.

By calculating the net credit for these options, you get the following credit, which is your maximum reward:

- Bear Call Spread Credit + Bull Selling Spread Credit

Since both spreads have the same distance, the maximum risk is the difference between the two strike prices minus the initial credit.

[(Exercise price difference × 100)] - Initial credit

[(80 - 70) - $ 240] = $ 760

Butterflies and condors have two levels of balance - one up and one down.

The once esoteric world of options is now present in the investment community. Yes, we may have heard cynical and negative statements about this mysterious derivative, "oh, so risky!" But, like any type of investment product, the risk is purely relative. And having a solid foundation and understanding of this product, often viewed negatively, is the key to mastering and maximizing this tool in the investment portfolio. The versatility of the options, which allows traders to take advantage of the three types of markets (high, low, and stagnant), has made option trading an extremely attractive tool for many. Formerly only available to institutional traders and investors, options trading has become widespread in the market, and the arrival of online brokers has made trading of these complex derivatives accessible to retail investors.

The investors in the stock options generally buy stock options in lieu of long and short positions. Even though these options are priced at a small fraction of the actual inventory, statistics have shown that most of these options are really worthless. In essence, this means a loss of 100% of the prepaid premium.

Does this make option trading extremely dangerous? It depends. In fact, you can use this leveraged product to generate passive income! Sounds good? Let me share some of the techniques that cautious investors use to generate passive income from trading options.

PUT OPTIONS

To hedge against the significant capital losses in their portfolios, especially in a downward trend, some investors would adopt a strategy of "protective sale" as a form of management technique of risk. This strategy essentially consists in maintaining a put option in addition to the investor's existing equity position, which decreases his risk of losing money if the value of the stock is unfavorable to him.

However, a put option expires with time. Therefore, to minimize its losses on its portfolio, the investor should continually buy put options to ensure his portfolio is secure.

For example, one person currently owns 1,000 ABC shares for $ 10 each. To protect his shares from unlimited risk, he may want to buy 10 sales contracts (because 1 option contract gives the buyer the right, not the obligation to sell 100 shares) at the exercise price of $ 9. for a premium. starting at $ 1.50 * 100 * 10 = $ 1500 (for ten option contracts). In the event that the value of ABC falls to $ 5, the investor is entitled to exercise his option contracts to sell his shares for $ 9 each.

GENERATE MONTHLY PROFITS WITH PUT OPTIONS

Although put options are primarily used by institutions and investors as a form of hedging tool, they can also serve as a means to generate passive income! By selling put options that expire in a month, you can regularly earn a premium (paid by the option buyer)!

Suppose an investor has an increase in ABC stock, which currently costs $ 50. To take advantage of rising or stagnant stock, he may actually sell a put option on a strike that is less than the actual value of the stock (for example). for example, $ 45) and win a prize for it. Be careful, however, by selling a put, the person is really "naked" in his position and exposed to unlimited losses.

For a conservative investor, he can decide to buy a new put option to attack even lower (e . G. $ 40) and pay a premium that is lower than the price he got from the sale of the previous option in the $ 45 exercise, which allows him to earn the difference between the two prices from the outset. In this scenario, the maximum investor losses are limited to $ 5 if the stock price falls below $ 40.

CALL OPTIONS

As with the put option, some investors who sell less than the market may buy put options to avoid exposure to a positive risk. However, most investors buy call options for speculative purposes. Potential positive returns augmented by the leverage offered by option trading make this tool extremely attractive to low-income investors who may want to make quick money and take advantage of a potential uptrend.

GENERATING MONTHLY PROFITS WITH CALL OPTIONS

Similar to the previous strategy of selling put options, the idea here is to sell call options that expire in a month.

Here is an example:

Suppose an investor has a delisting on the ABC stock, which currently costs $ 100. To take advantage of low or stagnant share, it can actually sell a call option in the event of the strike, then the value of the action (e.g., $ 105) and win a prize for it. Again, by trading a call option, the investor is exposed to unlimited losses.

A prudent investor can choose to buy a new option called for an attack more (e . G. $ 110) and pay a premium that is lower than the price he got from the sale of the previous option in the exercise of $ 105. This allows him to win the difference between the two prizes from the start. In this scenario, your maximum losses are limited to $ 5, even if the stock price exceeds $ 110.

COVERED-CALL STRATEGY

Unlike the previous strategy of selling calls without actually owning the actual stock, a hedged call strategy is adopted when an investor owns shares of the purchase he sells. This strategy is often utilized when an investor has a short-term, neutral view of the stock. As a result, the investor would continue to buy the stock while reducing the call option to generate additional earnings from the option premium.

Again, take the example of Apple Inc., which is currently valued at $ 705.02. Suppose an investor currently owns 200 Apple stocks and has a neutral view of the company in the short term (months). He can choose to sell 2 strike calls of $ 710 or $ 715 (if he is more risk-averse) to earn 2 * 15.2 * 100 =

$ 3040 and 2 * 12.95 * 100 = 2 $ 590, respectively. The following shows the potential result on the due date:

AAPL shares remain stable – option will expire worthlessly, and the power of investors will keep the premium acquired from the sale of the option.

AAPL Increase - If the stock price exceeds the strike, the option is exercised, and the investor's capital gains on his shares are limited to $ 710 or $ 715 (depending on the strike chosen).

AAPL shares fall - the option will expire worthlessly, and the investor will be able to retain the premium earned on the sale of the option.

This means that 2 of 3 scenarios would make the investor a winner! The only opposite side of this strategy would be to lose the upside potential due to the sale of the call option. Whatever it is, the majority of investors choose to sell your option at a strike, which they felt to ease the sale of their real actions. This makes this strategy a win-win situation!

Conclusion

The sale of put options or a call can be a great addition to a well-diversified portfolio as it let investors generate passive income regularly. Keep in mind, however, that put options expose you to unlimited risk if they are not protected.

For conservative or new investors, it is important first to recognize the maximum amount of risk you are willing to take on a trade and develop a strategy for selling and buying put / sell options (also known as the spread) to mitigate their losses.

There are no secrets in this world, there is only a lot of work and a lot of study. Reread this book at least 5 times because the information is a lot, and powerful.

If you don't, you won't understand the importance of this book.

All this works, during covid-19 I made money thanks to this method, so don't stop, read the book again and start earning!

I invite you to leave a positive review on amazon. If you do, I will notify you for future updates regarding this book and new information.

Thank you.

CPSIA information can be obtained
at www.ICGtesting.com
Printed in the USA
BVHW041646300421
606221BV00010B/1184

9 781801 141307